GOVERNMENT PROCEDURES AND OPERATIONS

VOTER IDENTIFICATION LAWS

ISSUES AND ANALYSES

Government Procedures and Operations

Additional books in this series can be found on Nova's website under the Series tab.

Additional e-books in this series can be found on Nova's website under the e-book tab.

GOVERNMENT PROCEDURES AND OPERATIONS

VOTER IDENTIFICATION LAWS

ISSUES AND ANALYSES

ALANNA SUMMERFIELD
EDITOR

nova publishers
New York

For permission to use material from this book please contact us:
Telephone 631-231-7269; Fax 631-231-8175
Web Site: http://www.novapublishers.com

Library of Congress Cataloging-in-Publication Data

ISBN: 978-1-63463-546-2

Published by Nova Science Publishers, Inc. † New York

CONTENTS

PREFACE

This book reviews what available literature indicates about voter ownership of and direct costs to obtain select IDs; what available literature and analyses of available data indicate about how, if at all, voter ID laws have affected turnout in select states; to what extent provisional ballots were cast due to ID reasons in select states; and what challenges may exist in using available information to estimate the incidence of in-person voter fraud.

Chapter 1 – The authority to regulate U.S. elections is shared by federal, state, and local officials. Congress has addressed major functional areas in the voting process, such as voter registration. However, the responsibility for administration of state and federal elections resides at the state level. In 2002 Congress passed the Help America Vote Act (HAVA), which requires states to request ID from first time voters who register by mail, when they register to vote or cast a ballot for the first time, and to permit individuals to vote a provisional ballot if they do not have the requisite ID. Numerous states have enacted additional laws to address how an individual may register to vote or cast a ballot. As of June 2014, 33 states had enacted requirements for all eligible voters to show ID before casting a ballot at the polls on Election Day.

Chapter 2 – This research report on Voter Identification Requirements in the 2004 election is part of a broader analysis that also includes a study of Provisional Voting, which has already been submitted to the EAC. Conducting the work was a consortium of The Eagleton Institute of Politics of Rutgers, The State University of New Jersey, and The Moritz College of Law of The Ohio State University.

The Eagleton Institute explores state and national politics through research, education, and public service, linking the study of politics with its day-to-day practice. It focuses attention on how contemporary political systems work, how they change, and how they might work better. Eagleton regularly undertakes projects to enhance political understanding and involvement, often in collaboration with government agencies, the media, non-profit groups, and other academic institutions.

In: Voter Identification Laws: Issues and Analyses
Editor: Alanna Summerfield
ISBN: 978-1-63463-546-2

Chapter 1

ELECTIONS: ISSUES RELATED TO STATE VOTER IDENTIFICATION LAWS*

United States Government Accountability Office

WHY GAO DID THIS STUDY

The authority to regulate U.S. elections is shared by federal, state, and local officials. Congress has addressed major functional areas in the voting process, such as voter registration. However, the responsibility for administration of state and federal elections resides at the state level. In 2002 Congress passed the Help America Vote Act (HAVA), which requires states to request ID from first time voters who register by mail, when they register to vote or cast a ballot for the first time, and to permit individuals to vote a provisional ballot if they do not have the requisite ID. Numerous states have enacted additional laws to address how an individual may register to vote or cast a ballot. As of June 2014, 33 states had enacted requirements for all eligible voters to show ID before casting a ballot at the polls on Election Day.

GAO was asked to review issues related to voter ID laws. This report reviews (1) what available literature indicates about voter ownership of and direct costs to obtain select IDs; (2) what available literature and (3) analyses of available data indicate about how, if at all, voter ID laws have affected turnout in select states; (4) to what extent provisional ballots were cast due to ID reasons in select states; and (5) what challenges may exist in using available information to estimate the incidence of in-person voter fraud.

GAO reviewed relevant literature to identify 10 studies that estimated selected ID ownership rates. GAO reviewed the studies' analyses and determined that these studies were sufficiently sound to support their results and conclusions. GAO also reviewed state statutes and websites to identify acceptable forms of voter ID in selected states and the price for certain forms of ID.

GAO also reviewed relevant literature and identified 10 other studies that estimated the effect of voter ID laws on turnout. GAO reviewed the studies' design, implementation, and

* This is an edited, reformatted and augmented version of the United States Government Accountability Office publication, GAO-14-634, dated September 2014.

analyses, and determined that the studies were sufficiently sound to support their results and conclusions. Further, GAO compared turnout in two states— Kansas and Tennessee—that changed ID requirements from the 2008 to 2012 general elections with turnout in four selected states—Alabama, Arkansas, Delaware, and Maine—that did not. GAO used a quasi-experimental approach, a type of policy evaluation that compares how an outcome changes over time in a treatment group that adopted a new policy, to a comparison group that did not make the same change. GAO selected states for evaluation that did not have other factors in their election environments that also may have affected turnout, such as significant changes to other election laws. GAO analyzed three sources of turnout data for the 2008 and 2012 general elections: (1) data on eligible voters, using official voter records compiled by the United States Elections Project at George Mason University, (2) data on registered voters, using state voter databases that were cleaned by a vendor through data-matching procedures to remove voters who had died or moved, and (3) data on registered voters, as reported to the Current Population Survey conducted by the U.S. Census Bureau.

GAO also analyzed data from Kansas and Tennessee election officials on the number of provisional ballots cast for ID reasons in the 2012 general election, and data from the Election Assistance Commission's Election Administration and Voting Survey on the number of provisional ballots cast in select states in 2008 and 2012.

GAO reviewed relevant literature and identified 5 studies that attempted to identify instances of in-person voter fraud. GAO reviewed the studies' analyses, and determined that these studies were sufficiently sound to support their results and conclusions. GAO also interviewed election officials in 46 states and the District of Columbia and officials from federal agencies that maintain federal crime data to determine how, if at all, instances of in-person voter fraud are tracked in state and federal databases.

WHAT GAO FOUND

The studies GAO reviewed on voter ownership of certain forms of identification (ID) documents show that most registered voters in the states that were the focus of these studies possessed the selected forms of state-issued ID, and the direct costs of required ID vary by state. GAO identified 10 studies of driver's license and state ID ownership, which showed that estimated ownership rates among all registered voters ranged from 84 to 95 percent, and that rates varied by racial and ethnic groups. For example, one study estimated that 85 percent of White registered voters and 81 percent of African-American registered voters in one state had a valid ID for voting purposes. The costs and requirements to obtain certain forms of ID, including a driver's license, state ID, or free state ID, vary by state. GAO identified direct costs for these forms of ID in 17 states that require voters to present a photo or government-issued ID at the polls and do not allow voters to affirm their own identities, and found that driver's license direct costs, for example, range from $14.50 to $58.50.

Another 10 studies GAO reviewed showed mixed effects of various forms of state voter ID requirements on turnout. All 10 studies examined general elections before 2008, and 1 of the 10 studies also included the 2004 through 2012 general elections. Five of these 10 studies found that ID requirements had no statistically significant effect on turnout; in contrast 4 studies found decreases in turnout and 1 found an increase in turnout that were statistically significant.

GAO conducted a quasi-experimental analysis to compare voter turnout in Kansas and Tennessee to turnout in the four comparison states that did not have changes in their voter ID requirements from the 2008 to 2012 general elections. In selecting these states from among 14 potential states that modified their ID requirements and 35 potential comparison states, GAO applied criteria to ensure that the states did not have other factors present in their election environments that may have significantly affected turnout. GAO selected states that did not experience contemporaneous changes to other election laws that may have significantly affected voter turnout; had presidential general elections where the margin of victory did not substantially change from 2008 to 2012 and all other statewide elections, such as U.S. Senate races, were non-competitive in both the 2008 and 2012 general elections; and ballot questions were not present, noncompetitive, or similarly competitive in both the 2008 and 2012 general elections. GAO analyzed three sources of data on turnout among eligible and registered voters, including data from official voter records and a nationwide survey. GAO's evaluation of voter turnout suggests that turnout decreased in two selected states—Kansas and Tennessee—from the 2008 to the 2012 general elections (the two most recent general elections) to a greater extent than turnout decreased in the selected comparison states—Alabama, Arkansas, Delaware, and Maine. GAO's analysis suggests that the turnout decreases in Kansas and Tennessee beyond decreases in the comparison states were attributable to changes in those two states' voter ID requirements. GAO found that turnout among eligible and registered voters declined more in Kansas and Tennessee than it declined in comparison states—by an estimated 1.9 to 2.2 percentage points more in Kansas and 2.2 to 3.2 percentage points more in Tennessee— and the results were consistent across the different data sources and voter populations used in the analysis.

To further assess the validity of the results of this analysis, GAO (1) compared Kansas and Tennessee with different combinations of comparison states and with individual comparison states, and (2) controlled for demographic characteristics that can affect turnout, such as age, education, race, and sex. GAO also conducted an analysis using survey data on registrants from Kansas and Tennessee and a nationwide comparison group of all states other than the selected comparison states. These additional analyses produced consistent results. GAO's estimates are limited to turnout in the 2012 general election in Kansas and Tennessee and do not apply to other states or time periods.

GAO also estimated changes in turnout among subpopulations of registrants in Kansas and Tennessee according to their age, length of voter registration, and race or ethnicity. In both Kansas and Tennessee, compared with the four comparison states, GAO found that turnout was reduced by larger amounts:

- among registrants, as of 2008, between the ages of 18 and 23 than among registrants between the ages of 44 and 53;
- among registrants who had been registered less than 1 year than among registrants who had been registered 20 years or more; and
- among African-American registrants than among White, Asian-American, and Hispanic registrants. GAO did not find consistent reductions in turnout among Asian-American or Hispanic registrants compared to White registrants, thus suggesting that the laws did not have larger effects among these subgroups.

A small portion of total provisional ballots in Kansas and Tennessee were cast for ID reasons in 2012, and less than half were counted. In Kansas, 2.2 percent of all provisional ballots in 2012 were cast due to ID reasons, and 37 percent of these provisional ballots were counted. In Tennessee, 9.5 percent of all provisional ballots in 2012 were cast due to ID reasons and 26 percent were counted. Provisional ballots cast for ID reasons may not be counted for a variety of reasons in Kansas and Tennessee, including the voter not providing valid ID during or following an election. GAO's analysis showed that provisional ballot use increased between the 2008 and 2012 general elections by 0.35 percentage points in Kansas and by 0.17 percentage points in Tennessee, relative to all other comparison states combined; these findings are not generalizable.

Challenges exist in using available information to estimate the incidence of in- person voter fraud. For the purposes of this report, "incidence" is defined as the number of separate times a crime is committed during a specific time period. Estimating the incidence of crime involves using information on the number of crimes known to law enforcement authorities—such as crime data submitted to a central repository based on uniform offense definitions—to generate a reliable set of crime statistics. Based on GAO's review of studies by academics and others and information from federal and state agencies, GAO identified various challenges in information available for estimating the incidence of in-person voter fraud that make it difficult to determine a complete picture of such fraud. First, the studies GAO reviewed identified few instances of in-person voter fraud, but contained limitations in, for example, the completeness of information sources used. Second, no single source or database captures the universe of allegations or cases of in-person voter fraud across federal, state, and local levels, in part because responsibility for addressing election fraud is shared among federal, state, and local authorities. Third, federal and state agencies vary in the extent they collect information on election fraud in general and in-person voter fraud in particular, making it difficult to estimate the incidence of in-person voter fraud.

In comments on draft report excerpts the Kansas, Tennessee, and Arkansas Secretary of State Offices disagreed with GAO's criteria for selecting treatment and comparison states and Kansas and Tennessee questioned the reliability of one dataset used to assess turnout. GAO notes that any policy evaluation in a non-experimental setting cannot account for all unobserved factors that could potentially impact the results. However, GAO believes its methodology was robust and valid as, among other things, GAO's selection of treatment and comparison states controlled for factors that could significantly affect voter turnout, and GAO used three data sources it determined to be reliable to assess turnout effects.

ABBREVIATIONS

ACTS II	Automated Case Tracking System II
ANES	American National Election Studies
ATT	average treatment effect for the treated
CCES	Cooperative Congressional Election Study
CPS	Current Population Survey
DMV	Department of Motor Vehicles
DOJ	Department of Justice

EAC	Election Assistance Commission
EAVS	Election Administration and Voting Survey
EOUSA	Executive Office for United States Attorneys
FJC	Federal Judicial Center
HAVA	Help America Vote Act
ID	identification
IDB	Integrated Database
LIONS	Legal Information Office Network System
MOV	margin of victory
NVRA	National Voter Registration Act
PACER	Public Access to Court Electronic Records
UOCAVA	Uniformed and Overseas Citizens Absentee Voting Act
USEP	United States Elections Project
USSC	United States Sentencing Commission

* * *

September 19, 2014

The Honorable Patrick Leahy
Chairman
Committee on the Judiciary
United States Senate

The Honorable Richard Durbin
Chairman
Subcommittee on the Constitution, Civil Rights and Human Rights
Committee on the Judiciary
United States Senate

The Honorable Charles Schumer
United States Senate

The Honorable Bernard Sanders
United States Senate

The Honorable Bill Nelson
United States Senate

As of June 2014, 33 states had enacted requirements for all eligible voters to show identification (ID) before casting a ballot at the polls on Election Day.[1] The authority to regulate elections in the United States is shared by federal, state, and local officials, contributing to the prevalence and diversity of these laws. Deriving its authority from various constitutional sources, depending upon the type of election, Congress has passed legislation addressing major functional areas in the voting process such as voter registration and prohibitions against discriminatory voting practices.[2] Nevertheless, the responsibility for the administration of state and federal elections resides at the state level, and state statutes regulate various aspects of elections, including registration and Election Day procedures. Within each state, responsibility for managing, planning, and conducting elections is largely a local process, residing with about 10,500 local election jurisdictions nationwide.

In 2002, Congress passed the Help America Vote Act (HAVA) in response to problems reported during the 2000 presidential election with respect to voter registration lists, absentee ballots, ballot counting, and antiquated voting systems.[3] Among other provisions, HAVA required states to request identification from first-time voters who register by mail, either when they register to vote or when they cast a ballot for the first time. HAVA also required states to permit individuals to vote a provisional ballot if they do not have the requisite identification or if they are not on the official list of registered voters. In the 12 years since Congress passed HAVA, states have implemented major election reforms, amended their election codes, or made other changes to their election procedures in order to comply with HAVA's provisions, including those related to voter ID for first-time voters. Numerous states have enacted additional laws to address how an individual may register to vote or cast a ballot.[4] In particular, many states have made substantive changes to their election codes or procedures related to voter ID requirements beyond those established by HAVA. Proponents of these ID requirements suggest that they may help prevent voter fraud and improve voter confidence in the election system, while opponents suggest that the requirements may create an undue burden for some voters.

In October 2012, we issued a report on state voter ID requirements for all eligible voters, including requirements to show identification prior to voting at the polls on Election Day and the types of documents that satisfy these requirements, provisions for no-excuse absentee voting by mail and in-person early voting, and requirements for voter registration drives conducted by nongovernmental organizations (third parties), among other things.[5]

You asked us to review the implications for voters of changes in state voter ID requirements, such as potential costs to voters and any effect on voter turnout for elections. This report addresses the following questions:

- What does available literature indicate about the proportion of voters who have selected ID documents, and what are the direct costs to voters to obtain documents needed to satisfy state voter ID requirements?
- What do existing studies indicate about how, if at all, voter ID laws have affected turnout?
- What does our analysis of available data indicate about how, if at all, changes in voter ID laws have affected turnout in selected states?
- To what extent were provisional ballots cast because of ID reasons and counted in two selected states during the 2012 election, and how did provisional ballot use in those states change after the adoption of voter ID laws?
- What challenges, if any, exist in using available information at the federal and state levels to estimate the incidence of in-person voter fraud?

In addition, we reviewed information related to the demographic characteristics of voters who voted and registered through different methods. This information can be found in appendix I.

To identify what available literature indicates about proportions of voters who have selected ID documents, we conducted a literature review to identify relevant studies. We identified 10 studies that estimate selected ID ownership rates through a review of online databases that catalog legal proceedings, peer-reviewed journal articles, conference proceedings, and research institute publications. Two GAO social scientists reviewed the 10 studies and determined that the design, implementation, and analyses of the studies were sufficiently sound to support the studies' results and conclusions based on generally accepted social science principles. To determine the direct costs to voters to obtain selected documents required to satisfy state voter ID requirements, we first reviewed state statutes and legislative websites to identify those states with requirements for all eligible voters to present identification documents that fall into one of three categories (1) photo only, government issued; (2) photo only, can be non-government issued; (3) non-photo, government issued.[6] We excluded states that allow all voters without ID to affirm their own identity at the polling place in order to cast a regular ballot, since there would be no cost to the voter. We also excluded states that allow non-photo, non-government forms of identification because these costs can vary widely and are difficult to obtain.[7] As of June 2014, we identified 17 states that met these criteria.[8] We reviewed state statutes, information provided by states to voters, and relevant state websites to identify acceptable types of voter ID in each state and the price for each selected ID. We confirmed price information for selected IDs with state officials to ensure accuracy.

To identify what existing studies indicate about how voter ID laws have affected turnout in selected states, if at all, we reviewed the literature on this topic. Specifically, we identified 10 studies that estimate the effect of voter ID laws on turnout. We identified these studies through a search of various online databases that catalog legal proceedings, peer-reviewed journal articles, conference proceedings, and research institute publications. Two GAO social scientists and a GAO statistician reviewed each of the 10 studies and determined that the design, implementation, and analyses of the studies were sufficiently sound to support the studies' results and conclusions based on generally accepted social science principles.

For our evaluation of available data to determine how, if at all, voter ID laws have affected turnout in selected states, we used a quasi- experimental approach. This approach is a type of policy evaluation that compares how an outcome changes over time in a "treatment" group that adopted a new policy, as compared with a "comparison" group that did not make the same change. As in controlled experiments, researchers using this approach analyze separate groups before and after one group changed a policy. We compared changes in voter turnout from the 2008 to the 2012 general election—the most recent general election cycle—in selected treatment states that implemented changes to voter ID requirements (Kansas and Tennessee) with selected comparison states that did not implement changes to their voter ID requirements (Alabama, Arkansas, Delaware, and Maine) during that time period. Our quasi-experimental comparison group design accounts for factors other than voter ID requirements that could affect voter turnout. We selected Kansas and Tennessee from among 14 potential treatment states and Alabama, Arkansas, Delaware, and Maine from among 35 potential comparison states. In making these selections, we took steps to ensure that states included in our analysis did not have other factors present in their election environments that may have significantly affected turnout. For example, we selected treatment and comparison states that had the following characteristics: did not experience contemporaneous changes to other election laws that may have significantly affected voter turnout on Election Day; had presidential general elections where the margin of victory did not substantially change from 2008 to 2012 and all other statewide elections, such as U.S. Senate races, were non-competitive in both the 2008 and 2012 general elections; ballot questions were not present, noncompetitive, or similarly competitive in both elections within a state; and had official voter history data that were sufficiently reliable for the purposes of our analysis.[9] We used three data sources for our analysis of voter ID requirement effects on voter turnout: official voter records in the United States Elections Project's (USEP) database; official voter records enhanced for improved accuracy by a vendor; and survey responses in the Current Population Survey (CPS).[10] For each of these sources, we reviewed documentation describing steps taken by the data managers to ensure data reliability and tested the data for anomalies that could indicate reliability concerns. We found each of the three sets of data sufficiently reliable for the purposes of our review. The results of our analysis of voter ID requirement effects on voter turnout cannot be generalized beyond Kansas and Tennessee. We provide additional details on the scope and steps of our analysis later in this report.

To determine how frequently provisional ballots were cast because of ID reasons and counted during the 2012 election for Kansas and Tennessee, the 2 selected states that modified voter ID requirements, we analyzed data from the Election Assistance Commission's (EAC) Election Administration and Voting Survey (EAVS) on the total number of ballots cast and the total number of provisional ballots cast in the 2012 general elections in those 2 states.[11] We also analyzed 2012 statewide data provided by election officials in the Kansas and Tennessee Secretaries of State offices on the number of provisional ballots cast for ID reasons and the number of provisional ballots cast for ID reasons that were counted, by state.[12] To determine how provisional ballot use in Kansas and Tennessee changed after those states' voter ID laws were changed, we analyzed EAVS data on the total number of ballots cast and the total number of provisional ballots cast in the 2008 and 2012 general elections in Kansas and Tennessee and in the 4 comparison states selected for objective two. We used these data to calculate the provisional ballot usage rate by state in 2008 and 2012. To assess the reliability of the 2008 and 2012 EAVS data as well as data provided to us by Kansas and Tennessee election officials, we analyzed the completeness of EAVS provisional ballot data for 2008 and 2012 and interviewed EAC officials and officials from the Kansas and Tennessee Secretaries of State offices regarding their data collection and quality control processes. We found the data to be sufficiently reliable for the purposes of our review. Our findings on provisional ballots are not generalizable beyond our specific treatment and comparison states.

To determine what challenges, if any, exist in using available information at the federal and state levels to estimate the incidence of in-person voter fraud, we first developed a standard definition of in-person voter fraud by analyzing relevant court cases to determine how courts have characterized in-person voter fraud, as well as activities that are not considered to be encompassed by the term.[13] For the purposes of this report, we have defined in-person voter fraud as involving a person who (1) attempts to vote or votes; (2) in person at the polling place; and (3) asserts an identity that is not the person's own, whether it be that of a fictional registered voter, dead registered voter, a false identity, or whether the voter uses a fraudulent identification. We shared our definition with Department of Justice (DOJ) and state election officials and integrated their feedback, as appropriate. We also conducted a literature review of relevant academic literature, organizational studies, peer- reviewed journals, books, and other regularly cited research published from 2004 through April 2014 to identify the extent to which these sources contain data on in-person voter fraud.[14] We identified and reviewed more than 300 studies to determine whether they (1) contained data related to in-person voter fraud and (2) included a description of the methodology used for collecting the data related to in-person voter fraud.[15] We identified five studies that met these criteria. Two GAO analysts and, as applicable, a GAO statistician reviewed each of the five studies and determined that the design, implementation, and analyses of the studies were sufficiently sound to support the studies' results and conclusions based on generally accepted social science principles. We found that these studies used various sources and methodologies in their efforts to provide estimates on in-person voter fraud.

At the federal level, we identified federal databases that contain information on investigations, prosecutions, and convictions of federal crimes, including the Legal Information Office Network System (LIONS) database, managed by DOJ's Executive Office for United States Attorneys (EOUSA); the Automated Case Tracking System II (ACTS II) database, managed by DOJ's Criminal Division; the Integrated Database, managed by the Federal Judicial Center (FJC) in the federal judiciary; and the Oracle database managed by the United States Sentencing Commission (USSC) in the federal judiciary.[16] We reviewed each database's associated codebooks and interviewed relevant federal officials from the four agencies who manage the databases to understand how, if at all, cases of in-person voter fraud are categorized and tracked within each database. On the basis of interviews with agency officials and the review of relevant court cases we conducted to develop a definition in-person voter fraud, we compiled a list of 14 possible federal statutory provisions under which our definition of in-person voter fraud could be prosecuted (see app. II).

At the state level, we interviewed election officials in 46 states and the District of Columbia.[17] We corroborated the information we gathered through these interviews by reviewing state statutes related to election fraud and in-person voter fraud and the documentation that officials from 27 states provided to us related to the incidence of election fraud. We reviewed the format and content of the documentation provided, as well as testimonial evidence from the original interviews and subsequent correspondence with state officials. This review allowed us to better understand the way in which the information was collected and compiled, and to identify any potential limitations associated with the provided information. We also reviewed how responsibility for addressing election fraud was distributed among various state and local agencies, in an effort to determine whether the information provided by the state represented a complete account of the in-person voter fraud allegations, investigations, prosecutions, or convictions that occurred within the state. More information on our objectives, scope, and methodology can be found in appendix II.

We conducted this performance audit from January 2013 to August 2014 in accordance with generally accepted government auditing standards. Those standards require that we plan and perform the audit to obtain sufficient, appropriate evidence to provide a reasonable basis for our findings and conclusions based on our audit objectives. We believe that the evidence obtained provides a reasonable basis for our findings and conclusions based on our audit objectives.

Background

The basic goal of the election system in the United States is that all eligible voters have the opportunity to cast their votes and have their valid ballots counted accurately. All levels of government share responsibility in the U.S. election process, and the election system is highly decentralized. States are responsible for the administration of their own elections as well as federal elections. Accordingly, states regulate various aspects of elections including registration procedures, absentee voting requirements, early voting requirements, establishment of polling places, provision of Election Day workers, testing and certification of voting equipment, and counting and certification of the vote.[18] At the federal level, Congress has the authority to affect the administration of elections in certain ways. Congress' authority to regulate elections derives from various constitutional sources, depending on the type of election.[19] Congress has enacted federal legislation to address voter registration, voter identification, absentee voting, accessibility provisions for the elderly and handicapped, and prohibitions against discriminatory practices, among other issues.

Further, just as responsibility for the overall U.S. election process is shared among various levels of government, the responsibility for identifying and investigating allegations of fraud may be shared by local, state, and federal authorities. Election fraud allegations may be reported to local, county, or state election officials; law enforcement; or county or state attorneys, among others. Depending on the state, any of a number of authorities may have, or share, jurisdiction to investigate and prosecute the allegations. Allegations of election fraud may also be investigated and prosecuted at the federal level.

Each of the 50 states and the District of Columbia has a unique electoral system, but the voting process in most states involves voter registration, absentee and early voting, Election Day voting, provisional voting, and vote counting and certification. See figure 1 for a description of this process.

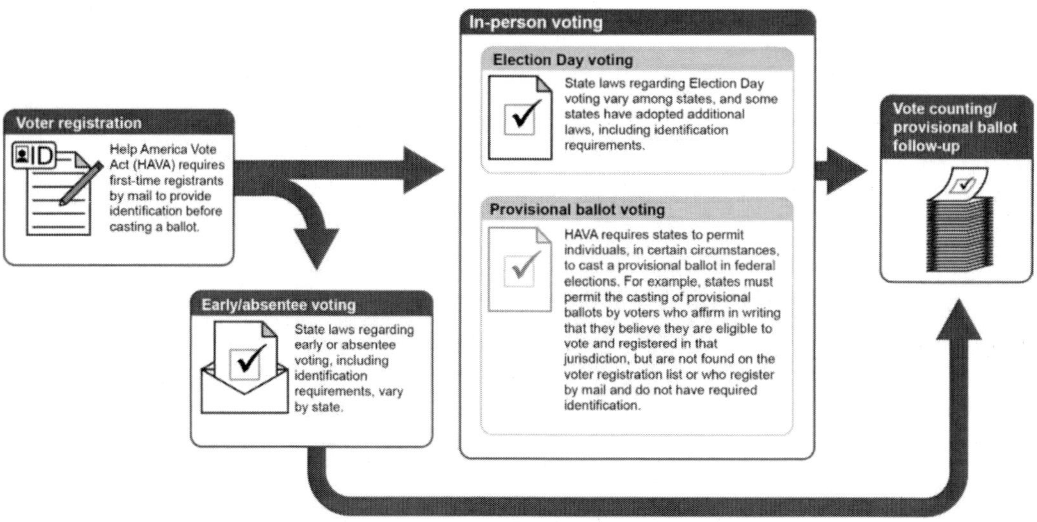

Source: GAO. | GAO-14-634.

Figure 1. The Voting Process.

Registration

States have established a variety of requirements for individuals to present identification when they register to vote. With the exception of North Dakota, all states and the District of Columbia generally require citizens to register before voting. Typically, state eligibility provisions require, at minimum, that a person be a U.S. citizen, at least 18 years of age, and a resident of the state, with some states requiring a minimum residency period. Citizens apply to register to vote in various ways, such as at motor vehicle agencies, by mail, at local voter registrar offices, or through third-parties.[20] Election officials process registration applications and compile and maintain the list of registered voters to be used throughout the administration of an election.

Although voter registration is not a federal requirement, Congress has passed two laws that regulate voter registration in those states that require it. The National Voter Registration Act of 1993 (NVRA), also known as the "motor voter" law, established registration procedures designed, in part, to "increase the number of eligible citizens who register to vote in elections for Federal office. . . protect the integrity of the electoral process . . . [and] ensure that accurate and current voter registration rolls are maintained."[21] The NVRA expanded the number of locations and opportunities for eligible citizens to apply to register to vote. In addition to any other method of voter registration provided for under state law, the NVRA prescribes three methods of registering voters for federal elections: (1) when they obtain a driver's license, (2) by mail using the federal voter registration form provided by the EAC, or (3) at offices that provide public assistance and services to persons with disabilities and other state agencies and offices.[22] In addition to accepting the federal mail-in voter registration form, states may develop and use their own mail-in voter registration forms provided that the form meets specified criteria.[23] For example, all registration forms must include an attestation by the applicant that he or she meets eligibility requirements and must be signed under the penalty of perjury.

In 2002, Congress passed HAVA, which requires states to collect specified types of identification from certain first-time voters who register by mail and establish a single, uniform, statewide, computerized voter registration list for conducting elections for federal office.[24] Under HAVA, states must require that registrants who apply by mail and who have not previously voted in a federal election in the state provide certain specified types of identification with their mail application, and if they do not provide such identification with their application, these first-time mail registrants are to provide the identification at the polls or a copy of such identification when voting by mail.[25] Under HAVA, in order not to show identification when voting, mail registrants must have provided either their driver's license number or at least the last four digits of their Social Security number when applying to register, which must match with an existing state identification record; or have provided in their application a copy of the following specified identification:

- a current and valid photo identification; or
- a copy of a current utility bill, bank statement, government check, paycheck, or other government documentation that shows the name and address of the voter.[26]

HAVA specifies that these are minimum requirements and should not be construed to prevent states from establishing election administration requirements that are stricter than

HAVA requirements as long as they are not inconsistent with certain other specified provisions.[27]

Voting

Absentee Voting or Early Voting

States have established alternatives for voters to cast a ballot other than at the polls on Election Day, including absentee voting and early voting.[28] All states and the District of Columbia have provisions allowing voters to cast their ballots before Election Day by voting absentee, with variations on who may vote absentee, whether the voter needs to provide an excuse, and the time frames for applying for and submitting absentee ballots.[29] As of the 2012 general election, most states—35 and the District of Columbia—provided an opportunity for voters to cast a ballot prior to Election Day without providing an excuse, either by no-excuse absentee voting or early voting, or both.[30] Some states also permitted registered voters to apply for an absentee ballot on a permanent basis so those voters automatically receive an absentee ballot in the mail prior to every election without providing an excuse or reason for voting absentee.

Voters who seek to cast an absentee ballot by mail may be subject to identification requirements. As we reported in October 2012, in some states, voters may be required to submit identifying information or a copy of acceptable identification along with their absentee ballot application, with their absentee ballot, or both.[31] The identifying information that voters are required to provide when voting absentee varies—with some states requiring that voters provide documentary identification, such as a driver's license number, Social Security number, or copy of an acceptable document, and other states requiring information that does not involve an underlying document, such as the voter's signature or date of birth.

In addition to allowing absentee voting, some states allow early voting. In general, early voting allows voters from any precinct in the jurisdiction to cast their votes in person without providing an excuse before Election Day either at one specific location or at one of several locations. Voters who choose to vote in-person during the designated early voting period may be subject to the same state voter identification requirements as voters who vote in-person on Election Day. As we reported in January 2012, implementation and characteristics of early voting—such as the dates, times, and locations—also vary among states, and in some cases, among the jurisdictions within a state.[32] Information on the demographic characteristics of early voters can be found in appendix I.

In-Person Voting on Election Day

As of June 2014, 33 states had enacted requirements for voters to show some form of ID at the polls on Election Day.[33] Such ID requirements have been cited as an attempt to help ensure the integrity of the voting process on Election Day at the polls in the event that ineligible voters may attempt to vote. Fourteen states and the District of Columbia do not have documentary identification requirements.[34] Figure 2 shows the year in which states enacted identification requirements since HAVA was enacted, as well as the year when states made changes to their identification requirements that resulted in a change in the type of acceptable ID (i.e., photo or non-photo) or the acceptable issuing authority (i.e., generally government-issued or nongovernment-issued).[35]

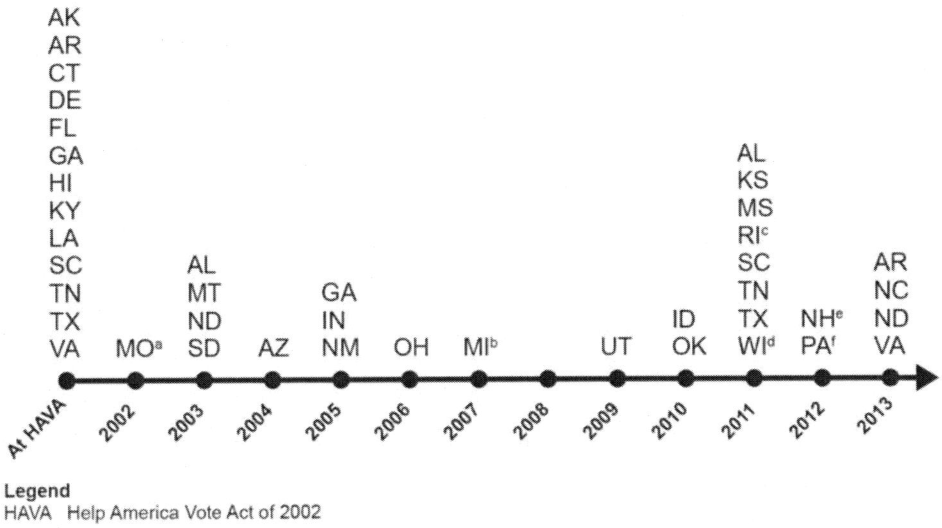

Source: GAO analysis of state statutes. | GAO-14-634.

Notes: Dates listed are generally when states enacted provisions, as opposed to when provisions went into effect or are legislated to go into effect. "At HAVA" indicates provisions were in effect at the time HAVA was enacted. States are repeated when they enacted laws that changed the type of document accepted (non-photo to photo) or acceptable issuing authority (nongovernment to generally government issued only). Colorado, Oregon and Washington vote-by-mail states and are not included in this figure.

[a] In 2006, Missouri also enacted a voter ID requirement that required government-issued photo identification to vote, but that provision was held to be unconstitutional by the Missouri Supreme Court and is no longer in effect.

[b] Michigan's voter ID law was enacted prior to HAVA, but due to an opinion by the Michigan Attorney General concluding that the requirement was unconstitutional, it was not enforced until after it was held to be constitutional by the Supreme Court of Michigan in 2007.

[c] Rhode Island's voter ID law, enacted in 2011, legislated additional requirements to go into effect in 2014. These changes will require photo identification only, as opposed to allowing documents that do not include a photograph, such as a birth certificate.

[d] Wisconsin enacted a new voter ID law that as of June 2014 was enjoined by federal and Wisconsin state courts.

[e] New Hampshire's voter ID law, which was enacted in 2012 and amended in 2013, provides for additional changes to go into effect in 2015.

[f] Pennsylvania's voter ID law was partially in effect for the 2012 election but has been permanently enjoined by the Pennsylvania Commonwealth Court. The Pennsylvania Governor issued a statement that the commonwealth will not pursue an appeal to the Pennsylvania Supreme Court to overturn the Commonwealth Court's decision.

Figure 2. States that Enacted Identification Requirements or Changed Acceptable Type of Document or Issuing Authority, by Year, from 2002 through 2013.

Of those states that have enacted voter ID laws beyond those required by HAVA, the forms of acceptable ID vary. Specifically, 20 states have enacted requirements that the ID provided contain a photograph of the voter, whereas 13 states have enacted requirements for a voter to provide identifying documentation that does not contain a photograph, such as the voter's Social Security card or a utility bill or a bank statement with the voter's name and address on it.[36] See figure 3 for a map of states that have enacted voter identification requirements, which may be in effect or scheduled to go into effect pursuant to legislation, regardless of litigation status, as of June 2014.

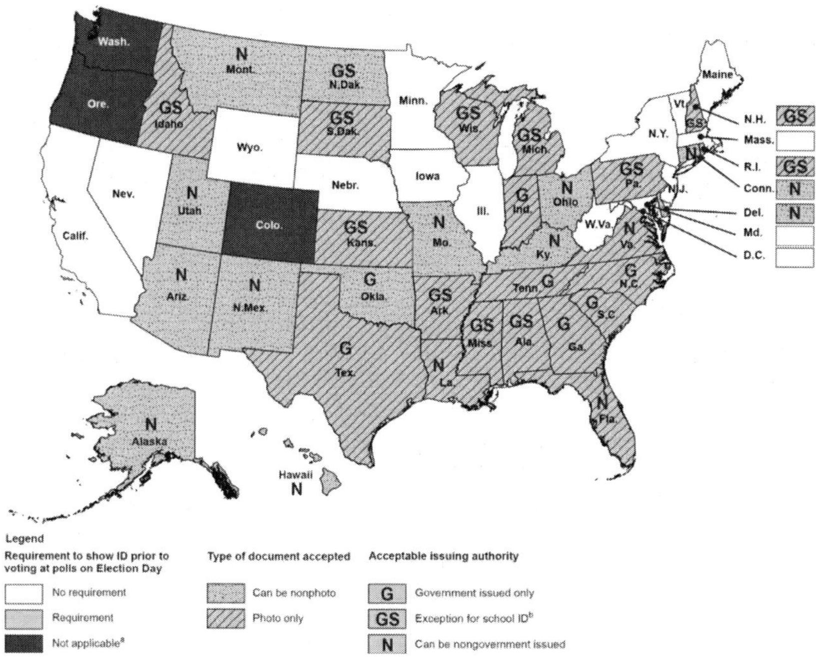

Source: GAO analysis of state statutes; Map Resources (map). | GAO-14-634.

Notes: This map includes states with enacted requirements that are currently in effect or scheduled to go into effect by legislation, regardless of the status of litigation. Some state laws may be enjoined pursuant to court order. In particular, as of June 2014, Pennsylvania's ID law was enjoined, Applewhite v. Commonwealth, 2014 WL 184988 (Pa. Commw. Ct. Jan. 17, 2014), as was Wisconsin's, Frank v. Walker, 2014 WL 1775432 (E.D. Wis. Apr. 29, 2104). New Hampshire's and North Carolina's new voter ID laws are scheduled to go into effect in 2015 and 2016, respectively.

[a] Colorado, Oregon and Washington are vote-by-mail states, but laws in these states require that there be places for voters to cast a ballot in person. Colorado law provides that voters who do not have acceptable identification may cast a provisional ballot. If it is verified that a voter who cast a provisional ballot is eligible to vote based on information the voter provided with the provisional ballot and a check of state databases, the provisional ballot will be counted. Oregon does not have identification requirements for voters who cast a ballot by mail or in person. Washington law has identification requirements applicable to voters who cast a ballot in-person, requiring that voters provide photo identification, or vote by provisional ballot (which will be counted if the signature on the ballot declaration matches the signature in the voter's registration record). For voters who cast a ballot by mail, the ballot will be counted if the signature on the ballot declaration matches the signature in the voter's registration record; there are no additional documentary identification requirements.

[b] In certain states, this exception applies to student IDs only, whereas in other states any identification issued by an education institution may be acceptable (e.g., employee ID). North Dakota additionally provides an exception for a long term care identification certificate (provided by a North Dakota facility) and Pennsylvania provides an exception for identification issued by a Pennsylvania care facility.

Figure 3. Map of States that Have Enacted Voter Identification (ID) Requirements, as of June 2014.

Provisional Ballots

Under HAVA, states are required to permit individuals, under certain circumstances, to cast a provisional ballot in federal elections. For example, voters who claim to be eligible to vote and registered in the jurisdiction they desire to vote in but whose names do not appear on the polling place registration list are to be allowed to cast provisional ballots in a federal election. In addition, if a voter does not have the requisite ID at the polls, HAVA requires that the voter be allowed to cast a provisional ballot. Under HAVA, election officials receiving provisional voter information are to determine whether such individuals are eligible to vote under state law. If an individual is determined to be eligible, HAVA specifies that such individual's provisional ballot be counted as a vote in that election in accordance with state law.

In states with voter ID requirements, there is variety in how states administer the provisional ballot processes when a voter does not have acceptable ID, including the way in which states determine whether the ballot will be counted. Of the 33 states that have an identification requirement for all eligible voters, 18 provide casting a provisional ballot as the only process for voters without acceptable identification.[37] Of these 18 states, 15 require some or all voters to provide the election authority with acceptable identification within a specified time period after the election as the only means to have the provisional ballot counted.[38]

Post-election Activities

Following the close of the polls on Election Day, election officials and poll workers complete steps such as securing equipment and ballots, transferring votes to a central location for counting and determining the outcome of the election. Votes counted include those cast on Election Day, absentee ballots, early votes (where applicable), and provisional ballots. While preliminary results are available usually by the evening of Election Day, the certified results are generally not available until days later.

Studies Show That Most Registered Voters Have State- Issued IDs; Direct Costs to Obtain Such IDs Vary among States

Studies Report that Majority of Registered Voters Have a Driver's License or State-Issued ID; ID Ownership Rates Vary by Race and Ethnic Group

We reviewed 10 studies that estimated rates of ownership of driver's licenses or state-issued IDs in selected states or nationwide.[39] Nine of these studies of driver's license and state ID ownership in selected states and the one nationwide survey showed that, depending upon the study, estimated ownership rates among registered voters ranged from 84 to 95 percent, as shown in table 1.[40] For example, in one of the studies, the North Carolina State Board of Elections estimated that up to 95 percent of registered voters statewide had a driver's license or state-issued ID as of March 2013, based on an analysis the board completed that matched voter registration and Department of Motor Vehicles (DMV) records.[41] In another study, focused on Indiana, researchers used a survey of registered voters and, according to that survey, estimated that 84 percent of registered voters statewide had a valid photo ID that could be used for voting purposes as of October 2007.[42] Three of the 10 studies also estimated ownership of selected IDs among individuals eligible to vote, but not necessarily registered to vote, and 2 of 3 reported slightly lower ID ownership rates among that population as compared with ownership rates for registered voters. The 10 studies we reviewed used either database queries or surveys to estimate selected ID ownership rates. Specifically, 6 of the 10 studies relied upon database queries where the researchers matched voter registration records to ID databases, such as driver's license and state ID databases, to estimate ID ownership rates. Four of the 10 studies used surveys to elicit responses on ID ownership from potential voters.

As shown in Table 1, estimates of ID ownership rates among racial and ethnic groups varied across the nine studies that analyzed such data. For example, according to seven of the studies, ID ownership among African- American registered voters was lower than among White registered voters in the population evaluated—nationwide, Georgia, Indiana, South Carolina, Texas, Wisconsin statewide, and Milwaukee County in Wisconsin. The eighth study found similar rates of ID ownership statewide between African-Americans and Whites in Pennsylvania, and the ninth study did not estimate rates of ownership among these demographic groups in North Carolina. ID ownership rates among Hispanic registered voters were also estimated to be lower than those of White registered voters in seven of the studies. The remaining three studies did not provide estimates of ID ownership rates among Hispanic registered voters.

Three studies included analysis that identified various factors that may affect ID ownership rates; the remaining studies did not provide analysis of factors potentially associated with ID ownership. The studies that analyzed factors reported several findings, including the following:

- **Transportation.** Bareto and others (2012) identified one factor that could affect ID ownership rates as access to transportation. In Pennsylvania, among eligible voters, 41.6 percent of individuals who reported that they do not have regular access to any kind of transportation reported lacking a valid photo ID, and 29.7 percent of those who reported not having a car, but reported access to some other kind of transportation, such as a bus, bicycle, or train, also reported lacking a valid ID. In comparison, 11.1 percent of those who reported having regular access to a car also reported lacking a valid ID.
- **Valid or expired IDs.** Bareto and others (2012) conducted analyses to determine if the rate of ownership of IDs was affected by whether respondents reported that their ID was valid or had expired. The authors found that large percentages of eligible voters in Pennsylvania stated in survey responses that they owned photo ID (98.6 percent). However, when asked follow-up questions about whether the photo ID had an expiration date and was current, the percentage of eligible voters with a non-

expired photo ID dropped to 87 percent. Similarly, Stewart (2013) reported that estimated rates of reported driver's license ownership declined by 11 percent nationwide (from 91 to 80 percent) when considering if the license was expired, or showed a different name or address than the one they had registered under.

- **Possession of underlying documents**. Bareto and others (2012) identified possession of required underlying documents as a factor that may affect ID ownership rates. According to their analysis of survey responses, an estimated 1.7 million eligible Pennsylvanians lacked necessary documentation to obtain valid photo ID as of July 2012. Necessary documentation included a proof of citizenship, identity, and Pennsylvania residency. Similarly, Bareto and Sanchez (2012) reported that an estimated 92,000 eligible voters in Milwaukee County, Wisconsin lacked the necessary documentary proof of citizenship, identity, and residency needed to apply for a Wisconsin driver's license or state ID card.

Table 1. Summary of Findings from Studies That Estimate Selected Identification (ID) Ownership

Study author and date published	Scope	Methods	Results: ID ownership overall[a]	Results: ID ownership among population sub-groups[b]
Ansolabehere. June 2012	Texas	Database queries matching records of registered voters to driver's license/ state ID card or gun permit records; results as of April 2012	86 percent of all registered voters had driver's license, state ID card, or gun permit	Holders of driver's license, state ID card, or gun permits: • 89 percent of registered Whites • 83 percent of registered Hispanics • 79 percent of registered African-Americans
Barreto, Nuño, and Sanchez. January 2009	Indiana	Survey of registered voters and adult non-registered residents, completed October 2007	• 84 percent of all registered voters had valid photo IDc • 81 percent of all eligible adults had valid photo ID	• 85 percent of all registered White voters and 83 percent of eligible White adults had valid photo ID • 81 percent of all registered African-American voters and 72 percent of eligible African-American adults had valid photo ID
Barreto and Sanchez. April 2012	Milwaukee County, WI	Survey of registered voters and adult non-registered residents, completed January 2012	91 percent of all registered and 91 percent of eligible voters had acceptable, non-expired photo ID[f]	• 94 percent of registered White and 93 percent of eligible White voters had acceptable, non-expired photo ID • 85 percent of registered African-American and 87 percent of eligible African-Americanj voters had acceptable, non-expired photo ID • 89 percent of registered Latino and 85 percent of eligible Latino voters had acceptable, non-expired photo ID

Table 1. (Continued)

Study author and date published	Scope	Methods	Results: ID ownership overall[a]	Results: ID ownership among population sub-groups[b]
Barreto, Sanchez, and Walker. July 2012	Pennsylvania	Survey of registered voters and adult non-registered residents, completed July 2012	• 87 percent of registered voters had valid photo ID[d] • 86 percent of eligible voters had valid photo ID	• 88 percent of registered and 86 percent of eligible Whites had valid photo ID • 86 percent of registered and 87 percent of eligible African-Americans had valid photo ID[e] • 83 percent of registered and 82 percent of eligible Hispanics had valid photo ID[e]
Beatty. April 2012	Wisconsin	Database queries matching records of DMV-issued driver's licenses and state ID cards with registered voter records[g]	89 percent of all registered voters had a valid driver's license or state ID	• 91 percent of White registered voters had a valid driver's license or state ID card • 84 percent of African-American registered voters had a valid driver's license or state ID card[e] • 75 percent of Hispanic registered voters had a valid driver's license or state ID carde • 84 percent of Asian-American registered voters had a valid driver's license or state ID card[e] • 94 percent of Native American registered voters had a valid driver's license or state ID card[e]
Bullock III and Hood III. March 2007	Georgia	Database queries matching records of DMV-issued photo ID (driver's license and state ID cards) with registered voter records; results as of October 2006	93 percent of all registered voters had valid identification	Probability of registered voter not possessing a valid driver's license or state ID card, by race: • White: 0.037 • African-American: 0.068e • Hispanic: 0.073[e] • Asian-American: 0.042[e]
Hood III. May 2012	Wisconsin	Database queries matching records of DMV-issued driver's licenses and state ID cards with registered voter records; results as of June 2012	91 percent of all registered voters had valid identification	Did not analyze results by population sub-groups
North Carolina State Board of Elections. April 2013	North Carolina	Database queries matching records of DMV-issued driver's licenses and state ID cards	95 percent of records matchedh	Numbers of registered voters who did not match ID records after all queries, by race (rates not provided in study): • White: 172,613

Study author and date published	Scope	Methods	Results: ID ownership overall[a]	Results: ID ownership among population sub-groups[b]
		with registered voter records; results as of March 2013		• African-American: 107,681 • Asian-American: 4,067 • Native American or Alaska Native: 3,773 • Other: 7,663 • Two or more races: 4,383 Undesignated: 18,463
Stewart. June 2012	South Carolina	Database queries matching records of DMV-issued driver's licenses and state ID cards, and passport and military IDs with registered voter records; results as of April 2012	93 percent of active registered voters possessed a valid driver's license or state ID card; 95 percent of active registered voters possessed a valid driver's license, state ID card, passport, or military ID	Percentage of active registered voters possessing a valid driver's license or state ID card, by race: • White: 94.5 percent • African American: 90.5 percent • Hispanic: 90.0 percent • Native American: 89.9 percent • Mixed: 85.6 percent • Other: 87.1 percent Percentage of active registered voters possessing a valid driver's license, state ID card, passport, or military ID, by race: • White: 96.1 percent • African-American: 91.7 percente • Hispanic: 93.3 percente • Native American: 91.7 percente • Mixed: 87.7 percente • Other: 91.6 percente
Stewart. Fall 2013	Nationwide	Survey of registered voters in each state and the District of Columbia March 2012	91 percent of registered voters had driver's license; 80 percent had valid license; 41 percent of registered voters had passport; 35 percent had valid passporti	• 93 percent of White registered voters had any driver's license, and 84 percent had a valid license • 79 percent of African American registered voters had any driver's license, and 63 percent had a valid license • 90 percent of Hispanic registered voters had any license, and 73 percent had a valid license • 41 percent of White registered voters had any passport, and 35 percent had a valid passport • 28 percent of African-American registered voters had any passport, and 25 percent had a valid passport • 49 percent of Hispanic registered voters had any passport, and 42 percent had a valid passport

Source: GAO analysis of studies that estimate ID ownership rates. | GAO-14-634

Notes: Full citations for these studies are listed in appendix III.

[a] Unless otherwise noted, all estimates are significant at least at the 0.05 level of statistical significance.

[b] Unless otherwise noted, all sub-group estimates and differences between White and other racial or ethnic groups are significant at least at the 0.05 level of statistical significance.

[c] Valid photo ID in Indiana, as defined in the survey, included a current driver's license, state ID card, or other government issued photo ID that includes the voter's full legal name.

[d] Valid photo ID in Pennsylvania, as defined in the survey, included non-expired photo IDs that listed the voter's name substantially conforming to the name on the voter registration roll.

[e] According to the study, difference from White significance not reported.

[f] Acceptable, non-expired photo ID in Wisconsin, as defined in the survey, included driver's license, state ID, military ID and passport, if they were current or had expired only after the previous statewide general election.

[g] The date of the database queries is not evident in the study.

[h] In order to determine the voters who have a North Carolina DMV-issued photo ID, the State Board of Elections used database queries to compare voter records with records in the North Carolina Department of Motor Vehicles customer database. The board used 29 queries, such as matches based on exact first and last name and Social Security number or driver's license number and date of birth. Using these queries, as voters were matched with records in the North Carolina Department of Motor Vehicles database, their records were removed from further queries, and only the remaining unmatched State Board of Elections records were used in subsequent queries. The State Board of Elections reported that 81 percent of records matched based on the first query only—exact first and last name and North Carolina Department of Motor Vehicles customer number—and 95 percent of records matched based on the end result of completing all 29 queries.

[i] Valid license is defined in this study as a driver's license that had not expired, showed the name under which the voter was registered, and listed the voter's current address. Valid passport is defined as one that had not expired and showed the name under which the voter was registered. The researchers determined voters with valid and non-valid driver's licenses and passports by including survey questions that asked respondents about each of these circumstances.

The studies that estimate ID ownership rates are subject to limitations, based on our review. First, the results of the nine state-level studies cannot be generalized beyond the states evaluated, as the results of those studies were based on state-specific data. Conversely, the remaining study, which was based on a nationwide survey, provides an estimate for the nation as a whole, but not for individual states. A second limitation is specific to those studies that use surveys to estimate ownership rates. Surveys of the public where respondents are asked to self-report whether or not they have valid identification, are registered to vote, or have voted are dependent on the extent to which respondents provide accurate responses, a fact that may lead to misrepresentations.[43] Instead of relying on respondents' self-reporting, in one study we reviewed, the authors attempted to address possible inaccuracies in survey respondents' reports of their voter registration status by obtaining a sample of registered voters from the state's public statewide voter file and cross-checking the list with the Secretary of State's office to verify registration status. Through this effort, the authors were able to validate the sample voters' reported registration status. However, the authors did not similarly validate survey respondents' reports on whether or not they owned valid ID. Studies that match voter registration records with driver's license or state-issued ID records rely on official records rather than potentially inaccurate information provided by survey respondents. However, official lists of registered voters may include registered voters who are ineligible to vote, because of reasons such as moving out of a jurisdiction, death, or a felony conviction. Voter registration records may not reflect these changes in eligibility status.[44]

Direct Costs to Obtain State-Issued ID Vary by State

Of the 33 states that had enacted a voter identification requirement as of June 2014, 17 states have requirements for voters to present photo or government issued ID at the polls prior to voting and do not allow voters to affirm their own identity in order to cast a regular ballot. The costs and requirements to obtain certain forms of ID, including a driver's license, nondriver state ID, or free state ID, vary by state.[45] All 17 states allow a driver's license or state-issued nondriver ID, among the most common types of ID presented to vote, as an acceptable form of ID.[46] Sixteen of the 17 states also provide a free ID to eligible voters.[47] However, there may be costs associated with obtaining the documents citizens must present to obtain a free ID. See figure 4 and appendix IV for more information about state ID requirements and the associated direct costs of selected IDs, as of July 2014.

The direct costs to obtain an ID that meets state voter ID requirements and the terms of acceptable IDs vary by state. Specifically, states may have different licenses based on age of the applicant and may provide a range of options with regard to the length of time a driver's license or other form of ID is valid. States may also charge other associated fees for drivers, which can affect the cost to the voter. For example, drivers in North Carolina pay $32 for an 8 year driver's license while drivers in Rhode Island pay $32 for a driver's license that is valid for a maximum of 5 years and an additional $26.50 fee for the required road test.[48] Citizens seeking to obtain a nondriver ID in Georgia can choose from either a 5- year ID card for $20 or an 8-year ID card for $32, and Kansas offers a 6- year nondriver ID for $14, plus an $8 photo fee.

A voter may be required to present documentation to obtain a driver's license, a nondriver ID, or a free ID. The types of documents that a voter would need to present to obtain a driver's license, a nondriver ID, or a free ID vary by state and could include various combinations of documents. Below we provide some examples:

- To obtain a driver's license in Indiana, a driver must provide various forms of documentation, including proof of identity; identity documents may include a U.S. birth certificate, a U.S. passport, or a U.S. consular report of birth abroad.
- In Kansas, any citizen can obtain a nondriver state ID at the Department of Motor Vehicles by providing proof of identity and Kansas residency.[49]
- To obtain a free ID in Alabama, voters without a photo ID are required to provide a nonphoto ID with full legal name and date of birth, documentation proving they are registered to vote in the state, and documentation showing name and address as reflected in the voter registration record.[50]

In general, examples of types of documents individuals can present to obtain a driver's license, nondriver state ID, or free ID could include a birth certificate, Social Security card, or other proof of identification or residency. Individuals may already have these documents, which can be used for other purposes, such as for enrolling in school, obtaining a passport, and obtaining a marriage certificate, among others. For individuals without these documents, the cost to obtain one of these documents to establish identity varies by state. Table 2 provides information on the costs, as of July 2014, of one type of document—the birth certificate—which, among the 17 states, is a common type of document individuals could present, among others, to obtain a driver's license, non-driver state ID, or free ID.[51]

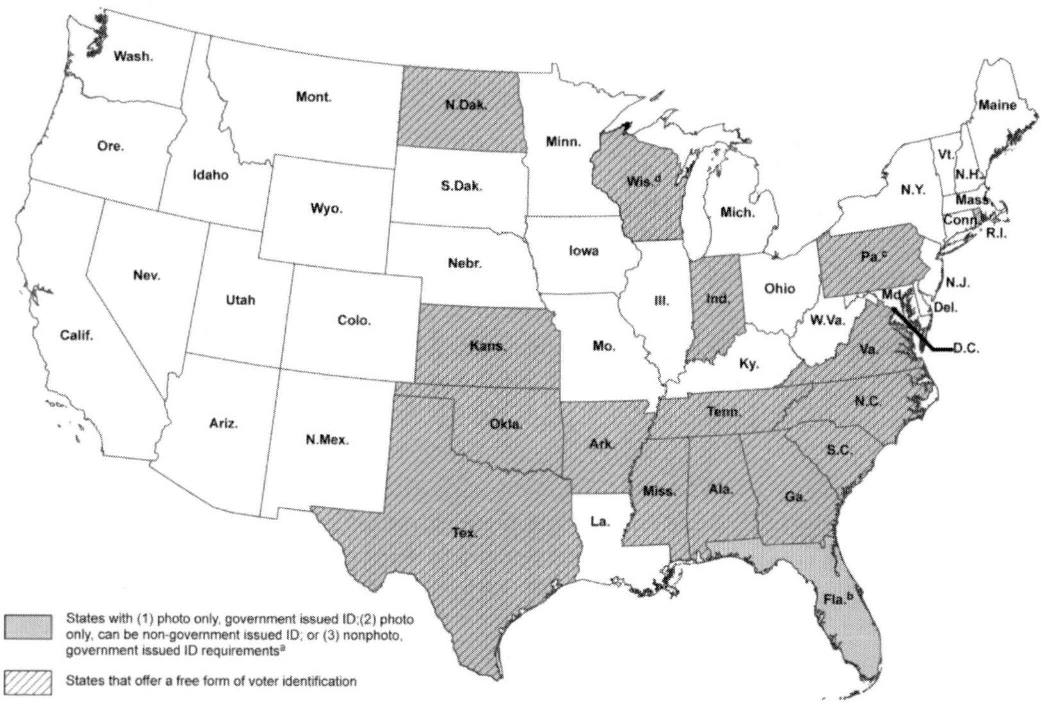

For additional details on Figure 4, please see appendix IV.

Source: GAO analysis of state information and data; Map Resources (map). | GAO-14-634.

Note: States with voter ID requirements that allow all voters to affirm their own identity at the polls and vote a regular ballot were excluded from our analysis.

The "nondriver identification" category does not include nondriver ID issued for voting purposes.

[a] As of June 2014, in effect or legislated to go into effect, regardless of litigation status. Government-issued ID includes states where there is an exception for a school ID.

[b] Florida allows as acceptable identification photo ID that may be nongovernment issued.

[c] Pennsylvania's voter ID law was partially in effect for the 2012 election but has been permanently enjoined by the Pennsylvania Commonwealth Court. Pennsylvania's Governor issued a statement that the commonwealth will not pursue an appeal to the Pennsylvania Supreme Court to overturn the Commonwealth Court's decision.

[d] Wisconsin enacted a new voter ID law that, as of June 2014, was enjoined by federal and Wisconsin state courts.

Figure 4. License and Nondriver State Identification (ID) Costs in Selected States, as of July 2014.

Table 2. Cost to Obtain Birth Certificate by State, as of July 2014

State	Cost of birth certificate
Alabama	$15[a]
Arkansas	$12
Florida	$9
Georgia	$25
Indiana	$10
Kansas	$15[b]
Mississippi	$15
North Carolina	$24
North Dakota	$7
Oklahoma	$15
Pennsylvania	$20
Rhode Island	$20
South Carolina	$12
Tennessee	$8[c]
Texas	$22
Virginia	$12
Wisconsin	$20

Source: GAO analysis of publicly available state birth certificate cost information. | GAO-14-634.

[a] A birth certificate may be provided at no cost for the purposes of obtaining required voter ID in Alabama.

[b] A birth certificate may be provided at no cost for the purposes of obtaining required voter ID in Kansas.

[c] Citizens born in Tennessee before 1949 are required to pay $15 to obtain a birth certificate.

STUDIES GENERALLY FOCUSED ON ELECTIONS PRIOR TO 2008 AND SHOWED MIXED EFFECTS OF VOTER ID REQUIREMENTS ON VOTER TURNOUT

We reviewed 10 studies that estimated effects of state voter ID requirements on turnout, nine of which examined earlier general elections, that is before the 2008 general election, and 1 study examined general elections from 2004 through 2012.[52] The studies used various approaches to estimate the effects of state voter ID requirements on turnout. In general, most of the studies used one data source, such as surveys or official voter records, to make their estimates, and 1 of the 10 studies used data from both surveys and official voter records. The studies, conducted by various researchers, showed mixed results and analyzed how various non-photo and photo identification laws affected turnout in presidential or congressional elections nationwide and in one state. The ID laws evaluated varied across states, ranging from requirements for voters to state their name to presenting a government- issued photo ID, and the assessment in 9 of the studies grouped and compared states according to ID law requirements.[53] These studies are useful for understanding potential effects of voter ID requirements on voter turnout; however, the studies face limitations in available data used in the analyses and the potential for other factors to obscure the effects of the requirements reviewed.

Researchers seeking to isolate the effect of voter ID laws must disentangle these effects from the many other factors associated with the decision to vote or with aggregate turnout in an election. In 9 of the 10 studies we reviewed, researchers combined data from all states to assess the effect of voter ID laws on turnout. In 7 of the 10 studies, researchers combined data across multiple elections. This approach helps ensure that enough data are available for analysis and potentially increases the breadth of the findings to more states and time periods. However, a broad analysis also introduces the possibility that factors varying across states or over time may explain turnout decisions, rather than voter ID laws themselves. For example, 1 study noted that changes to ballot access policies—such as absentee and early voting policies—and competitive elections during the time period examined could explain changes in voter turnout among voters subject to ID laws.[54] Studies that analyze turnout across multiple states and elections are vulnerable to bias from these kinds of alternative explanations that are unique to particular states and time periods; this vulnerability can be mitigated, in part, with attention to research design including appropriate statistical analysis and interpretation. In contrast, multiple-state studies that examine only one election period risk confounding the effects of election laws with existing differences across states that cannot be controlled for using readily available demographic data, such as differences in political culture.

As shown in table 3, of the 10 studies we reviewed, 5 found that state voter ID requirements had no statistically significant effects on voter turnout nationwide, and 5 studies found that changes in voter ID requirements had statistically significant effects on voter turnout. Among the 5 studies that showed statistically significant effects, 1 of the studies found an increase in voter turnout nationwide of 1.8 percentage points. The other 4 studies that showed statistically significant effects found that voter ID requirements decreased voter turnout, and the estimated decreases ranged from 1.5 to 3.9 percentage points.

In addition to evaluating potential effects of ID requirements on overall turnout, 5 of the 10 studies we reviewed examined effects of changes in voter ID requirements on various racial and ethnic sub-groups and provided estimates that we determined were sufficiently reliable for our reporting purposes. Of these 5 studies, 3 identified statistically significant effects of voter ID requirements for various racial and ethnic sub-groups and two did not find statistically significant effects.[55] The 3 studies that estimated statistically significant effects, and that we determined were sufficiently reliable, found different effects for minority voters, as compared with White voters:

- **Dropp (2013).** In his study estimating the effects of changes in voter ID requirements on voter turnout nationwide, Dropp estimated the effects on African-American, non-white, and White registered voters where voters' race was identified using a vendor's model to predict the race of registered voters listed in states' official voter record databases.[56] For the change in turnout between the 2004 and 2008 general elections, the study found no significant effects by race or ethnicity, with the exception of a 1 percentage point increase in state level turnout for Hispanics. For the 2006 to 2010 midterm elections, the study reported that the effect on state-level turnout was a 1 percentage point decrease for African-Americans, Whites, and non-Whites (estimated separately). For general elections held between 2004 and 2010, the study reported that the state level turnout effects identified were a 2 percentage point decline for African-Americans, a 1.25 percentage point decline for non-Whites, and 0.5 percentage point increase for Whites.[57]

- **Vercellotti and Andersen (2006 and 2009).** In their studies estimating the effects of voter ID requirements on voter turnout nationwide, Vercellotti and Andersen also estimated effects on African-American, Asian-American, Hispanic, and White voters by including survey respondents' self-reported ethnic or racial identities in their analysis. Using this method, the 2006 study found that the predicted probability that Hispanics would vote in states that required non-photo identification was about 10 percentage points lower than in states where Hispanic voters were required to give their names. According to the 2006 study, the difference was about 6 percentage points lower for African-Americans and Asian-Americans, and about 2 percentage points lower for White voters (the gap widened to 3.7 percentage points lower for White voters when comparing rates for photo identification with rates for stating one's name).[58] The 2009 study, which assessed the likelihood of voting among those living in states with an ID law first enacted in 2004, found that Hispanics in these states were 2 percent less likely to have reported voting in 2004.

The other 2 studies that examined effects of voter ID requirements for various racial and ethnic groups, did not find statistically significant effects.

- **Alvarez, Bailey, and Katz (2011 and 2008).**[59] In their study, Alvarez, Bailey, and Katz estimated the effects of changes in voter ID requirements on voter turnout for racial sub-groups by including survey respondents' self-reported ethnic or racial identities in their analysis. The authors estimated that the decrease in turnout of requiring photo IDs as compared with stating or signing names is larger for Whites than for non-Whites. Specifically, the results indicate a decrease in the probability of voting in states with photo ID requirements relative to those requiring voters to state their name is approximately 4 percentage points for Whites and approximately 2 percentage points for non-Whites. However, according to the information presented in the study, we determined that the results are too imprecisely estimated to support the conclusion that racial differences in the effects of voter ID requirements on voter turnout exist.
- **Milyo (2007).** In his study, Milyo estimated the effects of changes in voter ID requirements on voters in Indiana for minority groups by evaluating effects at the county level using U.S. Census Bureau data on the proportion of different races residing within each county.[60] Milyo estimated an increase in turnout of 0.07 percentage points for counties with a greater percentage of minority residents and 0.29 percentage points for counties with a greater percentage of populations in poverty, but reported that the estimates are not statistically significant.

Table 3. Summary of Studies on the Effects of Voter Identification (ID) Requirements on Overall Voter Turnout

Study authors	Time parameters	Data sources	Type of voter ID law evaluated	Scope of analysis	Election type	Direction and magnitude of effects of ID requirements on overall turnout[c]
No statistically significant effects on turnout						
Erikson and Minnite (2009)	2002 and 2006	Survey (Current Population Survey)	Range of requirements (state name to photo ID required)	Nationwide	Congressional	No effects
Muhlhausen and Sikich (2007)	2004	Survey (Current Population Survey)	Range of requirements (state name to photo ID required)	Nationwide	Presidential	No effects
Mycoff, Wagner, and Wilson (2007)	2000 to 2006	Official voter records and survey (American National Election Studies)	Range of requirements (state name to photo ID required)	Nationwide	Presidential and congressional	No effects
Mycoff, Wagner, and Wilson (2009)	2004 to 2006	Survey (Cooperative Congressional Election Survey)	Range of requirements (state name to photo ID required)	Nationwide	Congressional	No effects
Vercellotti and Andersen (2009)[a]	2004	Survey (Current Population Survey)	Range of requirements (non-photo to photo ID requirements)	Nationwide	Presidential	No effects
Statistically significant effects on turnout at aggregate or voter level						
Alvarez, Bailey, and Katz (2011 and 2008)[b]	2000 to 2006	Survey (Current Population Survey)	Range of requirements (state name to photo ID required)	Nationwide	Presidential and congressional	Decreased predicted probability of voting by 1.5 to 2 percentage points for voters in photo ID states compared with voters in states that required voters to state or sign their names

Study authors	Time parameters	Data sources	Type of voter ID law evaluated	Scope of analysis	Election type	Direction and magnitude of effects of ID requirements on overall turnout[c]
De Alth (2009)	2002 and 2006	Official voter records	Range of requirements (non-photo to photo ID requirements)	Nationwide	Congressional	Decreased county-level turnout—compared with states with no ID requirement, a 2.2 percentage point decline for non-photo ID requirements, and a 1.6 percentage point decline for photo ID requirements
Dropp (2013)	2004 through 2012	Official voter records	Range of requirements (state name to photo ID required)	Nationwide	Presidential and congressional	Decreased state-level turnout in states that changed ID requirements compared with those states with no ID requirements in midterm elections from 3.7 to 3.9 percentage points, with no effect on presidential elections[d]
Milyo (2007)	2002 and 2006	Official voter records	Photo ID requirements	Indiana	Congressional	Increased county level turnout from period prior to ID requirements— 1.8 percentage points

Table 3. (Continued)

Study authors	Time parameters	Data sources	Type of voter ID law evaluated	Scope of analysis	Election type	Direction and magnitude of effects of ID requirements on overall turnout[c]
Vercellotti and Andersen (2006)[a]	2004	Survey (Current Population Survey)	Range of requirements (state name to photo ID required)	Nationwide	Presidential	Lower state-level turnout—approximately 3 percentage points for states that required voters to show any ID compared with those states that required voters to state their namee

Source: GAO analysis of studies that estimate the effects of ID requirements on turnout. | GAO-14-634.

Notes: We identified these studies through a search of several online databases that catalog peer- reviewed journal articles, conference proceedings, and research institute publications for studies published from January 1, 2003 to May 2013, with subsequent searches to locate any additional material through March 2014. We had two social scientists and, as applicable, a statistician, review each of the 10 studies to determine whether the design, implementation, and analyses of the study were sufficiently sound to support the study's results and conclusions based on generally accepted social science principles. A variety of studies broadly examine aspects of the implementation of voter ID laws, but the sub-set of studies cited here estimate effects of voter ID laws on voter turnout. A description of our literature review methodology is provided in appendix II and full citations for studies listed here are provided in appendix III.

[a] We reviewed two studies by Vercellotti and Andersen evaluating potential ID law effects on voter turnout during the 2004 general election. They found differing results, generally because different methods of analysis were used. In their 2006 study, the researchers divided states into five groups, each with varying degrees of ID requirements, to assess effects of the requirements on turnout. The ID requirements ranged from stating one's name to providing a photo ID. In the 2009 study, the researchers divided states into three groups—states that required photo or non-photo ID requirements for the first time in the 2004 presidential election, states that had those requirements in a prior election, and all remaining states that did not require voter ID.

[b] We reviewed the published study (2011), as well as the working paper that led to the published study (2008).

[c] Unless otherwise noted, all estimates are significant at least at the 0.05 level of statistical significance.

[d] The study does not report standard errors, but states the differences are significantly distinguishable from zero.

[e] Significant at the 0.05 level of statistical significance, using a one-tailed statistical test.

The studies we reviewed identified various theories or factors that could help provide insights regarding the studies' varying estimated effects of changes in voter ID requirements on voter turnout. For example, Dropp (2013) and Gomez (2008) noted that changes in voter ID requirements could contribute to decreases in voter turnout by requiring voters to present necessary documents that certain segments of the population, who tend to be less familiar with the electoral system, are less likely to own than others. In contrast, Dropp (2013) has suggested that changes to ID laws could increase turnout by intensifying efforts by political campaigns and interest groups to help eligible voters obtain the required ID, which also could increase their propensity to vote.

Estimating the extent to which there may be effects, if any, of changes in voter ID laws on voter turnout is challenging, regardless of how the laws operate, because of limitations in the available data and the potential for other factors to obscure the effects of interest. For example, 7 of the 10 studies we reviewed used survey responses to estimate the effect of ID requirements on voter turnout.[61] In these studies, the authors used survey data from a representative sample of voting-age adults contacted shortly after a general election occurred in order to measure respondents' turnout and various other characteristics, such as race and age.[62] A key strength of surveys is that they can enable estimates of the effects of ID laws for subgroups of the population because they include more detailed demographic information than official voter files. However, political scientists have found that surveys produce higher estimates of turnout than official records maintained by election administrators. Possible explanations for this discrepancy between survey responses and actual records include memory limitations and respondents indicating they had voted when they had not, because of positive social attitudes toward voting among some groups of respondents.[63] Impact estimates of voter ID laws can be inaccurate if the survey respondents who are more likely to be affected by the laws are also more likely to report their turnout inaccurately (see app. VI).

Four of the studies we reviewed used official voter records obtained from election administrators to estimate the effect of changes in voter ID requirements on voter turnout. Official data should be the authoritative record of turnout. However, weaknesses in how voter records are maintained can also cause error and can lead to an underestimation of turnout as a proportion of registered eligible voters. In particular, official lists of registered voters do not necessarily identify those who are on the list of registered voters but ineligible to vote in any one election. A person may have been eligible to vote several years ago, and therefore was placed on the registration rolls, but subsequently moved out of the jurisdiction or state, died, or committed a crime that makes him or her ineligible to vote. Registration and voter history records may not reflect this change in eligibility, depending on the extent to which records are updated. When records are not current, a person may be categorized as a registered non-voter for a particular election, when in fact the person should not have been included in the eligible population for that election. In addition, election administrators may not always record a registered and eligible voter as having cast a ballot in official voter history files, because of record-keeping issues at polling places or central offices.[64]

Finally, the existing research provides limited evidence regarding the effects on turnout of the requirements for government-issued, photo IDs that states have adopted in recent years. All but 1 of the studies we reviewed analyzed turnout in elections from 2002 through 2006, but 6 of the 8 states with requirements for a voters to present a government- issued photo ID as of the 2012 general election implemented the requirements after the 2006 general election.[65] If ownership rates varied across various types of ID, impact estimates for prior elections and laws that allowed more forms of ID would not necessarily resemble estimates for more recent elections and ID laws that allowed fewer forms of ID.

Our Analysis Suggests that Decreases in General Election Turnout in Kansas and Tennessee from 2008 to 2012 Beyond Decreases in Comparison States Are Attributable to Changes in Voter ID Requirements

To examine the extent to which changes in voter ID requirements affected voter turnout in selected states, if at all, from the 2008 to 2012 general elections, we designed an evaluation that used multiple data sources, and we selected two treatment and four comparison states for evaluation. In comparison to most of the other studies which focused on elections prior

to 2008, our analysis focused on the extent of any changes in voter turnout from the 2008 to 2012 general elections—the two most recent general elections. Further, in comparison to most of the other studies, our analysis used multiple data sources, including both surveys and official voter records, and we selected treatment and comparison states by controlling for factors other than changes in voter ID requirements that could have affected turnout in the selected states. (App. V describes the design of this analysis in more detail.)

Data sources and quasi-experimental design. Because of concerns that surveys may overestimate and official voter records may underestimate voter turnout, we analyzed both types of data in order to assess the sensitivity of any results we would obtain from our analysis. The survey data we used were from the November 2008 and 2012 Voting and Registration supplements of the Current Population Survey (CPS), conducted by the U.S. Census Bureau. The CPS provided data for 92,360 respondents in 2008 and 94,311 respondents in 2012, after we selected only those respondents who said they were U.S. citizens of voting age and registered to vote. Political scientists use CPS data to study how the decision to vote is associated with individual characteristics, laws, political campaigning, and election administration practices.[66] The CPS measures registration and turnout, along with various demographic and economic variables, such as race, income, residential mobility, and population density.

In addition to survey data, we analyzed two versions of official voter turnout records for selected states. At the individual voter level, we analyzed official state data on registered voters and turnout history, sometimes known as voter registration and history files. We obtained these data from a commercial vendor who took steps to improve their reliability and to supplement the official state data with additional voter demographics from the U.S. Census Bureau and commercial sources (see app. VI). At the state level, we analyzed data provided by the United States Elections Project (USEP) at George Mason University. USEP data consist of vote or ballot totals reported by election administrators, along with estimates of the population of each state who are eligible to vote. This source provides an estimate of state-level turnout as a share of the eligible voting population, rather than of the registered voting population covered by the CPS and official voter databases.

We used a quasi-experimental comparison group design to account for factors other than voter ID requirements that could affect voter turnout. A quasi-experimental comparison group design is a type of policy evaluation that compares how an outcome changes over time in a "treatment" group that adopted a new policy with how an outcome changes in a "comparison" group that did not make the same change.[67] As in controlled experiments, researchers analyze separate groups before and after one group changed a policy.

The variation across states in the use of voter ID laws, along with their staggered adoption over time, makes a quasi-experimental analysis possible. Our treatment and comparison groups included all registered or eligible voters in selected states that did and did not modify ID laws in a certain time period. Within each group, we estimate how turnout changed by comparing time periods before and after the reform, and then we calculate how the change varied between groups, known as a difference- in-difference. If turnout changed by a greater amount in the states that adopted voter ID laws, evidence would suggest that ID laws affected turnout.

Quasi-experiments have a number of strengths for estimating the effects of election administration practices, as noted by academic studies.[68] The longitudinal nature of the analysis holds constant any differences between the treatment and comparison groups that do not change by large amounts over short periods of time. In our analysis, these could include differences across voters (and implicitly states) in age, education, income, race, political interest, residential mobility, state political culture, and partisanship, which may be correlated with both voter turnout and the presence of voter ID laws. Political science research has consistently shown that individual differences across citizens—and implicitly across the jurisdictions in which they live—largely explain the decision to vote or not to vote.[69] For this reason, a quasi-experimental design is well suited to estimating the effect of legal reforms designed to change the voting process, because it holds constant many of the most important confounding variables.

Treatment and comparison state selection. After reviewing voter ID requirements, legal changes, and election environments across states from 2002 through 2012, we selected Kansas and Tennessee as the treatment group and Alabama, Arkansas, Delaware, and Maine as the comparison group for our analysis.[70] The treatment group states had the following characteristics:

- They implemented government-issued photo ID requirements between the 2008 and 2012 general elections that also required voters to follow-up with election officials with acceptable ID in order to have their votes counted if they attempt to vote without acceptable ID.
- They did not experience contemporaneous changes to other election laws that may have significantly affected voter turnout on Election Day.
- They had presidential general elections where the margin of victory did not substantially change from 2008 to 2012 and all other statewide elections, such as U.S. Senate races, were non-competitive in both the 2008 and 2012 general elections.[71]
- There was a minimal presence of ballot questions in the 2008 and 2012 general elections.
- They had official voter history data that were sufficiently reliable for the purposes of our analysis.

The comparison group states had the following characteristics:

- They did not implement substantively amended voter ID laws between the 2008 and 2012 general elections.
- They had election cycles for statewide elected offices that were similar to those of the selected treatment states.
- They did not experience contemporaneous changes to other election laws that may have significantly affected voter turnout on Election Day.
- They had presidential general elections where the margin of victory did not substantially change from 2008 to 2012 and all other statewide elections, such as U.S. Senate races, were non-competitive in both the 2008 and 2012 general elections.
- Ballot questions were not present, noncompetitive, or similarly competitive in both elections within a state.
- Two of the four comparison states were geographically proximate to the treatment states.
- The states had official voter history data that were sufficiently reliable for the purposes of our analysis.

For a complete description of our design, including data sources and state selection process used, see appendix V.

Results of our analysis. According to the results of our quasi- experimental analysis, voter turnout decreased in Kansas and Tennessee from the 2008 to the 2012 general elections to a greater extent than turnout decreased in selected comparison states—Alabama, Arkansas, Delaware, and Maine. Our analysis suggests that the turnout decreases in Kansas and Tennessee beyond decreases in comparison states were attributable to changes in the two states' voter ID requirements. As shown in figure 5, turnout declined in all six of the states we analyzed between 2008 and 2012, but it declined by a larger amount in Kansas and Tennessee than in the four comparison states.[72] Compared with changes in turnout in all the comparison states combined, we estimate that turnout for eligible voters declined by an additional 3.0 percentage points in Kansas and by an additional 2.7 percentage points in Tennessee. Compared with changes in turnout in all the comparison states combined and depending on the source of turnout data analyzed, we estimate that turnout for the general population of registered voters declined by an additional 1.9 to 2.2 percentage points in Kansas and by an additional 2.2 to 3.2 percentage points in Tennessee. (See app. VI for a more complete description of our findings on voter turnout.) We designed our analysis to hold constant other factors that may have affected turnout; by doing so, our design increases the likelihood that decreases in turnout in Kansas and Tennessee are attributable to changes in voter ID requirements, rather than other factors such as changes in voter demographics, campaign mobilization, or other election administration laws.[73]

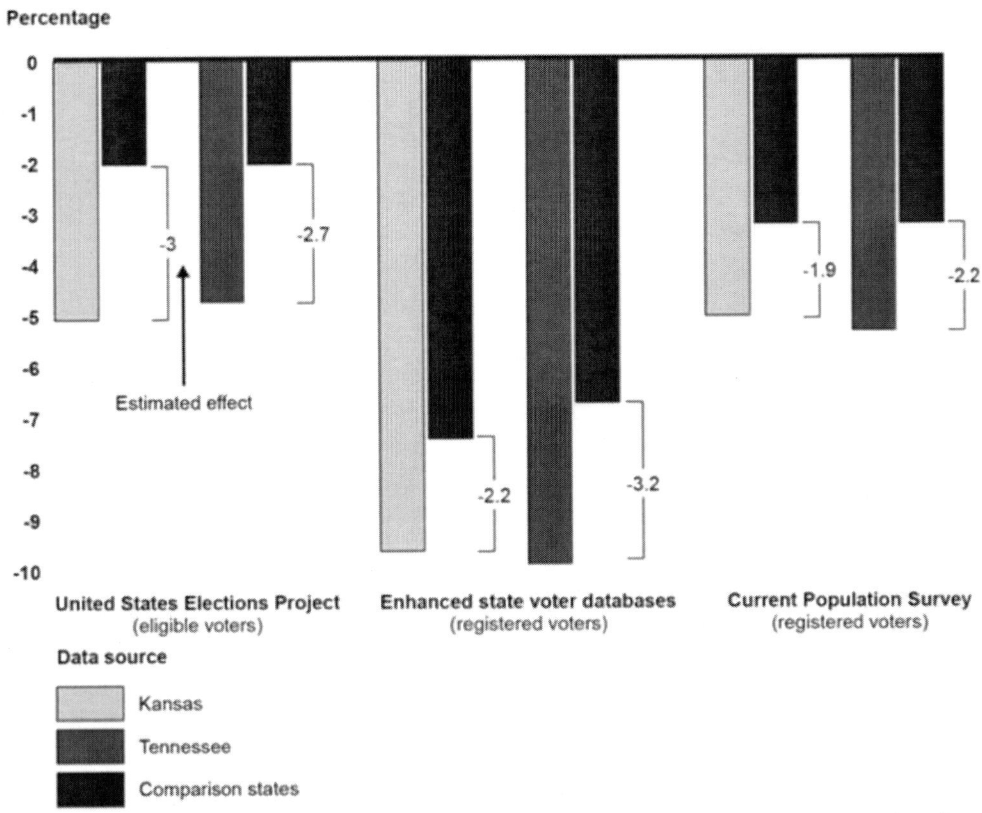

Source: GAO analysis of data from the United States Elections Project, state voter registration and history databases (commercially enhanced), and the Current Population Survey. | GAO-14-634.

Note: Change in turnout using enhanced state voter databases and the Current Population Survey are derived from multivariate statistical analyses (see app. VI, tables 16 and 21). Estimates of changes in ID requirement effects on voter turnout have a margin of error at the 95 percent confidence level. Depending on the source of the data, we estimated margins of error using statistical models or standard methods for calculating differences in proportions among independent samples (see app. VI). Specifically, the United States Elections Project estimates have a margin of error of +/- 0.12 percent for Kansas and +/- 0.09 percent for Tennessee. The enhanced state voter database estimates have a margin of error of +/- 0.12 percentage points for Kansas and +/- 0.09 percentage points for Tennessee. For the comparison state changes in turnout calculated from the enhanced state voter databases, we used weighting to make the distribution of voters in the comparison states similar to the distribution of voters in Kansas and Tennessee. Specifically, in this analysis, we weighted the distribution of comparison state voters in the categories of age, race, and registration year so that the distribution of registered voters was similar across these characteristics to the distribution in Kansas and Tennessee in 2012. We also limited our analysis to the subset of voters who were registered prior to the 2008 election and potentially eligible to vote in either election. This weighting approach was completed only for the analysis using the enhanced state voter database. The Current Population Survey estimates have a margin of error of +/- 3.5 percentage points for Kansas and +/- 2.8 percentage points for Tennessee.

Figure 5. GAO Analysis of the Effects of Voter Identification (ID) Requirement Changes on Turnout in the 2012 General Election in Kansas and Tennessee.

To validate the results of our analysis, we (1) compared Kansas and Tennessee with both different combinations of comparison states and individual comparison states, and (2) controlled for demographic characteristics that can affect turnout. According to these additional analyses, we found that greater turnout decreases in Kansas and Tennessee compared with individual and different combinations of comparison states, and controlling for demographic characteristics, were most likely attributable to changes in voter ID requirements rather than other factors.

Multiple comparisons. We compared turnout changes in Kansas and Tennessee with turnout changes in various combinations of comparison states using the three datasets, to determine if any particular comparison state or combination of comparison states could bias our results. According to our analysis of the different data sets, we found that the decrease in turnout was greater in both Kansas and Tennessee than the turnout decreases for different combinations of comparators. For example, using USEP data, we found that turnout declined in Kansas 3.1 percentage points more than the pooled decline of Alabama and Arkansas.[74] Similarly, we found that turnout in Tennessee declined 2.9 percentage points more than the pooled decline in Alabama and Arkansas. We also found similar patterns of declines in turnout when Kansas and Tennessee were compared with individual states. For example, according to CPS data, the turnout decline in Kansas was 2.3 percentage points greater than the decline in Alabama, 3.5 percentage points greater than the decline in Arkansas, 5.6 percentage points greater than the decline in Delaware, and 4.7 percentage points greater than the decline in Maine.[75]

Demographic controls. We included demographic controls in our analysis when analyzing changes in turnout using CPS data. The CPS data allow for additional demographic data to be included in our analysis, which permits us to determine if turnout changes persist when other demographic factors are considered. We also specified a model that allowed different rates of change in turnout between 2008 and 2012 for different demographic subgroups, to control for the possibility that trends in turnout may not be parallel within demographic groups if political campaigns or interest groups disproportionately encouraged turnout among some groups in one year but not another, even though our design ensures that overall levels of competition were similar at the state level (see app. VI). After making these adjustments for age, education, employment status, family income, marital status, race, and sex, we found that the greater decreases in turnout in Kansas and Tennessee persisted. We estimated that turnout in Kansas decreased by 1.9 percentage points more than turnout decreased in all comparison states and turnout in Tennessee decreased by 2.2 percentage points more than turnout decreased in all comparison states. We obtained similar results after applying similar controls in an analysis of voter-level data from the commercially enhanced state voter databases (see app. VI).

Our analysis of the enhanced state voter databases provided sufficient numbers of records to reliably estimate the effects of changes in state voter ID laws separately for various sub-groups of age, race or ethnicity, and length of voter registration. To estimate the extent to which changes in voter ID laws affected turnout among these sub-groups, we estimated the difference-in-difference separately for each sub-group, and compared how these estimates varied across sub-groups. According to this analysis, we found that changes in turnout were larger among registrants who were younger, African-American, or recently registered in our two treatment states, relative to the comparison states pooled, and our analysis suggests that these changes are attributable to the states' changes in voter ID laws, because we held other factors constant that could have otherwise affected turnout. The differences between groups described below are each statistically distinguishable from zero. Our estimates by sub-group appear in figure 6, and margins of error for each estimate provided are listed in appendix VI.

- **Age**. In Kansas, the turnout effect among registrants who were 18 years old in 2008 was 7.1 percentage points larger in size than the turnout effect among registrants between the ages of 44 and 53. The change in turnout in Tennessee was reduced among 18 year-old registrants by 1.3 percentage points more than among 44 to 53 year- olds. The same effects among registrants between the ages of 19 and 23 were 3.6 percentage points larger in Kansas and 1.2 percentage points larger in Tennessee.
- **Race or ethnicity.** In both Kansas and Tennessee we found that turnout was reduced by larger amounts among African-American registrants, as compared with Asian-American, Hispanic, and White registrants. We estimate that turnout was reduced among African- American registrants by 3.7 percentage points more than among Whites in Kansas and 1.5 percentage points more than among Whites in Tennessee. However, we did not find reductions in turnout among Asian-American or Hispanic registrants, as compared with White registrants, thus suggesting that the laws did not have larger effects on these registrants.[76]
- **Length of registration.** In Kansas, the reduction in turnout for people registered to vote within 1 year prior to Election Day 2008 was 5.2 percentage points larger in size than for people registered to vote for 20 years or longer prior to Election Day 2008. In Tennessee, the effect on turnout for people registered to vote within 1 year prior to Election Day 2008 was 4.6 percentage points larger than the effect for people registered to vote for 20 years or longer prior to Election Day 2008. The effect of ID laws changes may vary according to length of registration, for several reasons. For example, more recently registered voters may be less familiar with the requirement for establishing their identities at the polls and may be less likely to have current identification documents. Alternatively, longer registrants may be more familiar with the voting process and more likely to pay attention to changes in requirements. Length of registration may also serve as an approximate measure of the time period a voter has remained in a community as a registered voter, to the extent that people register to vote when they move into a state, such as when obtaining a new driver's license. A short period of registration, for example, is a possible indicator of a voter who may have recently moved into a community. Moreover, length of registration should be no longer than length of residence, since people must be legal residents of a state to become registered voters.[77]

Figure 6 shows our analysis of the estimated effects of voter ID requirement changes on turnout in the 2012 general election in Kansas and Tennessee by age, race, and length of registration.

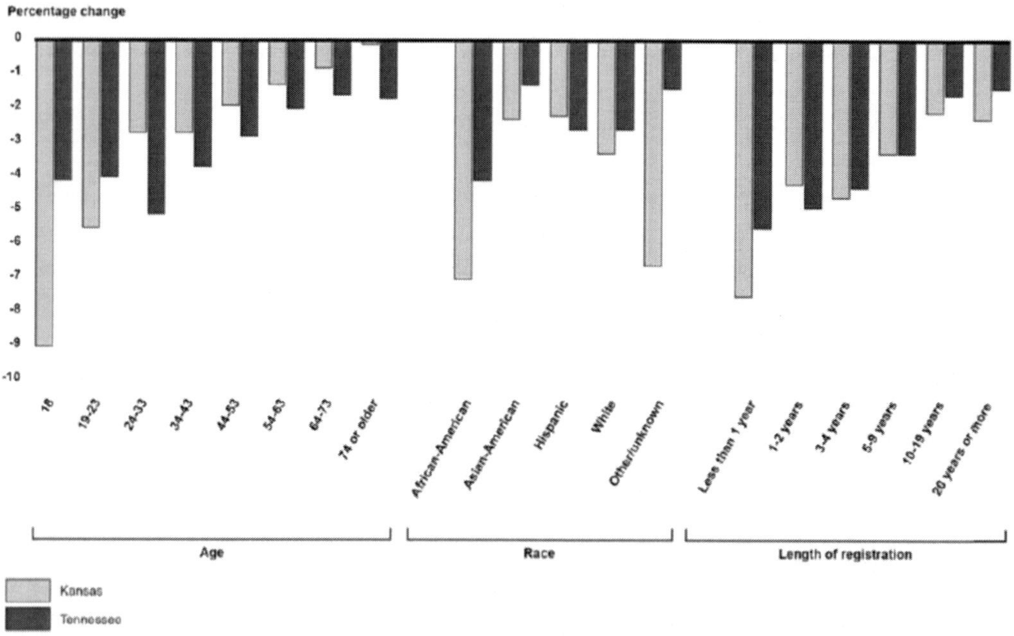

Source: GAO analysis of state voter registration and history databases (commercially enhanced. | GAO-14-634.

Figure 6. GAO Analysis of the Effects of Voter Identification (ID) Requirement Changes on Turnout in the 2012 General Election in Kansas and Tennessee by Age (as of 2008), Race, and Length of Registration.

Although the design of our analysis effectively controls for a variety of alternative explanations and sources of bias, several limitations may apply.

Our results cannot be generalized beyond Kansas and Tennessee. Our impact estimates are limited to changes in turnout among Kansas and Tennessee eligible or registered voters between the 2008 and 2012 general elections and do not necessarily apply to other states or time periods. Our results cannot be generalized to states that adopted substantially different ID requirements, particularly states that allow forms of ID such as utility bills, bank statements, and affidavits. To reliably generalize our findings, replication of our analysis is necessary for other ID laws, states, time periods, and subgroups of voters.

The recent adoption of the ID laws we analyzed in Kansas and Tennessee further limits the generalizability of our results. The effects we estimated between the 2008 and 2012 general elections—with 2012 being the first general presidential election when the laws were in effect—may not persist over time if, in the future, voters adjust to requirements that were new in 2012 and obtain the necessary ID. In contrast, efforts by political and government entities to inform voters about newer ID laws in the first election after adoption may have the effect of mitigating the laws' effects. In subsequent elections, these efforts may wane, and the impact of the ID law changes on turnout may increase.[78] This type of education campaign may affect voter turnout in ways that are difficult to measure and may change over time.[79]

Quality of comparison states. The validity of our impact estimates largely depends on the quality of the matched comparison states we selected. In principle, the comparison states provide examples of turnout rates that Kansas and Tennessee might have had if these states had not adopted requirements for government-issued photo IDs (also known as counterfactual potential outcomes).[80] We believe our comparison analyses are sufficiently strong, because our choice of comparison states holds constant a number of factors, including voter characteristics that do not change substantially over time (e.g., sex and race); election schedules; campaign competition for state and federal offices and ballot questions; changes to other election administration laws; and, to a lesser extent, election day weather conditions and broadcast media exposure. As previously described, to mitigate the risk of bias in selecting a matched comparison group, we calculated impact estimates for various combinations of treatment and comparison states and obtained similar results.

Alternative explanations. Alternative factors may explain the change in turnout between our treatment and comparison states, despite the many factors that are held constant by our choice of states, time periods, and statistical methods. Examples of such unobserved factors include voter mobilization campaigns for state legislative and municipal elective offices, local ballot propositions, and changes to state laws and practices beyond those we reviewed. We believe these factors are likely to be idiosyncratic and not likely to systematically affect the change in turnout for all voters in the treatment states more strongly than in the comparison states, because of a wide variety of local factors that may influence local and state legislative voter mobilization efforts. Nevertheless, any policy evaluation in a non-experimental setting, such as ours, cannot account for all unobserved factors that could bias or confound impact estimates with certainty.[81]

Limited number of treatment and comparison states. By selecting treatment and comparison states where other factors that affect turnout are unlikely to be operating, we have a higher level of confidence that our results do not reflect the impact of factors that were not held constant. However, the cost of this design approach is less precise estimates of how voter ID requirement changes affect turnout, because a smaller number of voters, states, and time periods produce fewer data for statistical analysis and generally larger margins of error. Generally, with larger volumes of data for use in a statistical analysis, estimates may be produced with smaller margins of error. However, given the large variation in state election environments that can affect turnout, there is a risk that a broader analysis that included additional states and time periods would produce more precise yet biased estimates of the effects of changes in voter ID requirement on voter turnout.

A Small Portion of Total Provisional Ballots in Two States Were Cast for ID Reasons in 2012, and Less Than Half Were Counted

Provisional ballots are cast by voters at the polls whose eligibility to vote is unclear and must be determined at a later date by election officials. In Kansas and Tennessee, as in other states that use provisional ballots, voters may cast a provisional ballot for a variety of reasons. For example, a voter may lack sufficient ID to meet the state's or HAVA's requirements,[82] or a voter's name may not appear on the voter registration list where he or she intended to vote.[83]

In both Kansas and Tennessee, a voter who casts a provisional ballot for ID reasons must provide appropriate identification at a later time specified by law to ensure that his or her ballot is counted.[84] If a voter does not provide appropriate identification during the specified time period, the provisional ballot is not counted. In Kansas, a voter who casts a provisional ballot must provide a valid form of identification to the county election officer in person or provide a copy by mail or electronic means before between 8:00 a.m. and 10:00 a.m. on the Monday following an election, when the county board of canvassers meets. At this meeting, the county election officer presents copies of identification received from provisional voters and the corresponding provisional ballots, and the board determines the validity of a voter's identification and whether the ballot will be counted. In Tennessee, in order to have a provisional ballot counted, the voter must provide evidence of identification to the administrator of elections at the county election office or other designated location by the close of business on the second business day after the election. The voter must also sign an affidavit affirming that he or she is the same person who cast the provisional ballot.[85]

If a provisional ballot is cast for multiple reasons, one of which is that the voter does not have appropriate photo identification, the reason actually recorded may vary between the two states. Kansas officials in the Secretary of State's office stated that the county election officer is responsible for deciding which reason is assigned to the provisional ballot, and this determination may vary depending upon individual circumstances. Tennessee officials in the Secretary of State's office stated that in this situation, poll workers are instructed to categorize the provisional ballot as having been cast for lack of a photo ID, and to use an orange provisional ballot designated for this purpose.

Table 4. Provisional Ballot Totals and Rates in 2012 General Election for Kansas and Tennessee

State	Total ballots cast	Total provisional ballots	Percentage of total ballots that were provisional	Total provisional ballots cast for ID reasons	Percentage of total provisional ballots that were cast for ID reasons	Total provisional ballots cast for ID reasons that were counted	Percentage of provisional ballots cast for ID reasons that were counted	Percentage of provisional ballots cast for non-ID reasons that were counted
Kansas	1,115,281	38,865	3.48	838	2.16	306	37	65
Tennessee	2,480,182	7,089	0.29	673	9.49	178	26	23

Source: GAO analysis of the 2012 Election Administration and Voting Survey (EAVS) conducted by the U.S. Election Assistance Commission (EAC) and 2012 election data provided by the Kansas and Tennessee Secretaries of State. | GAO-14-634.

We analyzed data from the 2012 EAVS conducted by the EAC and 2012 election data provided to us by the Kansas and Tennessee Secretary of State offices to determine the number of provisional ballots cast in the 2012 general election and the extent to which provisional ballots were counted.[86] According to our analysis, few provisional ballots were cast for ID reasons in Kansas and Tennessee in 2012, relative to total provisional ballots cast and total ballots cast. In Kansas, 1,115,281 total ballots were cast in the 2012 general election; of those ballots, 38,865 were provisional ballots and, according to data provided by the Kansas Secretary of State's office, 838 of those provisional ballots, or 2.2 percent, were cast for ID reasons. In Tennessee, 2,480,182 total ballots were cast in the 2012 general election; of those ballots, 7,089 were provisional ballots and, according to data provided by the Tennessee Secretary of State's office, 673 of those provisional ballots, or 9.5 percent, were cast for ID reasons. In Kansas, 37 percent of provisional ballots cast for ID reasons ultimately were counted, and in Tennessee 26 percent were ultimately counted. Provisional ballots cast for ID reasons may not be counted for a variety of reasons in Kansas and Tennessee, including the voter not providing a valid ID during or following an election. Table 4 provides additional information on the numbers and types of ballots cast and the percentage of provisional ballots counted in Kansas and Tennessee in the 2012 general election.

Table 5. Change in Provisional Ballot Usage between 2008 and 2012 General Elections, in Treatment and Comparison States

State	Percentage of total ballots that were provisional in 2008	Percentage of total ballots that were provisional in 2012	Change in provisional ballot usage between 2008 and 2012 general elections[a]
Kansas	3.18	3.48	0.30
Tennessee	0.17	0.29	0.12
Alabama	0.47	0.29	-0.18
Arkansas	0.20	0.24	0.04
Delaware	0.09	0.11	0.01
Maine	0.05	0.04	-0.01
Alabama/Arkansas pooled[b]	0.34	0.27	-0.07
Delaware/Maine pooled[b]	0.07	0.07	0.00
All comparison states pooled[b]	0.26	0.21	-0.05

Source: GAO analysis of U.S. Election Assistance Commission's Election Administration and Voting Survey (EAVS) 2008 and 2012 data from jurisdictions in selected states that provided data in response to EAVS in both 2008 and 2012. | GAO-14-634.

Notes: This table includes only those jurisdictions that provided data to state officials in response to the EAVS in both 2008 and 2012. The full EAVS data sets for 2008 and 2012 include jurisdictions that did not report data in 1 or both years. Those jurisdictions that did not provide data in both years have been excluded from the analysis.

[a] The change in provisional ballot usage between 2008 and 2012 may not equal the percent of total ballots that were provisional in 2012 minus the percent of total ballots that were provisional in 2008 due to rounding in subtraction.

[b] "Pooled" rates of provisional ballot use reflect the grouped states' combined total provisional ballots divided by the grouped states' combined total ballots cast. Because of the quasi-experimental design of our study, we assume that the comparison states are interchangeable and thus can be pooled together to create an additional group for analysis. The larger size of this pooled group reduces the statistical uncertainty of our estimates.

Using the EAVS data, we also analyzed the extent to which the use of provisional ballots changed, if at all, between the 2008 and 2012 general elections in Kansas and Tennessee and relative to our comparison states of Alabama, Arkansas, Delaware, and Maine. Delaware, Kansas, and Tennessee provided data to the EAVS for all jurisdictions in their state in each year, but data were missing for some jurisdictions in the other states.[87] In our analysis, data for Alabama, Arkansas, and Maine include only data from jurisdictions in those states that reported data on provisional ballot usage for both the 2008 and 2012 general elections. Our analysis shows that the rate of provisional ballot usage, overall, increased slightly between the 2008 and 2012 general elections in Kansas and Tennessee. The rate of provisional ballot usage also increased slightly in Arkansas and Delaware, though the increases were smaller than in Kansas and Tennessee. Table 5 describes the change in provisional ballot usage between the 2008 and 2012 general elections in treatment and comparison states.

Our analysis of changes in provisional ballot usage rates between the 2008 and 2012 general elections in the treatment and comparison states showed that Kansas and Tennessee increased their usage of provisional ballots by 0.35 percentage points and 0.17 percentage points, respectively, between the two elections, relative to all other comparison states combined, as shown in table 6. These quasi-experimental, "difference-in-difference" estimates control for other factors that could have affected election outcomes such as the presence of competitive races for statewide or federal offices, voter characteristics that do not change substantially over time (e.g., race), controversial ballot questions, and the voter mobilization activities of campaigns. For these reasons, our analysis suggests that the increased usage of provisional ballots in Kansas and Tennessee from the 2008 to 2012 general elections relative to the comparison states is attributable to changes in those two states' changes in voter ID requirements. Moreover, positive effects on provisional ballots are consistent with our findings that decreases in voter turnout in Kansas and Tennessee in the 2012 general election beyond decreases in the comparison states were attributable to those two states' changes in voter ID requirements, as casting a provisional ballot that is ultimately not counted is one way in which turnout could have decreased.[88] However, our choice of comparison states was not specifically designed to account for unique factors changing between 2008 and 2012 that could explain the change in provisional ballot usage, such as changes to state systems of registering voters and requirements for when provisional ballots must be cast. As a result, factors other than new voter ID laws may have contributed to the increase in provisional ballot usage.[89] These findings are not generalizable beyond our specific treatment and comparison states.

In addition, we analyzed the EAVS data to determine how provisional ballot rates changed over time in our treatment and comparison states using data reported by all jurisdictions in those states (e.g., to include all jurisdictions responding to the EAVS in either 2008 or 2012). We conducted this additional analysis to determine if missing data affected the results of our analysis in which we excluded jurisdictions that did not report data for both the 2008 and 2012 EAVS. In our second analysis, we obtained results similar to those in our first analysis, indicating that our exclusion of jurisdictions with missing data did not affect our conclusion that provisional ballot usage increased in Kansas and Tennessee from the 2008 to the 2012 general election relative to comparison states. Appendix VII provides more detailed information on the results of this additional analysis.

Table 6. Comparison of Change in Provisional Ballot Usage between 2008 and 2012 General Elections in Treatment and Comparison State Groups

State	Kansas (%)	Tennessee (%)
Alabama/Arkansas pooleda	0.37 (0.047)	0.18 (0.013)
Delaware/Maine pooleda	0.30 (0.046)	0.12 (0.011)
All comparison states pooled[a]	0.35 (0.046)	0.17 (0.011)

Source: GAO analysis of U.S. Election Assistance Commission's Election Administration and Voting Survey (EAVS) 2008 and 2012 data from jurisdictions in selected states that provided data in response to the EAVS in both 2008 and 2012. | GAO-14-634.

Notes: Entries in parentheses are 95 percent margins of error (e.g., +/- 0.047 percentage points). This table analyzes data from jurisdictions that provided data in response to the EAVS in both 2008 and 2012. The full EAVS data sets for 2008 and 2012 include jurisdictions that did not report data in 1 or both years. Those jurisdictions that did not provide data in both years have been excluded from the analysis.

[a] "Pooled" rates of provisional ballot use reflect the grouped states' combined total provisional ballots divided by the grouped states' combined total ballots cast. Because of the quasi-experimental design of our study, we assume that the comparison states are interchangeable and thus can be pooled together to create an additional group for analysis. The larger size of this pooled group reduces the statistical uncertainty of our estimates.

CHALLENGES EXIST IN USING AVAILABLE INFORMATION TO ESTIMATE THE INCIDENCE OF IN- PERSON VOTER FRAUD

A variety of factors affect efforts to estimate the incidence of in-person voter fraud, making it difficult to produce complete estimates.[90] For the purposes of this report, incidence is defined as the number of separate times a crime is committed for a specific time period. Estimating the incidence of crime generally involves using information on the number of crimes known to law enforcement authorities—such as crime data submitted to a central repository within states based on uniform offense definitions—to generate a reliable set of crime statistics. However, even when crime data are centrally collected, the true incidence of crime can be difficult to determine due to the potential for crimes not to be reported.[91] We have reported that crimes of fraud, in particular, are difficult to detect, as those involved are engaged in intentional deception.[92] For example, in the areas of Medicare fraud and Internal Revenue Service refund fraud involving identity theft, we have reported that reliable estimates of the extent of such fraud are not known.[93] In addition, with regard to identity fraud, in March 2002 we reported that no single hotline or database captured the universe of identity theft victims and that it was difficult to fully or accurately measure the prevalence of identity theft.[94] Although not necessarily the same as other types of fraud, the incidence of in-person voter fraud can be difficult to estimate. We reviewed studies conducted by academic researchers and others on efforts to identify instances of in-person voter fraud. We also reviewed information from federal and state agencies on election fraud. Based on our review of these information sources, we found that various challenges and limitations in information available for estimating the incidence of in- person voter fraud make it difficult to determine a complete estimate of such fraud.[95] For example, based on our own review of federal and state information sources, we identified challenges such as there is no single source of information on possible instances of in-person voter fraud and variation exists among federal and state sources in the extent to which they collect information on election fraud.

The studies we reviewed identified few instances of in-person voter fraud, and while they provide information on efforts to estimate in-person voter fraud, limitations in the populations studied and sources used make it difficult to use these studies to determine a complete estimate of the incidence of in-person voter fraud. In particular, we reviewed five research studies,[96] five studies by state agencies, and information provided by DOJ. The five studies by researchers we reviewed as part of our literature review used various methods and sources of information to identify instances of in-person voter fraud. Table 7 describes the approaches used in each study and the limitations we or the studies' authors identified.

These five studies provide useful information on efforts to identify instances of in-person voter fraud among the populations studied and sources used. However, as shown in table 7, the studies have limitations that affect their usefulness in estimating the complete incidence of in- person voter fraud. For example, two of the studies sought to identify actual instances of in-person voter fraud, but there are limitations in the completeness of information contained within the sources of information used, such as information from federal or state data sources and newspaper articles.[97] The three remaining studies used proxy measures for determining whether in-person voter fraud may exist, including sample surveys of voters, aberrations in voter turnout patterns, and votes cast in the names of deceased individuals.[98] These measures are indicators of whether in-person voter fraud may have occurred within the populations studied, but do not precisely or directly estimate how frequently in-person voter fraud occurs. These challenges limit the extent to which information from these studies can be used to determine a complete estimate of the incidence of in-person voter fraud.

Five states provided us with investigative studies that focused on specific types of election fraud.[99] The studies matched official records of voting activity to other data sources, and then investigated any identified discrepancies. Of the studies states provided to us, one included some information on allegations of in-person voter fraud; the four remaining state studies generally focused on issues such as double-voting, voting by ineligible voters such as non-citizens or felons, or instances of absentee ballot fraud, activities which fall outside our definition of in- person voter fraud. The one study that included some information on allegations of in-person voter fraud examined instances of votes cast in the name of deceased persons in one state. It examined about 200 questioned votes that were cast in the November 2010 election and ultimately determined that all but 5 of the questioned votes could be attributed to errors by state or local officials—including clerical errors, data matching errors, errors in scanning voter registration forms, and the issuance of absentee ballots in the wrong name—or to applications for absentee ballots by voters who died before the election. For the remaining 5 allegations, the study could not conclusively determine whether in-person voter fraud occurred. In conducting this study, the South Carolina State Law Enforcement Division reviewed documentation of the questioned votes, such as poll lists and voter registration records, to determine whether the questioned votes occurred as a result of clerical error, such as marking the wrong individual as having voted, or for some other reason, such as fraud.[100] This study provides useful information on the results of a review of votes cast in the name of deceased persons in one election in one state. However, as the study focused on the investigation of a specific type of alleged in-person voter fraud—votes cast in the name of deceased persons—it does not provide information needed for estimating the overall incidence of in-person voter fraud.

Table 7. Summary of Findings and Methods from Studies That Attempted to Identify Instances of In-Person Voter Fraud

Study author and date published	Scope	Methods	Results	Limitations
Ahlquist, Mayer, and Jackman. October 2013	Nationwide	Used a survey list experiment to detect fraud, particularly voter impersonation fraud. In this method, commonly used in survey research to detect sensitive behaviors, survey respondents were randomly assigned to one of two groups and were presented with a list of activities they may have engaged in during the prior election (such as attending a rally, or reading about the election in the news). In one version of the experiment, one list included engaging in in-person voter fraud ("casting a ballot under a name that was not my own"); the other list was identical but did not include in-person voter fraud. Instead, the second list included an activity respondents were unlikely to have engaged in ("I attended a political fundraising event for a candidate in my home town."). Respondents were asked how many of these activities, rather than which specific activities, they had engaged in. The researchers hypothesized that the difference between the numbers of items selected by respondents in the two groups would provide an indication of the prevalence of in-person voter fraud.	No significant indicators of voter impersonation fraud in the 2012 general election.	The authors note that their findings were necessarily limited to the prevalence of voters casting fraudulent ballots, not the number of fraudulent ballots cast. In principle a tiny number of people could have cast many thousands of fraudulent ballots, but the authors viewed that as unlikely because casting in-person ballots, fraudulent or otherwise, is time intensive. The authors note that their survey has limited statistical power. The authors state that a much larger sample would be required to detect a very small difference between the two groups evaluated for the study. If the incidence of voter fraud is rare, the study sample is not large enough to detect it with statistical certainty. The authors estimate that a sample of 260,000 individuals would be required to reliably detect low levels of voter fraud, such as 1 percent. The authors' sample included 1,000 U.S. citizens age 18 and over.

Table 7. (Continued)

Study author and date published	Scope	Methods	Results	Limitations
Christensen and Schultz. January 2014	Ohio; Miami, Florida; and Dagget County, Utah	Used a five-step methodology that combined both qualitative and statistical analysis of voting records. Specifically, to determine the extent to which evidence of in-person voter fraud existed, the authors looked at orphan votes and voters with the lowest propensity to vote based on official turnout data in local jurisdictions within three states. The authors defined orphan votes as votes cast in a low- profile election by a voter who did not vote in the preceding and subsequent high-profile elections. Propensity to vote in a specific election was calculated using that person's past and future voting record and other voter characteristics. After identifying jurisdictions with unusual patterns of orphan and low-propensity voters, the authors conducted extensive research to assess whether the observed anomaly had an innocent explanation (such as university housing when encountering multiple new registrants at the same address).	No suspicious anomalies found in voting patterns.	The authors assume that fraudulent ballots will be created in a coordinated fashion by the perpetrators of the fraud, using the names of unlikely voters (i.e., orphan or low propensity voters). The authors note that this assumption is generally valid because of the severe consequences for any campaign if even a small number of votes are cast in the names of people who later attempt to vote. The authors indicate that the older the elections, the fewer the number of actual voters in that election that were included in their analysis, since voting and registration records are publicly available only for those voters currently registered to vote. We determined that the method used is not based entirely on statistical calculations, but requires professional judgment as to the likelihood that jurisdictions with suspicious numbers of orphan and low propensity voters experienced fraud or that there is a plausible alternative explanation other than fraud to account for the results.
Hood III and Gillespie. March 2012	Georgia	Used data mining and record linkage techniques to match registration and voter history files to listings of recently deceased individuals to search for fraudulent votes	Five questionable votes cast in the November 2006 general election in Georgia.	The authors indicate that the county registrars associated with the 5 questionable votes did not respond to their requests for information; if provided, information from

Study author and date published	Scope	Methods	Results	Limitations
		being cast on behalf of such registrants. Process involved (1) linking registration and death files by county, manually eliminating cases where race or ethnicity, sex, or middle name did not match; (2) matching the remaining cases of deceased registered voters to Georgia's voter history database in order to identify individuals voting in the November 2006 election; (3) checking the validity of the records by cross-referencing these cases with the Social Security Death Index; and (4) systematically investigating each of the resulting cases through examination of absentee ballot request forms and certification forms signed by in-person voters, generally obtained from county registrars.		the registrars may have clarified the status of the 5 questionable votes identified.
Minnite. 2010	Federal court records and data from 4 states	Analyzed 10 years of federal court records and data from 4 states to search for instances of voter fraud.	Forty eight individual voter defendants charged with violating federal election laws from 1996-2005. These cases may or may not include instances of in-person voter fraud. One possible state-level case of in-person voter fraud in New Hampshire.	According to the author, multiple state offices share responsibility for handling complaints and for investigating and prosecuting voter fraud allegations, making obtaining complete information on all potential instances of voter fraud difficult. The author notes that federal case information is difficult to review because the nature of a crime can be difficult to identify in charging documents, records may be duplicates because some data are annual and

Table 7. (Continued)

Study author and date published	Scope	Methods	Results	Limitations
				cases extend across fiscal years, data entry errors exist, and the coding schemes in the database reviewed were not reliable.
News21. August 2012	Nationwide	Made public records requests to federal, state, and local election and law enforcement officials and reviewed court documents, official records, and media reports to collect information on over 2,000 election fraud cases from 2000 to 2011 in an attempt to determine how many involved in-person voter fraud.	10 confirmed cases of in-person voter fraud among the over 2,000 election fraud cases identified.	According to News21 documentation, News21 submitted public records requests to each of the 50 states' departments of elections and secretaries of state. News21 also contacted each state's attorney general and nearly 1,000 additional county district attorneys. Some state officials did not respond to the request for information, and some jurisdictions did not provide any information to News21 because their computer systems lacked the capability to search for election fraud cases. In some states' responses to News21, important details about the case, including the circumstances of the alleged fraud, were missing, and News21 was unable to categorize the type of election fraud or the responsible party, such as a voter or election official.

Source: GAO analysis of studies that attempted to identify instances of in-person voter fraud among the populations studied and sources used. | GAO-14-634.

In addition, with regard to DOJ, in July 2014, the department submitted a declaration as part of a court filing in litigation regarding a state voter ID law.[101] In that declaration, the Director of the Elections Crimes Branch of the Public Integrity Section of the Criminal Division stated that a review of data from DOJ's case management systems—the Automated Case Tracking System (ACTS II) managed by DOJ's Criminal Division and the Legal Information Office Network System (LIONS) managed by the Executive Office for U.S. Attorneys (EOUSA)—and certain publicly available and related court records indicated that there were no apparent cases of in-person voter impersonation charged by DOJ's Criminal Division or by U.S. Attorney's offices anywhere in the United States, from 2004 through July 3, 2014.[102] We were not able to obtain more detailed information on DOJ's methodology, because the case was ongoing at the time of our review.

For the purposes of our review, we obtained and reviewed information from federal and state agencies, as well those studies noted above that attempted to determine instances of in-person voter fraud, to determine the extent to which information from these sources could be used to estimate the incidence of in-person voter fraud. Based on our review of these information sources, we found that limitations with these available sources make it difficult to determine a complete estimate of in-person voter fraud. The key factors we identified that made this difficult include that there is no single source of information on possible instances of in-person voter fraud and that variation exists among federal and state sources in the extent to which they collect information on election fraud.

No single source of information on possible instances of in-person voter fraud. As with other types of fraud, there is no single source or database that captures the universe of allegations or cases of in-person voter fraud across federal, state, and local levels, making it difficult to determine a complete estimate of the incidence of in-person voter fraud. This is in part due to the fact that responsibility for addressing election fraud is shared among federal, state, and local authorities. As discussed earlier in this report, state and local authorities are responsible for the administration of state and federal elections, and state statutes regulate various aspects of elections, including activities associated with election fraud broadly, and in-person voter fraud specifically. For election fraud committed during federal elections, states and localities share jurisdiction with federal authorities, including DOJ's Criminal Division and United States Attorneys' Offices.[103] Within any given state, various state and local agencies may be responsible for identifying, investigating, and prosecuting election fraud, and information may not be shared among the entities. For example, allegations of election fraud may be reported to any combination of local, county, or state election officials; law enforcement; or county or state prosecutors, among others. Similarly, the investigation and prosecution of these allegations may be conducted by local or state law enforcement or prosecutors. Of the 46 states that responded to our requests for interviews, state election officials in 34 states reported that multiple agencies or units are responsible for identifying and investigating allegations of election fraud.[104] Of those states, officials in 28 states reported that local or county officials are at least partially responsible for addressing election fraud. In another 3 states, state officials reported that local or county officials are exclusively responsible for identifying and investigating allegations of election fraud. In these 31 states where local or county officials have some responsibility for addressing election fraud, allegations, investigations, prosecutions, and convictions are not necessarily reported to officials at the state level. For example, election officials in 1 state reported that allegations made at the county level can be referred directly to the county attorney without ever involving state- level officials. Given the multiple entities that may be involved in indentifying, investigating, or prosecuting in-person voter fraud, it is difficult to obtain data sufficient to support an incidence determination.

Two of the studies we reviewed that used federal and state sources to attempt to identify instances of in-person voter fraud also faced challenges as a result of the shared responsibility for addressing election fraud. For example, News21, an educational journalism program, gathered, organized, and analyzed reported cases of election fraud. News21 contacted state and local officials in all 50 states to compile a database of cases involving election fraud from 2000 through 2011.[105] In some cases, state and local officials contacted referred News21 to the county district attorneys, who then referred them back to the secretary of state or department of elections. Similarly, Minnite found that multiple state offices share responsibility for handling complaints in these states and that policies for investigating and prosecuting voter fraud complaints are not uniform within these states.

Federal and state agencies vary in the extent to which they collect information on election fraud. Federal and state agencies vary in the extent to which they collect and maintain information on election fraud in general and in-person voter fraud in particular, making it difficult to estimate the incidence of in-person voter fraud. For example, at the federal level, various databases may include information on federal investigations, prosecutions, and convictions involving in-person voter fraud. In particular, we identified four federal databases that could contain such information. Two of these databases are managed by DOJ components—the LIONS database and the ACTS II database; the other two databases are managed by components of the federal judiciary—the Integrated Database, managed by the Federal Judicial Center (FJC) and an Oracle database, managed by the United States Sentencing Commission (USSC).[106] These four databases potentially contain the universe of all federal in-person voter fraud investigations, prosecutions, and convictions that have been reported to these entities. However, given the types of data maintained on cases in each database, officials from each agency said it would be challenging to identify these cases because there is no specific code for identifying or tracking in-person voter fraud in the four databases. For example, the FJC's Integrated Database stores information on criminal cases filed in federal district court, and the USSC's Oracle database collects information solely on defendants convicted for federal crimes. Although each of these two databases has codes that identify type of criminal offense, neither has any specific code for election crimes.

Further, from our interviews with officials from the four federal agencies, we identified 14 different statutory provisions under which in-person voter fraud may be prosecuted. However, under each of these 14 statutes, a variety of conduct other than in-person voter fraud may be prosecuted, making searching by statute within a database over inclusive.[107]

States also varied in the extent to which they collected and maintained information on election fraud more broadly or in-person voter fraud in particular.[108] Of the 46 states we interviewed for our review, 27 states provided documentation to us related to election fraud, and this documentation was in a variety of formats. For example, seven states that became aware of fraud allegations through hotlines or online complaint forms provided us with spreadsheets containing information such as the date of the complaint, the name and contact information of the individual making the complaint, or an open-ended narrative field describing the alleged election law violation. Most of the documentation provided by the 27 states was not sufficiently detailed for us to determine whether in- person voter fraud was involved. In addition, 5 of the 27 states provided documentation that was focused on instances of election fraud that had been determined to warrant investigation or prosecution by a specific unit within the state responsible for addressing election fraud or by the state's attorney general. These states' documentation did not necessarily include all allegations of election fraud made to state-level authorities, because reports made to local authorities were not necessarily included.[109] As a result, the documentation we reviewed did not provide a complete picture of instances of in-person voter fraud within the state, even where documentation was provided to us.

The literature we reviewed identified similar challenges associated with variation in the data states collected on in-person voter fraud. For example, News21 analyzed 2,068 election fraud cases from 2000 through 2011, but acknowledged limitations with the data it received. According to the study, some state officials did not respond to requests for information, and some jurisdictions did not provide any information to News21because jurisdiction officials reported that their computer systems lacked the capability to search for election fraud cases. In some states' responses to News21, important details about the case were missing, including the circumstances of the alleged fraud. In these cases, News21 could not categorize the type of election fraud or the responsible party, such as a voter or election official.

AGENCY AND THIRD PARTY COMMENTS AND OUR EVALUATION

We provided a draft of this report to DOJ, EAC, FJC, and USSC for their review and comment. None had comments on the draft report.

We also provided excerpts of the draft report to the Secretaries of State Offices of each of the six treatment and comparison states we selected for our review. The excerpts for each treatment state–Kansas and Tennessee–included a full description of the methodology we employed in our study to select the treatment and comparison states and the findings that specifically pertained to each state regarding the costs of selected voter ID documents, the effects of changes in voter ID requirements on turnout and the overall number of provisional ballots cast, and the total number of provisional ballots cast and counted for ID reasons. The excerpts for each of the comparison states–Alabama, Arkansas, Delaware, and Maine—included a description of the methodology we employed to select the comparison states, and those findings that pertained to each state regarding the costs of selected voter ID documents, if applicable, and changes in provisional ballot usage between the 2008 and 2012 elections.[110] The Secretary of State Offices of Arkansas, Kansas, and Tennessee provided written comments on the excerpts provided to them for review, which are incorporated in the report as appropriate. The Office of the Secretary of State of Alabama provided technical comments on the excerpt provided for review, which we incorporated as appropriate. State election officials in Delaware and Maine reviewed the report excerpts and had no comments.

Overall, the Secretary of State Offices in Kansas and Tennessee stated that they believe that the report is flawed, and Tennessee officials noted that they do not confirm the data we used. The Secretary of State Offices from these two states disagreed with the methodology of our study, raising two common points of disagreement. First, the Offices in both states disagreed with aspects of the design of our study, specifically the criteria we used to select treatment and comparison states. Kansas and Tennessee asserted that their states were different from the states with which they were being compared, and thus our comparisons were flawed. Kansas and Tennessee stated that the larger declines in turnout that we found in their states, versus declines in the comparison states, could be explained by factors other than changes in their states' voter ID laws, occurring in either their own states or the comparison states. The Secretary of State's Office in Arkansas also raised a number of concerns regarding the criteria we used to select it as a comparison state, including that there was no election for any statewide office in 2008 and 2012, there was no major party opposition in the 2008 races, and there was a change in political climate between 2008 and 2012. Second, the state election offices in both Kansas and Tennessee questioned the validity of one of the data sources we used to measure turnout—the voter history and registration data that we purchased from Catalist LLC. Tennessee questioned the reliability of these data, stating that the vendor is not a neutral party, but an explicitly "progressive" data firm and its list of clients includes a number of organizations opposed to voter ID laws. Tennessee also stated that the Secretary of State's Office had no record of Catalist obtaining data from the Secretary of State after 2010, and thus could not attest to the accuracy or reliability of the 2012 data supplied to us by Catalist. Further, both Kansas and Tennessee questioned the validity of the vendor's estimates of registrants' race, which are based on an algorithm supplied by a third party. The Secretary of State's Offices in both states therefore took issue with our analyses that showed greater declines in turnout among African-American registrants in their respective states than among African-American registrants in the comparison states.

In addition, Tennessee raised two other issues of disagreement. First, it noted that our analyses of changes in voter turnout by age and race using the Current Population Survey (CPS) as a data source are inconsistent with official sub-group analyses reported by CPS. Second, regarding our analysis of provisional ballot usage, Tennessee stated that it believes we ignored unique factors that contributed to the increased use of provisional ballots in that state, compared to use of provisional ballots in the comparison states.

We address each of these comments below.

Selection of Treatment and Comparison States

Regarding the design of our study, we believe that we used appropriate criteria, and correctly applied the criteria to select our treatment and comparison states. As we discuss on pp. 46-47 of our report, and pp. 128-133 of appendix V, after we identified states for the treatment group, we then applied additional selection criteria to ensure that the treatment group states we selected did not have other changes that could plausibly account for any changes in voter turnout between the 2008 and 2012 general elections.[111] Specifically, in selecting Kansas and Tennessee as our treatment states, we selected states that did not experience changes in other election laws or practices between 2008 and 2012 that could substantially affect turnout and had similar election environments in 2008 and 2012 in terms of, for example, competitiveness of races and presence and competitiveness of ballot initiatives, among other things. As described in table 10 on pp. 132-133, we first conducted a legal analysis for each of the potential treatment states to determine if relevant election laws or procedures changed contemporaneously with the changes to the potential treatment states' ID laws. In its response, Tennessee noted that officials responsible for the administration of elections changed substantially at the state and local levels, and approximately thirty pieces of legislation were passed during the time between the 2008 and 2012 elections. Tennessee also noted that the political climate in the state changed substantially from 2008 to 2012, with the Tennessee House of Representatives majority party switching in 2008. We did not consider changes in administrative positions in election offices as part of our selection criteria, as we did not identify literature or research showing that such changes are likely to significantly affect voter turnout. We also reviewed changes to Tennessee election legislation and determined that none of the changes was likely to substantially affect turnout based on our legal review of those changes.[112] In addition, according to academic research on voting behavior in American politics, the party control of state legislatures is not is not among the variables identified as being associated with turnout in presidential general elections.

In addition to our legal analysis, we collected data on the competitiveness of statewide and federal elections in the potential treatment states in order to ensure that changes over time in voter mobilization efforts by campaigns were not likely to affect voter turnout in 2008 or 2012. We considered a race to be competitive if the margin of victory was fewer than 20 percentage points. As discussed on pp. 130-131 of our report, and shown in Table 12 on p. 139, using a number of indicators of competitiveness, including whether a statewide race (such as for U.S. Senate or Governor) was held in the state in 2008 or 2012, or the margin of victory for races that were held—the presidential race, races for U.S. Senate and U.S. House of Representative, races for other statewide offices, and ballot questions—our analysis indicated that Kansas and Tennessee had generally noncompetitive general election environments in both 2008 and 2012.

In their responses, Kansas and Tennessee stated that the 2012 election was particularly non-competitive in their respective states, and further, that the states we chose as comparison states had higher levels of competition in 2012, making these states inappropriate comparators. Kansas noted that it had no statewide political campaigns in 2012 other than the presidential campaign, and presidential campaigns typically are not active in Kansas; for example, Kansas noted there were no get-out- the-vote efforts in 2012. Tennessee noted, among other things, that the strength of the U.S. Senate campaigns differed in 2008 and 2012, and that the state drew minimal campaign dollars from the presidential campaigns to drive turnout in 2012. Kansas and Tennessee also stated that salient electoral issues in 2012 in Alabama, Arkansas, Delaware, and Maine made them inappropriate comparators. For example, Kansas noted that Maine had a race for U.S. Senate in 2012, whereas Kansas did not, and Tennessee noted that Arkansas, Alabama, and Maine all had controversial issues on their ballots in 2012.

The discussion below explains how we considered these factors when applying our methodology and why we believe our approach is appropriate for selecting treatment states and comparison states. We selected comparison states where the patterns in electoral competition did not substantially change from the 2008 to the 2012 general election and were similar to the patterns in the treatment states. Differences between the treatment and comparison states in any one year do not bias impact estimates, so long as these differences are constant across years, and the statistical properties of the difference-in-difference methods we use to estimate impact ensures that factors that may vary over time would not bias our estimates, as we discuss on pp. 146-147. Further, as we discuss on pp. 133-143, we used several criteria to choose states which matched Kansas and Tennessee in election cycles and the competitiveness of statewide races. We attempted to match U.S. Senate and gubernatorial election schedules in comparator states with those of Kansas and Tennessee, so as to avoid choosing states having mobilization efforts different from the treatment states that might differentially drive turnout. We examined the competitiveness of the presidential races, races for statewide offices, and ballot initiatives in the comparison states we selected by examining the margins of victory in these races. Table 12 on p. 139 shows the results of efforts to match comparison states with treatment states in terms of the margins of victory, indicating that the states generally matched election cycles, and, where they did not, margins of victory for races held were greater than 20 percent. On pages 141-142, we also discuss in detail our analysis of statewide ballot races in the 4 comparison states, to ensure that there were no particularly salient or competitive ballot questions that might have affected voter turnout inconsistently across both elections (i.e., contributed to increased turnout in 2008 but not 2012, or vice versa).

Our process to select comparison states was similar to the process we used to select treatment states. We repeated our legal analysis for each potential comparison state to ensure that none of these states experienced changes in election law and procedures from 2008 to 2012 that could have substantially affected turnout. Arkansas, in its response, noted that the state passed a number of measures impacting absentee voting; during our selection process we reviewed the amendments identified and determined that these changes and others enacted were unlikely to substantially affect turnout.[113]

Moreover, Kansas stated that it is not appropriate to compare Kansas to states that had any statewide race, such as Maine. In selecting the four comparison states, we selected two states—Alabama and Arkansas— that also had no U.S. Senate races in 2012, no gubernatorial races in either 2008 or 2012, and no competitive presidential races, like Kansas. Although Alabama and Arkansas had races for U.S. Senate in 2008, neither race was competitive, with margins of victory equal to 27 and 59 percent, respectively, and therefore were unlikely to have experienced unusually high turnout. For similar reasons, we believe that our other two comparison states, Delaware and Maine, remain appropriate comparators, because their U.S. Senate races in 2012 were not competitive, with margins of victory equal to 37 and 21 percent, respectively. Nevertheless, to test the robustness of our results to alternative choices of comparison states, we estimated the effect of ID laws using different combinations of comparison states and obtained consistent results across the multiple comparisons.

Tennessee also noted that its U.S. Senate race in 2012 was non- competitive compared to the race in 2008. Our test for evaluating U.S. Senate races among potential treatment states was either that a race was not held because 2008 or 2012 was not a U.S. Senate election year in the state or that a U.S. Senate race that was held had at least a 20 percent margin of victory, indicating that the race was not competitive and not likely to experience unusually high turnout. In the case of Tennessee, U.S. Senate races were held in both 2008 and 2012, each with a 34 percent margin of victory, indicating similar levels of competitiveness and consequential effect on voter turnout. As with Kansas, when conducting our analysis related to voter turnout, we used multiple combinations of treatment and comparison states, as well as a nationwide comparison group, to determine if our results were consistent across the selected states. As shown in appendix VI, the results are consistent across multiple comparisons.

With regard to Tennessee's specific concerns about ballot issues in Alabama, Arkansas, and Maine, we examined ballot questions as part of our selection process for treatment and comparison states. We collected data on the margin of victory for all statewide ballot questions in each state, and systematically searched news media and other electronic information databases to ensure that there were no particularly salient or competitive ballot questions that might affect voter turnout inconsistently across both elections (i.e., contributed to increased turnout in one year but not the next, or vice versa). As a result, we selected comparison states that had no ballot questions, noncompetitive questions, or similarly competitive questions present in both the 2008 and 2012 general elections, as described in appendix V. The relevant question for our analysis regarding comparison state qualifications is how the election environments compared within each state between the 2008 and 2012 general elections, rather than whether each comparison states' election environment was similar to Tennessee in 2012. This is because we compared changes in turnout within each comparison state to changes in turnout within Kansas and Tennessee to determine whether or not there were any effects of voter ID law changes. We conducted extensive sensitivity tests of our results by comparing Kansas and Tennessee to individual comparison states, multiple groups of comparison states, and a nationwide comparison group, and found our results to be consistent.

Further, Tennessee noted that in 2012, Alabama had an amendment dealing with health care reform and an amendment dealing with racial segregation and poll taxes on the ballot. Tennessee noted that both amendments should have increased turnout. In analyzing the competitiveness of Alabama's ballot initiatives in 2008 and 2012, we found that the initiatives were similarly competitive in both years. Specifically, we found that in 2012, 11 questions were on the ballot, and 3 were competitive, whereas in 2008, 6 questions were on the ballot and 5 were competitive (that is, where the margins of victory were less than 20 percent). The presence of several competitive ballot questions in both 2008 and 2012 created a similar potential for overall voter mobilization and engagement in both years. Further, according to our analysis, the ballot question on health care reform cited in Tennessee's comments has a margin of victory of 18 percent (close to our criteria of 20 percent being considered noncompetitive), while the ballot question on eliminating specific race based language in the Alabama Constitution was noncompetitive, with a margin of victory of 21 percent. Nevertheless, to ensure that our overall analysis of any effects of voter ID law changes by race or ethnicity were not affected by individual state-level issues, we conducted our analysis using other comparison states, which yielded similar effects.

Tennessee also noted that Arkansas had controversial gambling issues and a marijuana issue on the 2012 ballot, which, in their view, makes Arkansas an inappropriate comparator. Arkansas also noted the presence of these initiatives, stating that the controversial gambling initiatives were physically on the 2012 ballot, but due to Arkansas Supreme Court rulings close to Election Day, the votes cast were not counted. Arkansas noted that many voters probably were not aware of the court's decision to not count the votes and the fact that both issues were on the ballot could have impacted turnout. In reviewing Arkansas' ballot initiatives in 2008 and 2012, we found that Arkansas voter turnout was not likely to have been affected to a greater degree in 2012 or 2008 by ballot questions because each election had one competitive, salient ballot question race, with the remaining questions either noncompetitive or not on salient topics, as discussed in appendix V. The competitive and salient question was related to medical marijuana in 2012 (margin of victory of 3 percent), as noted in Tennessee's comment, and to limiting adoptions to married cohabitants in 2008 (margin of victory of 14 percent). This scenario of similarly salient and competitive ballot questions in both the 2008 and 2012 general elections suggests that ballot questions likely would have affected turnout similarly in both elections. In addition, our review of the 2008 ballot question media coverage in Arkansas indicated substantial campaigning related to the ballot question on limiting adoptions to married cohabitants, suggesting that voter mobilization efforts in the 2008 general election were not unlike efforts in 2012, when the medical marijuana question was on the ballot.

With regard to the two 2012 gambling initiatives noted by Tennessee and Arkansas, our analysis of statewide ballot questions that could affect turnout was based on officially reported results. In this case, we did not evaluate the gambling initiatives since votes for those initiatives were cast, but not counted, and were subsequently not reported in the official 2012 Arkansas general election results. We acknowledge the possibility that the initial salience and subsequent confusion about the gambling initiatives could have affected turnout. However, our use of multiple comparison states controls for the bias specific to any particular comparison. Our analysis of voter turnout included versions that excluded Arkansas, the results of which mirrored our general findings, as shown in appendix VI.

Tennessee also noted that Maine had the issue of same sex marriage on the ballot in 2012, and believed that a significant amount of money was spent to support and oppose the measure. We found that five ballot questions were on Maine's 2012 general election ballot, two of which were competitive. Three questions were on the 2008 general election ballot, two of which were competitive. The presence of competitive and salient ballot questions in both years suggests that voter mobilization was unlikely to have been higher in one of the elections versus the other. However, consideration of Maine's 2012 same-sex marriage initiative, as well as competitive imbalances between the 2008 and the 2012 general elections in Maine's two congressional districts, led us to conduct our analysis both with and without Maine included among our comparison states to ensure the validity of our findings. Our results were consistent under both approaches to the analysis, as described in appendix VI, suggesting that our results are robust to concerns about Maine's election environment.

Finally, Tennessee noted that Delaware is an inappropriate comparison state because it had Joe Biden on the ballot as Vice President in 2012. Joe Biden was on the ballot in Delaware as a vice presidential candidate in both 2008 and 2012, and thus we believe his candidacy would likely have had similar effects in both elections and would not have affected our results.

In summary, we believe that our use of two treatment states and multiple comparison groups strengthens our findings and makes them robust to potential sources of bias in any particular state or year. This design allowed us to analyze turnout changes in our treatment groups against several plausible comparators. In addition, the CPS data allowed us to conduct a version of the analysis including all states other than Kansas or Tennessee, as described in appendix VI.

A nationwide comparison group mitigates any bias caused by choosing particular comparison states, because the potentially biasing factors, such as the voter mobilization due to campaigns or ballot propositions, would need to have been systematically unbalanced over time in the remaining 48 states and the District of Columbia. Using this nationwide comparison group, we obtained results similar to those using the states we chose to purposively control for specific factors that can change over time, such as electoral competition and other changes to election administration laws.

Selection and Use of Data Sources

The Secretary of State Offices in Kansas and Tennessee took issue with the validity of the voter history and registration data we purchased from Catalist LLC., one of three data sources we used to analyze voter turnout. Tennessee noted that it had no record of Catalist's purchasing data from the state since 2010. According to Catalist, the firm acquired the Tennessee voter file directly from the Tennessee Secretary of State's Office on February 19, 2014.

This file included voter history data for the 2012 general election. Tennessee also noted that Catalist's stated progressive goals and clients make its data invalid. We took steps to assess the reliability of the data we used from Catalist and found the data sufficiently reliable for the purposes of our review. For example, we reviewed assessments of Catalist data reliability conducted by other researchers and, as we note on pp. 160-161 of our report, political scientists have extensively analyzed the reliability of Catalist's data on voter registration and turnout history, and have specifically examined the potential for political bias.

This independent, third-party research, published in two peer-reviewed journals of academic research that focus on methods of political analysis, found no evidence of systematic bias in the data Catalist provides.[114] In one of these publications, peer reviewers accepted Catalist data as sufficiently unbiased and reliable to validate another common source of data on voter turnout—post-election surveys of the general population. In addition, a study that used Catalist data was submitted as evidence by the Department of Justice in its case against Texas before a 3-judge panel of the U.S. District Court for the District of Columbia in June 2012.[115]

In addition to review by third-parties, we independently assessed the reliability of the data and took measures to ensure that the use of data from this particular source would not bias our results. First, we used other data sources—the CPS and the United States Elections Project—to produce parallel impact estimates when possible. Using these other data sources, we found results consistent with those using Catalist data, as described in appendix VI. Second, we assessed the data's reliability and found it sufficiently reliable for our purposes, as described in appendix VI.

The steps we took included reviewing documentation on the completeness and consistency of the voter files compared to official election results; comparing estimates of the change in turnout to estimates from other data sources; and interviewing Catalist staff regarding the entity's data management processes and controls.

Kansas and Tennessee also questioned whether Catalist accurately estimates a registrant's race. Specifically, Kansas and Tennessee asserted that our analysis of turnout among African-American registrants was flawed, due to the potential inaccuracy of these estimates. Two of the states used in our analysis—Alabama and Tennessee—include registrants' race in their voter registration and history databases. These data are included in official versions of voter registration and history databases, and are preserved in the versions of the databases we purchased from Catalist.

The remaining four states we analyzed— Arkansas, Delaware, Kansas, and Maine—have not collected racial data on almost all registrants as part of their databases. For these registrants, Catalist estimates race using an algorithm supplied by a commercial firm.

As part of our analysis, we assessed the reliability of Catalist's estimated racial data, derived by the algorithm, and found them sufficiently reliable for the purposes of our review. To assess the reliability of these racial estimates, we received a custom validation from Catalist, which compared the estimated race of registrants in North Carolina to the actual race that registrants report to state election officials.

This analysis found that approximately 70 to 90 percent of registrants, depending on racial group, coded by Catalist as "likely" or "highly likely" to self-identify with a certain racial group did, in fact, identify with that group in official records. Academic research has found similar levels of reliability. One study matched racial estimates from Catalist's voter files to a nationwide survey, in which respondents were allowed to identify with various racial groups. For at least 93 percent of survey respondents, Catalist's estimates matched the race that respondents identified for themselves.

Our review of the evidence allowed us to conclude that Catalist's estimates of race were sufficiently reliable for the purpose of calculating impact estimates for various racial subgroups. However, we also assessed the sensitivity of our results to potential racial misclassification by estimating effects separately for Alabama and Tennessee, where 98.8 and 63.4 percent of the racial data, respectively, are provided by registrants directly. In addition, several versions of the analysis include only registrants with self-reported race and/or age in these states. We obtained results similar to those we obtained using estimated racial data in Arkansas, Delaware, Kansas, and Maine.

Tennessee also stated that CPS data contradict our assertion that Tennessee saw a decline in voter participation among 18 to 24 year-olds in the 2012 general election. First, Tennessee stated that the CPS demonstrates that turnout among 18 to 24 year-olds was not statistically different from the national average in 2012, but that turnout among this group was statistically lower than the national average in 2008. Second, Tennessee stated that in 2008, prior to passage of Tennessee's photo ID law, the CPS estimated that 59 percent of Non-Hispanic Blacks voted in Tennessee, but that in 2012, after the implementation of the photo ID law, 61 percent of Non-Hispanic Blacks voted. Tennessee asserts that the CPS supports higher turnout among the Non-Hispanic Black registrants, rather than a decline. However, our analysis focuses on the question of whether changes in turnout from 2008 to 2012 in our treatment states were similar to changes from 2008 to 2012 in our comparison states, not whether a subgroup in one state experienced a change in turnout over that time. Additionally, our findings with respect to subgroups were estimated from a statistical model based on the complete, respondent- level public release file of CPS data. We did not use state-level CPS data published by the Census Bureau. Notably, the Census Bureau measures turnout as a proportion of registered voters who say they voted, did not vote, or "don't know" whether they voted. In contrast, our analysis adopts a common approach of treating the last group as having missing data. Therefore, the published state-level CPS data cited by Tennessee do not contradict our analysis and are not directly comparable.

Tennessee also stated that our draft report referred to individuals 18 and younger and that no one under the age of 18 at the time of the election was allowed to vote in Tennessee. We revised our description of age group ranges analyzed in the report to reflect those age ranges as of 2008. Our analysis and results were not affected by the age group description revisions.

Additional Comments

The Tennessee Secretary of State's office also stated that our report is incomplete regarding the factors that caused an increase in the usage of provisional ballots in Tennessee. According to Tennessee, to compare the 2008 provisional numbers to the 2012 provisional numbers and attribute the increase in the usage of provisional ballots to changes in voter ID requirements ignores relevant factors specifically unique to Tennessee. Tennessee cited changes to its provisional ballot statute in 2011 that allowed voters to cast provisional ballots under additional circumstances and subsequent election official training as factors that it states increased provisional ballot use. We acknowledge that increased training and additional circumstances under which voters may have been permitted to cast provisional ballots may have affected provisional ballot usage in Tennessee. While we noted in our report that such factors might exist generally, we have included Tennessee's perspectives on why provisional ballot usage increased in particular in Tennessee in relevant sections of our report.

Further, with regard to data jurisdictions in Arkansas reported to EAVS on provisional ballots, Arkansas noted that some counties may have misunderstood what is required in EAVS and suggested that the data may need to be reexamined. We determined that some local election jurisdictions in some states, such as some jurisdictions in Arkansas, did not consistently report provisional ballot information to the EAVS for both the 2008 and 2012 elections. To increase the reliability of our analysis, we analyzed provisional ballot data only for jurisdictions that reported provisional ballot information in both 2008 and 2012 and, separately, for all jurisdictions that reported provisional ballots in one or both years. In our analyses we obtained similar results, indicating that our exclusion of jurisdictions with missing data did not affect our conclusions.

In addition, Kansas noted that, in its view, the analytically correct comparison for Kansas in 2012 would be in Kansas in 2000, the last time there were no U.S. Senate or statewide offices on the ballot.

Kansas stated that in 2000, statewide turnout in Kansas was 66.7 percent and turnout in 2012 was 66.8 percent. Rather than comparing changes in turnout between general elections within one state, we used a difference- in-difference approach to compare how changes in turnout in our treatment states from the 2008 to the 2012 general elections compared to changes in turnout in our comparison states for the same elections, as a difference-in-difference approach is a more robust method for analyzing whether changes in voter ID laws had any effect on turnout on the treatment states because we controlled for other factors that could affect turnout. Thus, our difference-in-difference approach controls for all factors that changed in similar ways over time in the states analyzed. Comparisons within Kansas between the 2000 and 2012 elections would confound any effect of voter ID laws, which changed during this period, and various other factors that also changed, such as salient political issues, voter mobilization efforts by campaigns and interest groups, and changes to other election administration policies.

Overall, we believe that the design and implementation of our study were rigorous, due to the careful selection of appropriate treatment and comparison states, the use of three different sources of turnout data, and the application of a number of statistical techniques to control for competing explanations for our results.

Our overall findings of greater turnout declines in treatment states than in comparison states are consistent across the three datasets we used, occurred in both of our treatment states in comparison with multiple constructions of the comparison group, and withstood multiple tests of the sensitivity of our results. This gives us confidence that the findings are most likely attributable to changes in voter ID requirements rather than other factors.

However, as we have noted on pp. 55-56, any policy evaluation in a non- experimental setting such as ours, cannot account for all unobserved factors that could impact the results. For example, Kansas stated that photo ID laws are intended to reduce or eliminate fraudulent voting, and if lower overall turnout occurs after implementation of a photo ID law, some of the decrease may be attributable to the prevention of fraudulent votes. We have noted in our report the challenges in estimating the incidence of in-person voter fraud, which would make any analysis of the effect of voter ID laws in preventing in-person voter fraud difficult. Given these difficulties, we did not attempt to test this explanation in our study, and thus we cannot rule it out as a reasonable contributor to some of the turnout declines we found.

Rebecca Gambler
Director, Homeland Security and Justice

Nancy Kingsbury, Ph.D.
Managing Director, Applied Research and Methods

APPENDIX I. DEMOGRAPHIC CHARACTERISTICS OF VOTERS WHO VOTED AND REGISTERED THROUGH DIFFERENT METHODS

Voter Demographics by Method of Voting

States have established alternatives for voters to cast a ballot other than at the polls on Election Day, including absentee voting and early voting.[116] All states and the District of Columbia have provisions allowing voters to cast their ballots before Election Day by voting absentee, with variations on who may vote absentee, whether the voter needs to provide an excuse, and the time frames for applying for and submitting absentee ballots.[117] As of the 2012 general election, 27 states and the District of Columbia allowed voters to cast an absentee ballot by mail without an excuse; 33 states and the District of Columbia had laws providing for early voting; and Oregon and Washington were vote-by-mail states. Using data from the Voting and Registration Supplement to the U.S. Census Bureau's Current Population Survey (CPS), we identified the proportions of voters in different demographic categories that reported that they voted (1) in person on Election Day; (2) in person before Election Day; (3) by mail on Election Day; or (4) by mail before Election Day. Our analysis covered the 2008, 2010, and 2012 elections, and included the following demographic characteristics:

- race,
- education,
- age,

- income,
- employment status,
- residential mobility,[118] and
- sex.

Additional details regarding our methodology can be found in appendix II. Our analysis showed that the majority of individuals within each demographic category voted in person on Election Day. The detailed results of our analysis can be found in figures 7-13 below.

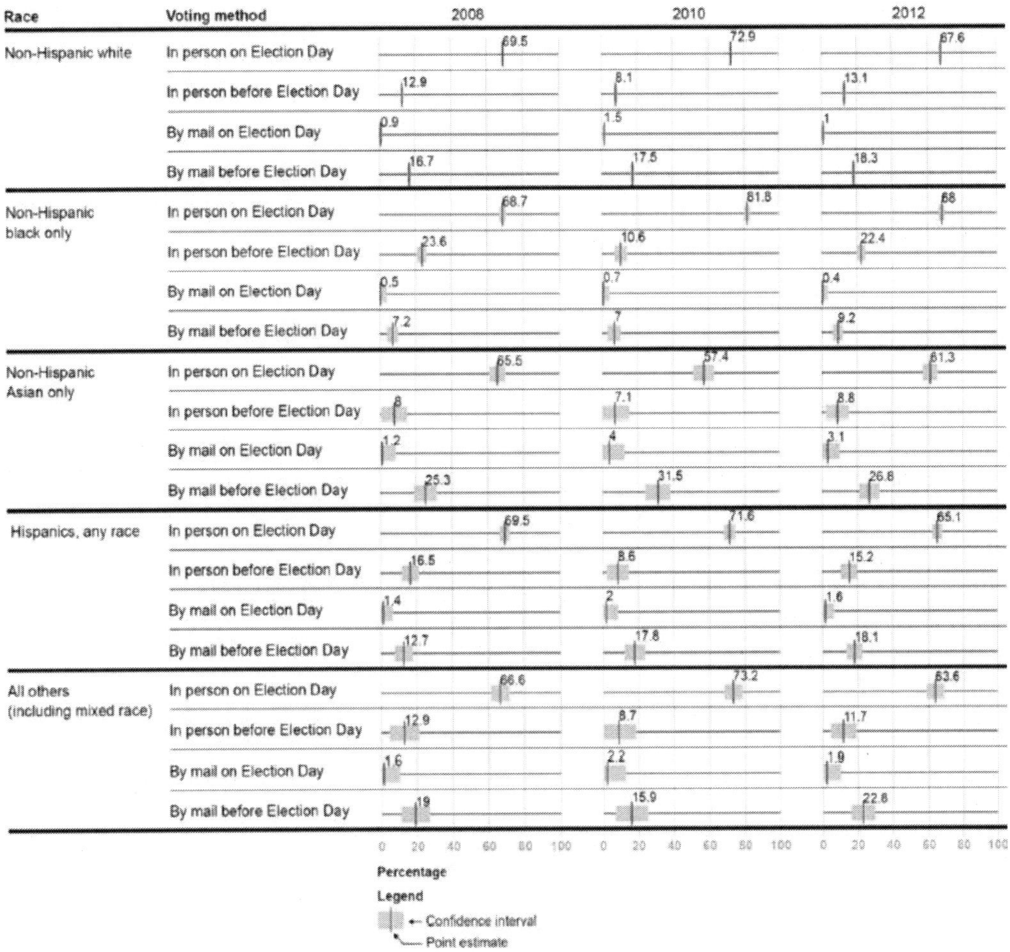

Source: GAO analysis of U.S. Census Bureau's Current Population Survey Data. | GAO-14-634.

Figure 7. Voting Method by Race in the 2008, 2010, and 2012 General Elections.

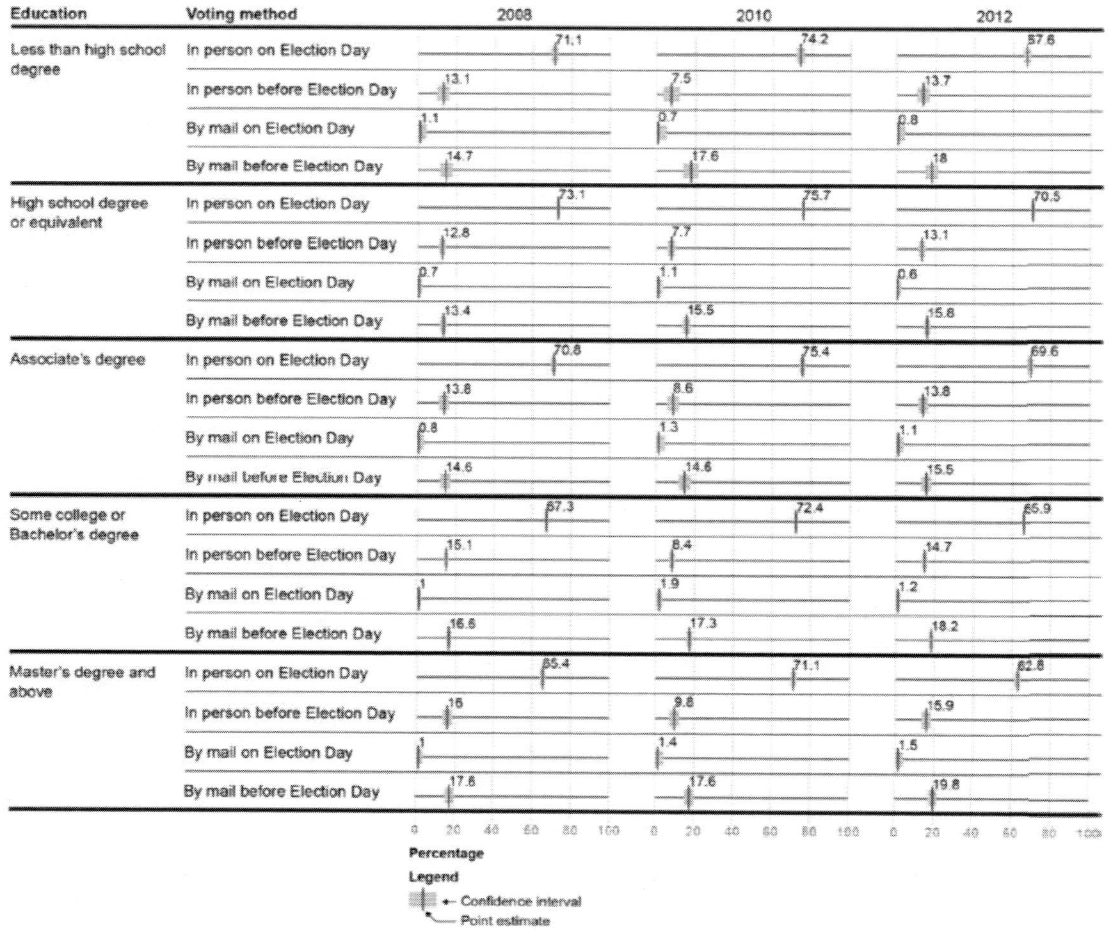

Source: GAO analysis of U.S. Census Bureau's Current Population Survey Data. | GAO-14-634.

Figure 8. Voting Method by Education Level in the 2008, 2010, and 2012 General Elections.

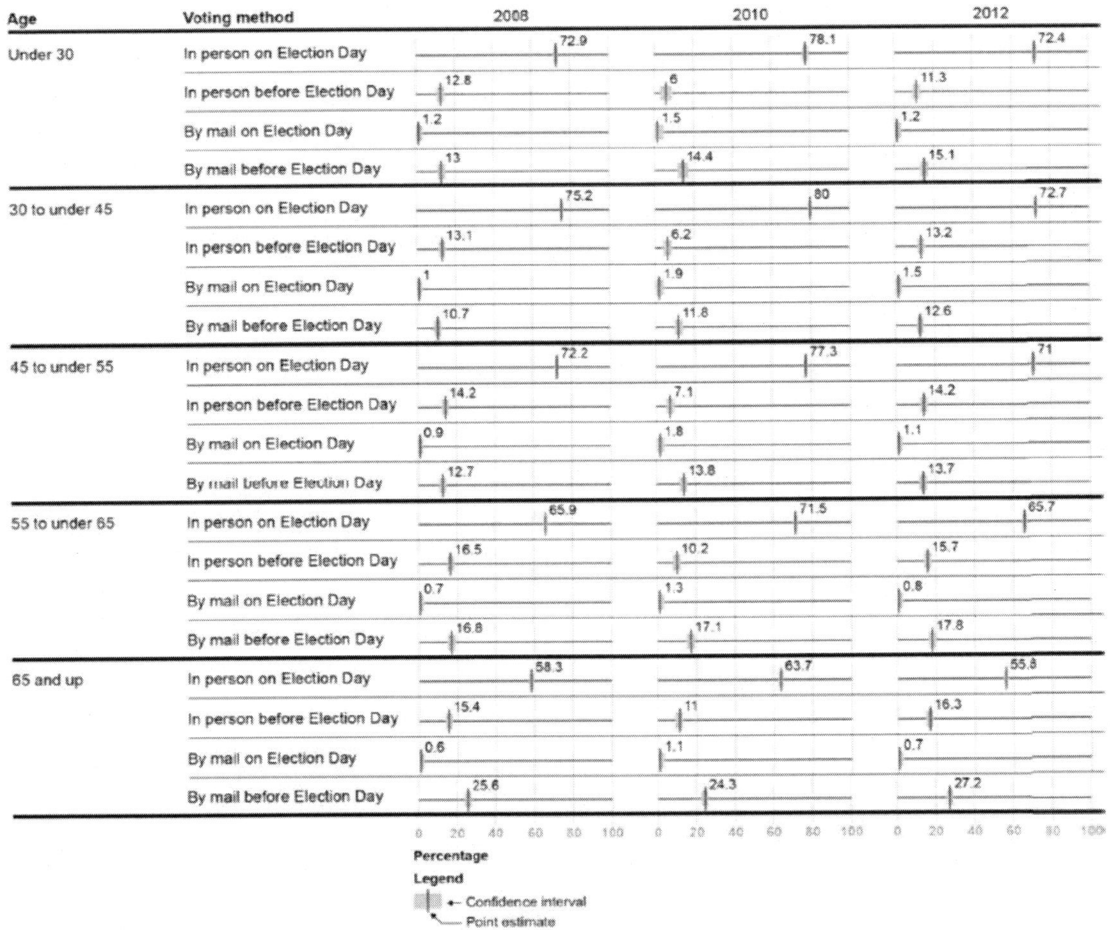

Source: GAO analysis of U.S. Census Bureau's Current Population Survey Data. | GAO-14-634.

Figure 9. Voting Method by Age in the 2008, 2010, and 2012 General Elections.

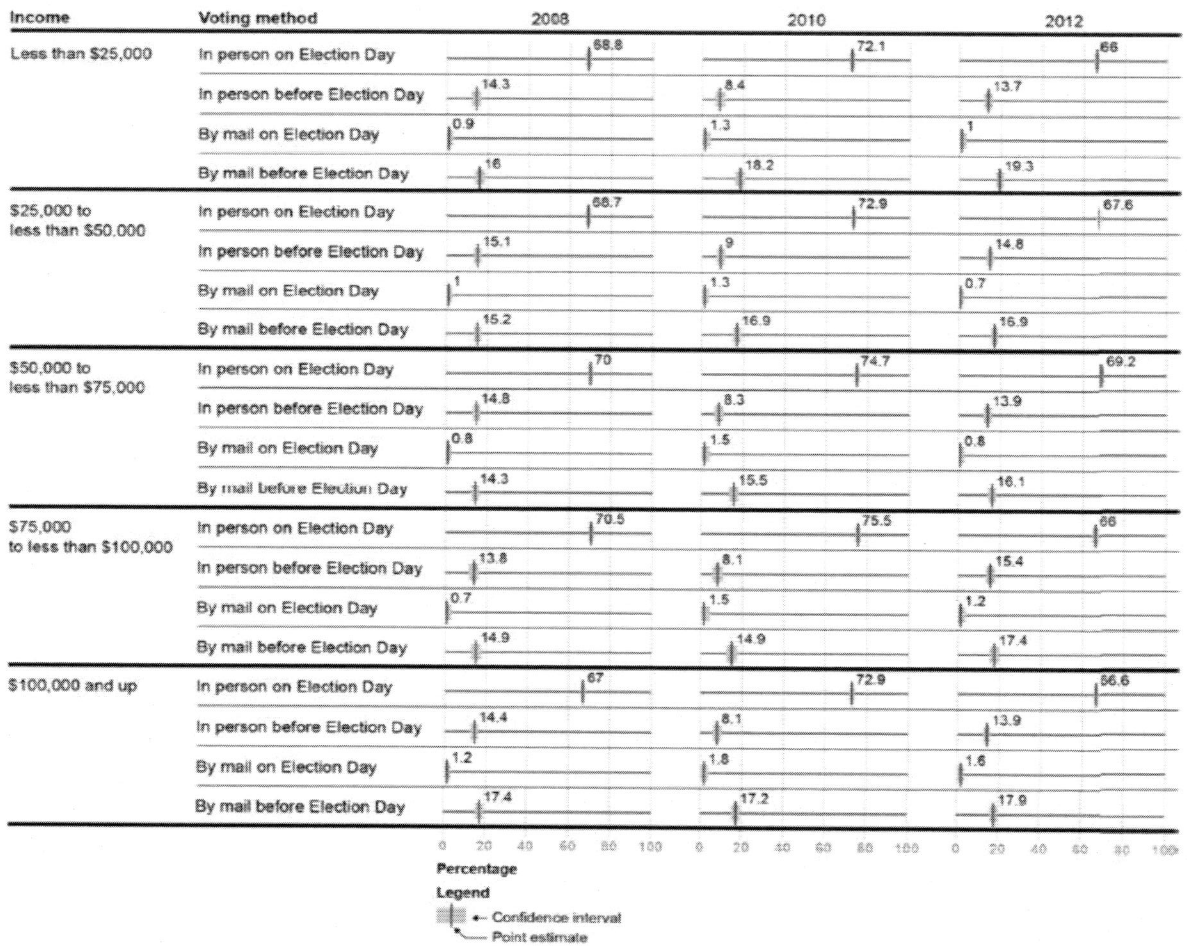

Source: GAO analysis of U.S. Census Bureau's Current Population Survey Data. | GAO-14-634.

Figure 10. Voting Method by Income Level in the 2008, 2010, and 2012 General Elections.

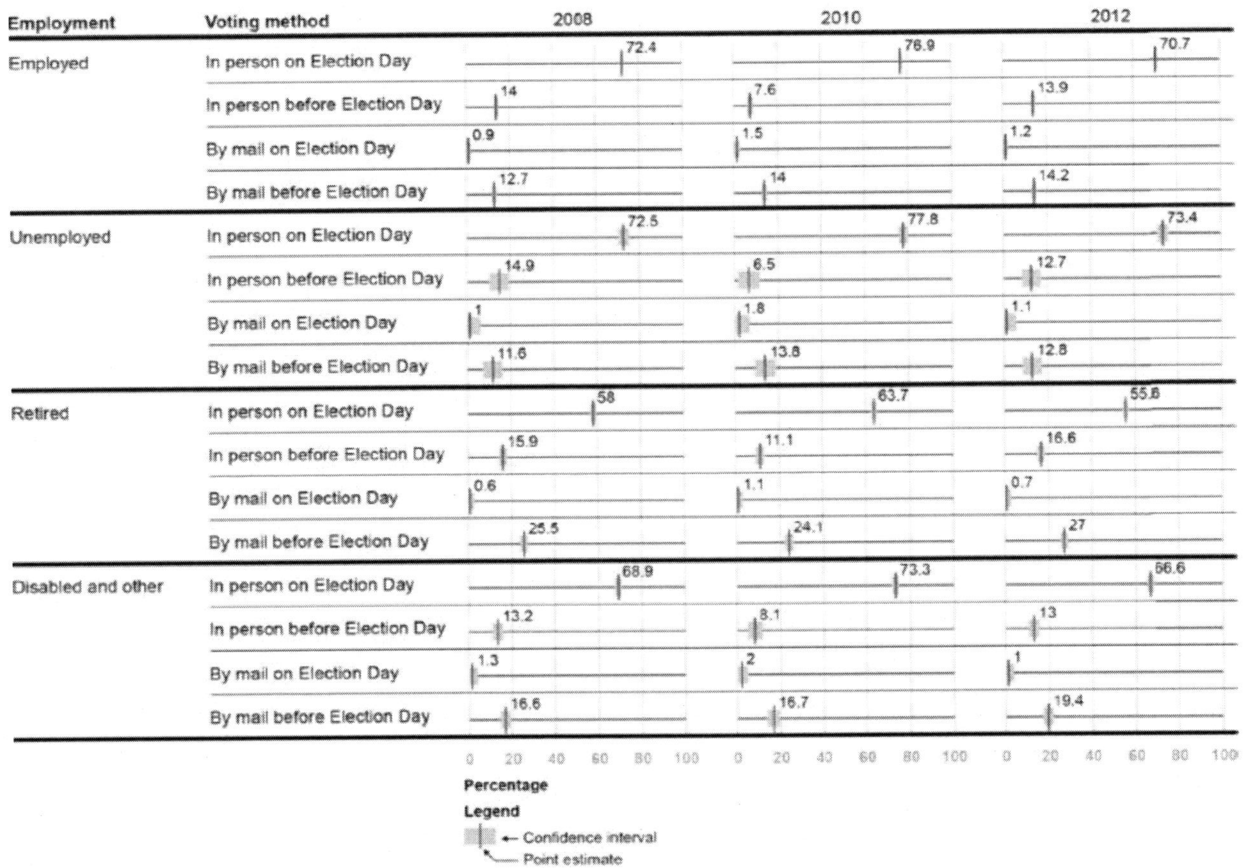

Source: GAO analysis of U.S. Census Bureau's Current Population Survey Data. | GAO-14-634.

Figure 11. Voting Method by Employment Status in the 2008, 2010, and 2012 General Elections.

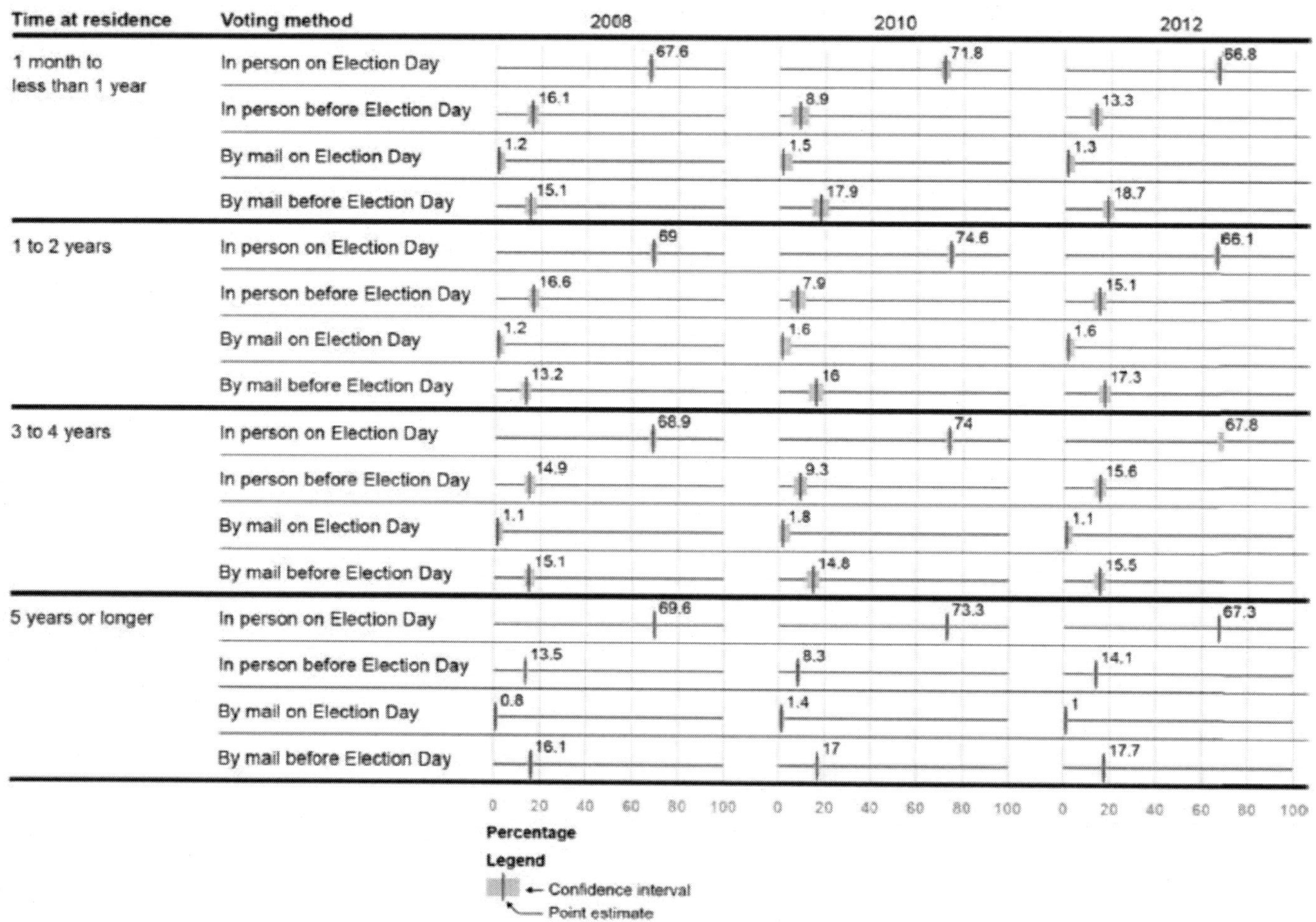

Source: GAO analysis of U.S. Census Bureau's Current Population Survey Data. | GAO-14-634.

Figure 12. Voting Method by Length of Time at Residence in the 2008, 2010, and 2012 General Elections.

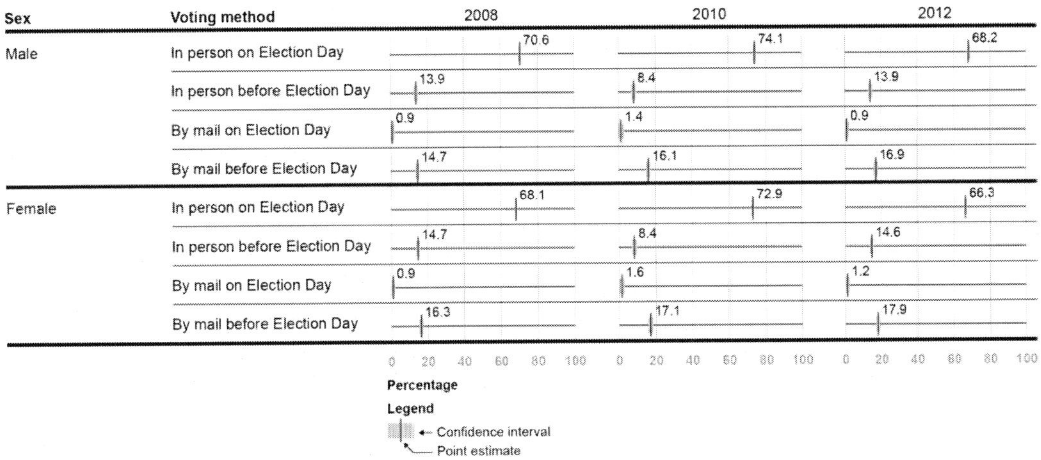

Source: GAO analysis of U.S. Census Bureau's Current Population Survey Data. | GAO-14-634.

Figure 13. Voting Method by Sex in the 2008, 2010, and 2012 General Elections.

Voter Demographics by Method of Registration

With the exception of North Dakota, all states and the District of Columbia generally require citizens to register before voting. Citizens apply to register to vote in various ways, such as at motor vehicle agencies, by mail, at local voter registrar offices, or through third-parties.[119] We reported in October 2012 that 30 states and the District of Columbia imposed some requirement on organizations that conduct voter registration drives. As of October 2012, 17 states did not impose any requirements on third- party voter registration; that is, persons and organizations may generally conduct voter registration drives without restriction. In addition, 2 states— New Hampshire and Wyoming—did not allow third-party voter registration drives. Using data from the Voting and Registration Supplement to CPS, we identified the proportions of registered citizens in different demographic categories that reported that they had registered to vote (1) at a government office (including a department of motor vehicles (DMV), a public assistance agency such as a Medicaid or Food Stamps office, or a town hall or county/government registration office) or a polling place; (2) by mail or online; (3) through a registration drive or at a school, hospital or campus; or (4) stated that they did not know how they registered or used another method. Our analysis covered the 2008, 2010, and 2012 elections, and included the following demographic characteristics:

- race,
- education,
- age,
- income,
- employment status,
- residential mobility,[120] and
- sex.

Additional details regarding our methodology can be found in appendix II. We found that respondents in most demographic groups were more likely to report having registered at a government office than through other methods.[121] The detailed results of our analysis can be found in figures 14-20 below.

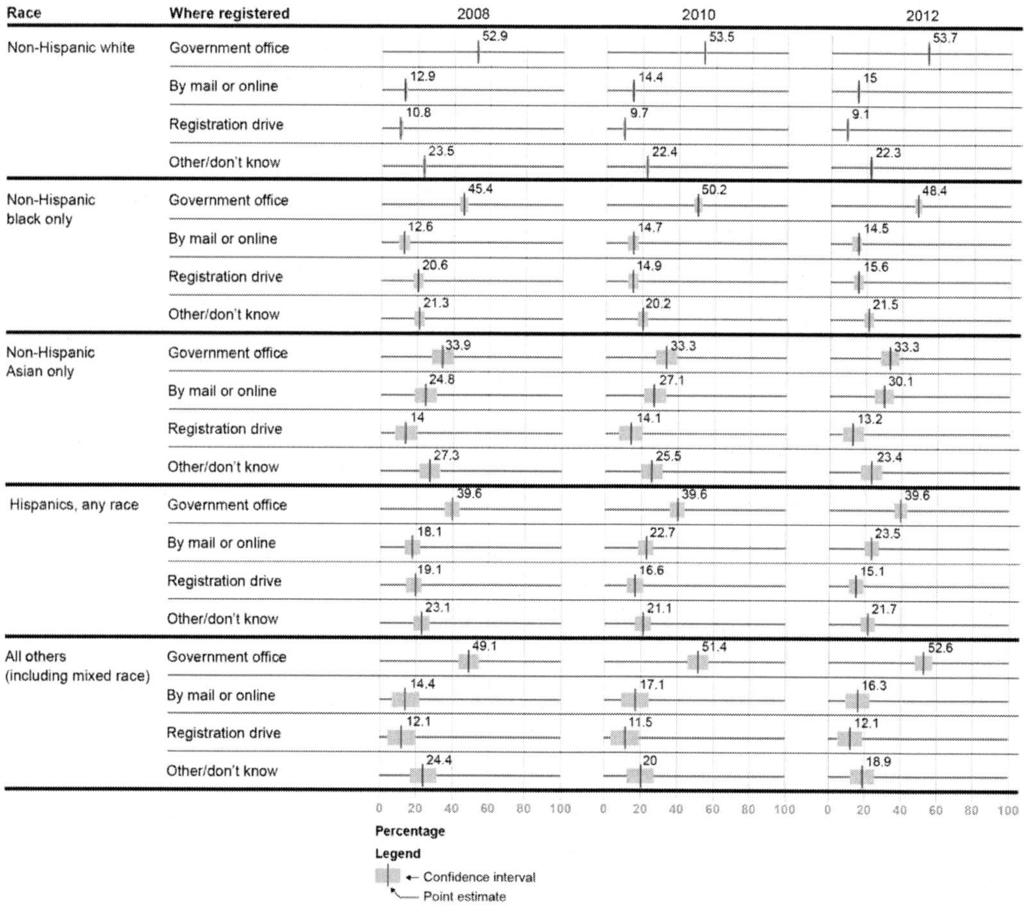

Source: GAO analysis of U.S. Census Bureau's Current Population Survey Data. | GAO-14-634.

Figure 14. Registration Method by Race in the 2008, 2010, and 2012 General Elections.

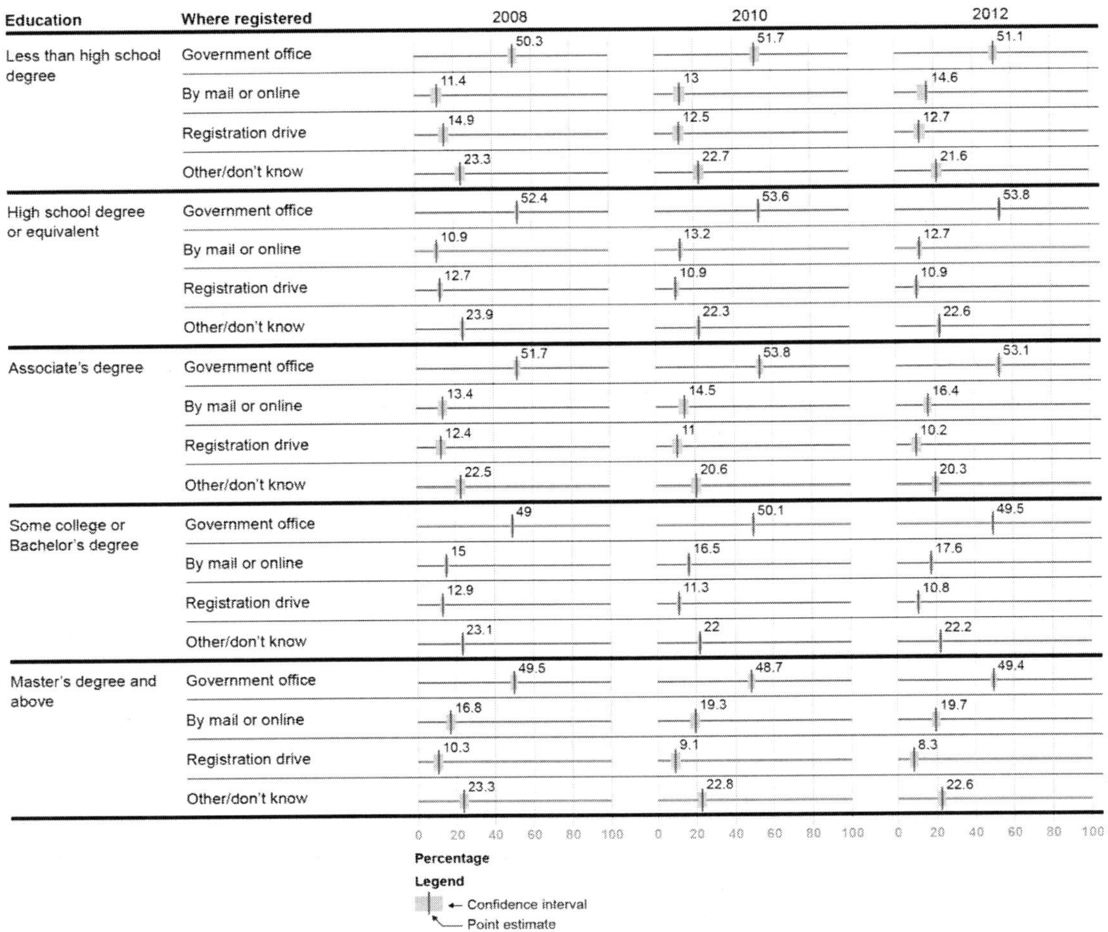

Source: GAO analysis of U.S. Census Bureau's Current Population Survey Data. | GAO-14-634.

Figure 15. Registration Method by Education Level in the 2008, 2010, and 2012 General Elections.

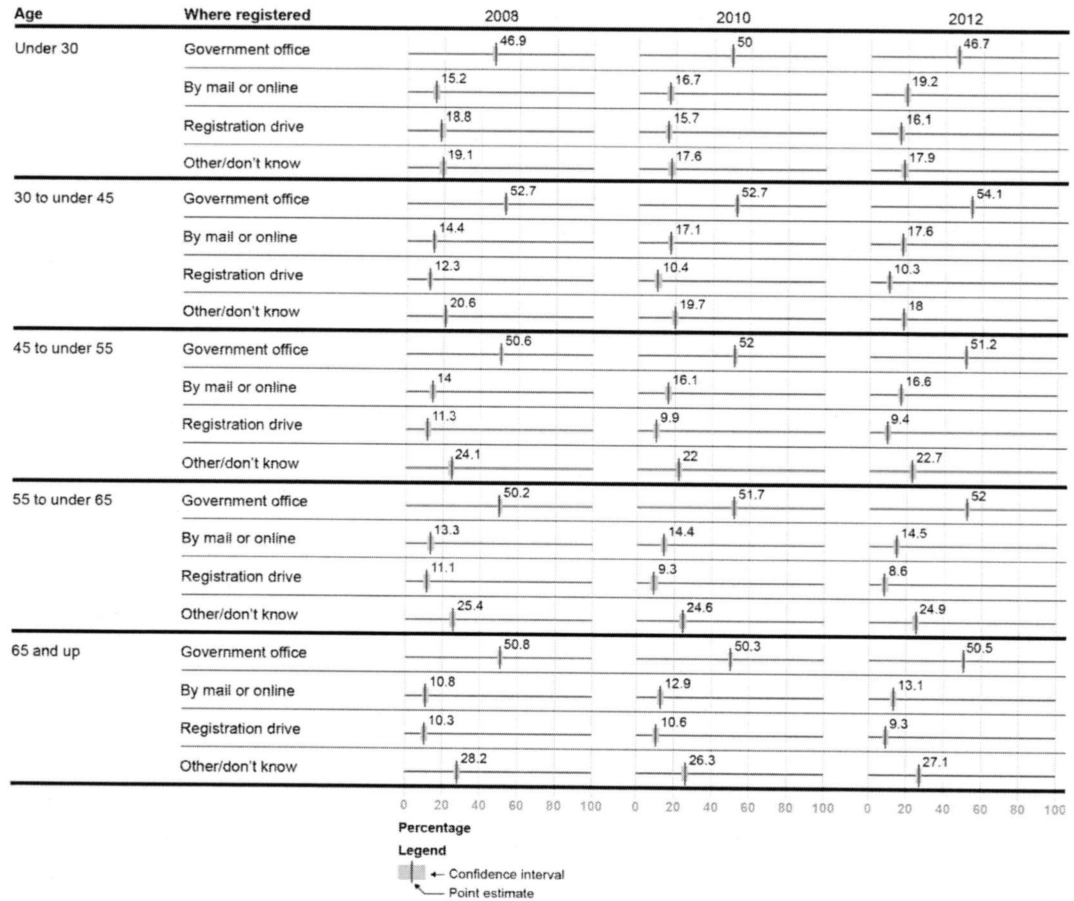

Source: GAO analysis of U.S. Census Bureau's Current Population Survey Data. | GAO-14-634.

Figure 16. Registration Method by Age in the 2008, 2010, and 2012 General Elections.

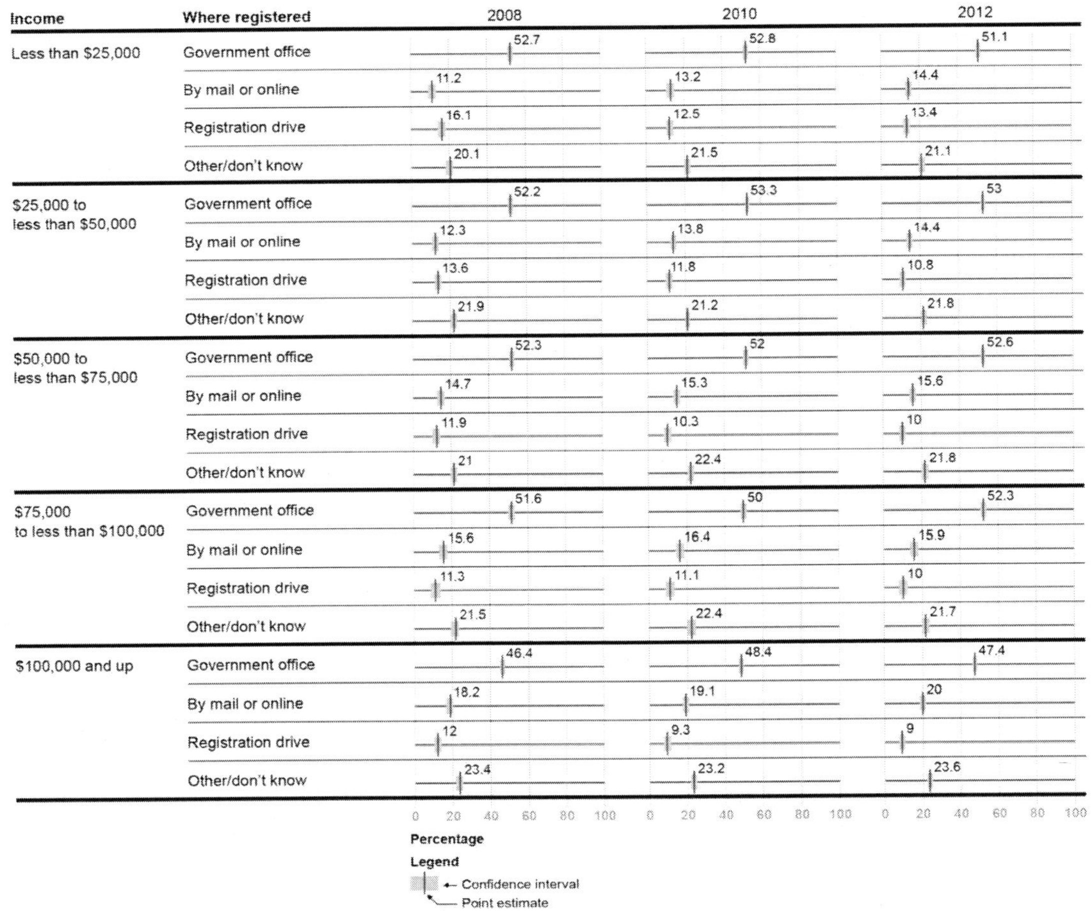

Source: GAO analysis of U.S. Census Bureau's Current Population Survey Data. | GAO-14-634.

Figure 17. Registration Method by Income Level in the 2008, 2010, and 2012 General Elections.

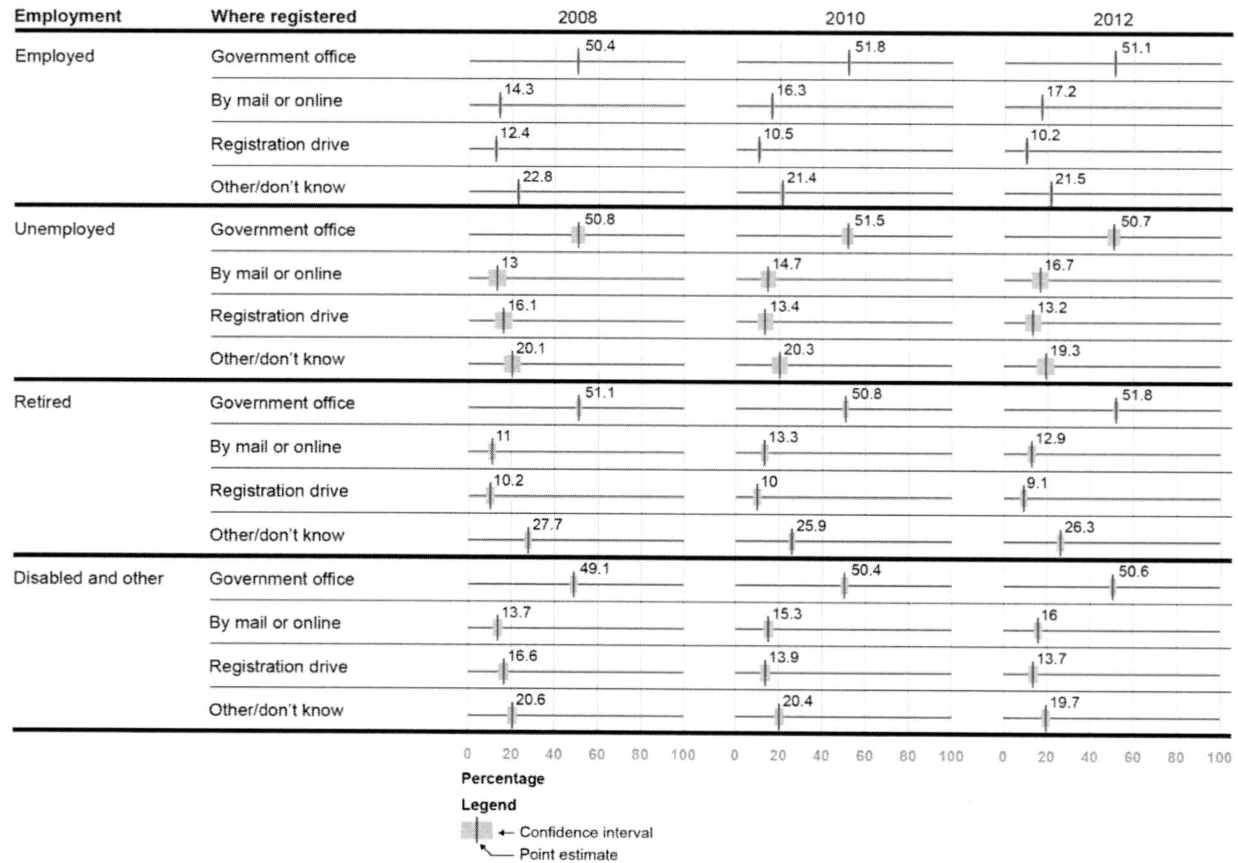

Source: GAO analysis of U.S. Census Bureau's Current Population Survey Data. | GAO-14-634.

Figure 18. Registration Method by Employment Status in the 2008, 2010, and 2012 General Elections.

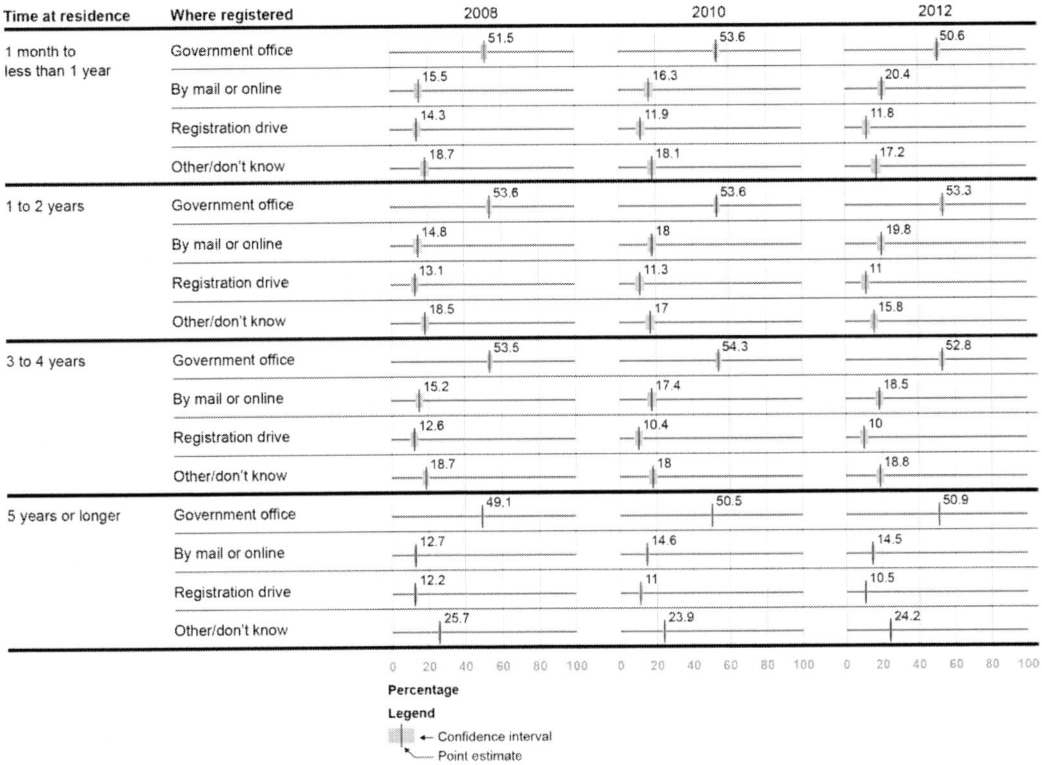

Source: GAO analysis of U.S. Census Bureau's Current Population Survey Data. | GAO-14-634.

Figure 19. Registration Method by Length of Time at Residence in the 2008, 2010, and 2012 General Elections.

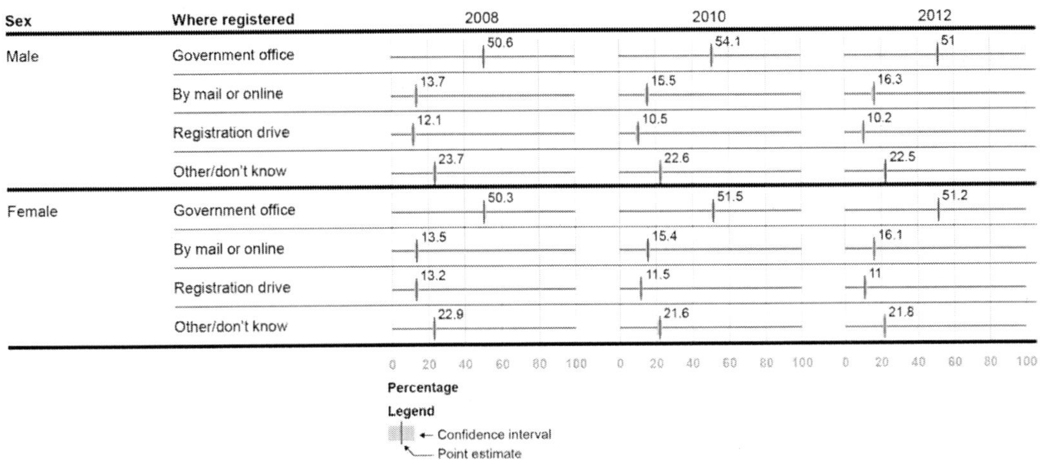

Source: GAO analysis of U.S. Census Bureau's Current Population Survey Data. | GAO-14-634.

Figure 20. Registration Method by Sex in the 2008, 2010, and 2012 General Elections.

Appendix II. Objectives, Scope, and Methodology

Objectives

This report addresses the following questions:

1. What does available literature indicate about the proportion of voters who have selected identification (ID) documents, and what are the direct costs to voters to obtain documents needed to satisfy state voter ID requirements?
2. What do existing studies indicate about how, if at all, voter ID laws have affected turnout?
3. What does our analysis of available data indicate about how, if at all, changes in voter ID laws have affected turnout in selected states?
4. To what extent were provisional ballots cast because of ID reasons and counted in two selected states during the 2012 election, and how did provisional ballot use in those states change after the adoption of voter identification laws?
5. What challenges, if any, exist in using available information at the federal and state levels to estimate the incidence of in-person voter fraud?

In addition, this report provides information related to the demographic characteristics of early voters and voters registered through third parties. This information can be found in appendix I.

Proportion of Voters Who Have Selected ID Documents and Direct Costs to Voters to Obtain Documents Needed to Satisfy Voter ID Requirements

To determine what existing studies indicate about the proportion of voters who have selected ID documents, we first conducted a literature review. We targeted our literature search to databases that index peer-reviewed journals such as *Political Analysis, Election Law Journal*, and *Judicature*. We also broadened our search beyond articles published in peer-reviewed journals to identify studies such as dissertations, conference proceedings, or studies issued by research institutes or government agencies. For example, we conducted both subject and keyword searches in Academic OneFile, Article First, Dissertation Abstracts, Online, ECO, JSTOR, NTIS, ProQuest, PolicyFile, PsycInfo, Social SciSearch, and Worldcat. We performed these searches and identified studies from January 1, 2003, to May 2013, with subsequent searches to locate any new studies through March 2014.

In addition to performing searches of literature databases, we reviewed the dockets of court cases that we identified as involving challenges to state voter ID requirements in order to identify studies submitted to the courts that may provide information on proportions of voters that have selected forms of ID. Specifically, we identified relevant studies submitted in the following cases: *Applewhite v. Pennsylvania,* No. 330 MD 2012 (Pa. Commw. Ct.); *Frank v. Walker*, No. 11-01128 (E.D. Wis.); *Texas v. Holder*, No. 12-00128 (D.D.C.); *League of United Latin American Citizens v. Deininger*, No. 12-00185 (E.D. Wis.); *South Carolina v. United States,* No. 12-203 (D.D.C.).

Through our literature search, we identified 10 studies that provided sufficiently sound information on proportions of voters who have selected ID documents.[122] A GAO social scientist read and assessed each study, using a standardized data collection instrument. The assessment focused on information such as the types of IDs examined, the research design and data sources used, and methods of data analysis and subgroups analyzed. The assessment also focused on the quality of the data used in the studies as reported by the researchers, any limitations of data sources for the purposes for which they were used, and inconsistencies in reporting study results. A second GAO social scientist reviewed each completed data collection instrument to verify the accuracy of the information included. We determined that the studies were sufficiently sound to support their results and conclusions.

To determine the direct costs to voters to obtain selected documents required to satisfy state voter ID requirements, we first reviewed state statutes and legislative websites to identify those states that had enacted requirements for all eligible voters attempting to vote to present identification documents that fall into one of three categories (1) photo only, government issued; (2) photo only, can be nongovernment issued; (3) nonphoto, government issued.[123] We excluded states that allow voters without ID to cast a regular ballot by affirming their own identity at the polling place, since there would be no cost to the voter in this situation. We excluded states that allow nonphoto, nongovernment forms of identification because costs to obtain these types of documents can vary widely and are difficult to obtain.[124] As of June 2014, 17 selected states met these criteria.[125]

We reviewed state statutes, voter education material, and relevant official state websites to identify those types of ID required in each of the 17 states to satisfy the states' voter ID requirements. All selected states accepted driver's licenses, the most commonly used form of identification at the polls, and nondriver state IDs. During the course of our evaluation, we reviewed state websites that contained information on costs for driver's licenses and nondriver state IDs in the 17 states. The state websites we reviewed included those for states' departments of motor vehicles, departments of public safety, departments of driver services, and departments of transportation, among others. Using information obtained from these websites, we compiled the costs of driver's licenses and nondriver state IDs for the 17 selected states. We also collected information on any additional fees associated with obtaining one of these forms of identification.[126] To confirm the accuracy of these costs, we contacted the appropriate state officials in each state.

While researching driver's license and nondriver ID costs in the 17 states, we also obtained information on which of these 17 states provide some type of free identification card to voters who do not own one of the forms of ID required to be presented at the polls before voting. Each state that provides a form of free ID has its own requirements for voters to obtain the free ID. We examined official state websites and identified these requirements, which may include providing proof of identity, proof of residency, Social Security number, and verification of voter registration, among other requirements. In cases where additional documentation, such as a birth certificate, is necessary to prove identity, we identified the cost of these documents through official state websites. We confirmed the requirements for free voter identification and the cost of required documents with state officials.

Information from Selected Studies on Any Effects of State Voter ID Laws on Turnout

To determine what existing studies and available data indicate about how voter ID laws have affected turnout in selected states, if at all, we reviewed the literature on this topic and analyzed turnout data in selected states. Specifically, for the review of existing studies, we targeted our literature search to databases that index peer-reviewed journals such as *Political Analysis, Election Law Journal,* and *Judicature*. We also broadened our search beyond articles published in peer-reviewed journals to identify studies such as dissertations, conference proceedings or studies issued by research institutes or government agencies. For example, we conducted both subject and keyword searches in various databases, including Academic OneFile, Article First, Dissertation Abstracts, Online, ECO, JSTOR, NTIS, ProQuest, PolicyFile, PsycInfo, Social SciSearch, and Worldcat. We performed these searches and identified articles from January 1, 2003 to May 2013, with subsequent searches to locate any additional material through March 2014. In addition to searches of literature databases, we reviewed the dockets of court cases that involved challenges to state voter ID requirements, such as those listed in our description above for identifying studies that estimate proportions of voters with selected ID documents, in order to identify studies submitted to the courts that assessed the effects of state voter ID requirement on turnout. During the course of this review, we did not identify any studies submitted to the courts that provide relevant data on the effects of voter ID laws on turnout.

Through our literature search, we identified 10 studies that provide sufficiently sound information on possible effects, if any, of state voter ID requirements on voter turnout.[127] A GAO social scientist read and assessed each study, using a data collection instrument. The assessment focused on the research design and data sources used, methods of data analysis and subgroups analyzed, the primary conclusions, and limitations that could affect those conclusions based on generally accepted social science principles.[128] The assessment also focused on the quality of the data used in the studies as reported by the researchers and our observations of any problems with missing data, any limitations of data sources for the purposes for which they were used, and inconsistencies in reporting study results. A second GAO social scientist reviewed each completed data collection instrument to verify the accuracy of the information included. A GAO statistician also reviewed each study and completed the data collection instrument. We determined that these studies were sufficiently sound to report their results; however, we discuss limitations associated with these studies' methodologies in this report.

Our Evaluation of Available Data on Any Effects of Changes in State Voter ID Laws on Turnout in Selected States

For our evaluation of available data to identify how, if at all, changes in voter ID laws may affect turnout, more detailed information on our scope and methodology is presented in appendixes V and VI. In summary, we selected treatment states—Kansas and Tennessee—that implemented changes to their voter ID requirements between the 2008 and 2012 general elections. We also selected comparison states—Alabama, Arkansas, Delaware, and Maine—

that did not implement changes to voter ID requirements during the same time period. When selecting these states for our analysis, we sought to minimize the presence of other factors that could affect voter turnout, such as other changes to election laws and election competitiveness. We then compared treatment and comparison state changes in voter turnout from the 2008 to 2012 general elections to determine what effect, if any, changes in state voter ID laws had on voter turnout in the treatment states of Kansas and Tennessee. Our findings are not generalizable to states beyond Kansas and Tennessee.

Provisional Ballot Use

To determine how frequently provisional ballots were cast because of ID reasons and counted in selected states during the 2012 election, we analyzed data from the Election Assistance Commission's (EAC) Election Administration and Voting Survey (EAVS) on the total number of ballots cast and the total number of provisional ballots cast in the 2012 general elections in Kansas and Tennessee.[129] More detailed information on our criteria for selecting Kansas and Tennessee is provided in appendix V. We also analyzed 2012 statewide data provided to us by Kansas and Tennessee election officials on the number of provisional ballots cast for identification reasons and the number of provisional ballots cast for identification reasons that were counted during the 2012 general election. To determine the reliability of the EAVS and state data, we interviewed EAC officials and officials from the Kansas and Tennessee Secretary of State offices regarding their data collection and quality control processes. We determined that the EAVS data collection procedures were sufficiently strong to identify and correct duplicative or illogical data. In addition, we reviewed the data provided by Kansas and Tennessee and published by the EAC to describe the proportion of jurisdictions providing complete provisional ballot data. We found the data to be sufficiently reliable for the purposes of determining how frequently provisional ballots were cast because of ID reasons and counted in Kansas and Tennessee.

To determine how provisional ballot use in Kansas and Tennessee changed from the 2008 to 2012 general elections, we analyzed EAVS data on the total number of ballots cast and the total number of provisional ballots cast in the 2008 and 2012 general elections in Kansas and Tennessee and in the four comparison states selected for objective three—Alabama, Arkansas, Delaware, and Maine. For details on how we selected the four comparison states, see appendix V. We used these data to calculate the provisional ballot usage rate—the total number of provisional ballots cast for any reason divided by the total number of all ballots cast—by treatment states and comparison states in 2008 and 2012. To assess the reliability of the 2008 and 2012 EAVS data, we analyzed the completeness of EAVS provisional ballot data for the 2008 and 2012 general elections and interviewed EAC officials regarding their data collection and quality control processes. We determined that between 0.2 and 28.9 percent of local election jurisdictions in three of our six treatment and comparison states had missing data in the 2008 or 2012 EAVS report. Three of our selected states had complete data for all jurisdictions within the state, for both years. To overcome this potential limitation, and to determine how provisional ballot use changed between the 2008 and 2012 general elections, we conducted analyses in two different ways. First, we used EAVS data from all the local election jurisdictions in the treatment and comparison states where nonmissing data useful for our calculations (total ballots cast, total provisional ballots cast) were available for both 2008 and 2012, omitting those local election jurisdictions where data for one or both years were missing. We also analyzed EAVS data from all the local jurisdictions in the treatment and comparison states where data were available from EAVS in either 2008 or 2012, or both years. We present the first analysis in the body of our report and the second analysis in appendix VII. The results of both analyses are similar, regardless of the inclusion or exclusion of local election jurisdictions with data missing for 1 year but not the other. Consequently, we found the EAVS data to be sufficiently reliable for the purposes of our review. Our findings on provisional ballots are not generalizable beyond our specific treatment and comparison states.

Available Information on the Incidence of In-Person Voter Fraud

To determine what challenges, if any, exist in using available information at the federal and state levels to estimate the incidence of in-person voter fraud, we developed a standard definition of in-person voter fraud for purposes of this report and conducted a literature review to identify relevant studies. At the federal level, we reviewed federal databases containing federal crime investigation and court information and interviewed relevant Department of Justice (DOJ) and judicial branch officials. We also contacted state election officials and reviewed information they provided to identify any challenges in using the information they provided to estimate the incidence of in-person voter fraud.

Definition of In-Person Voter Fraud

The offense of "in-person voter fraud" is not readily defined in law, and, according to DOJ and EAC officials, their agencies do not have a definition of the term "in-person voter fraud."[130] However, several federal and state court decisions have discussed the concept of in-person voter fraud. We used these court cases to develop a definition of in-person voter fraud for the purposes of this report: In-person voter fraud involves a person who (1) attempts to vote or votes; (2) in person at the polling place; and (3) asserts an identity that is not the person's own, whether it be that of a fictional registered voter, a dead registered voter, a false identity, or whether the voter uses a fraudulent identification.

To develop this definition, we analyzed relevant court cases to determine how courts have characterized in-person voter fraud, as well as activities that are not considered to be encompassed by the term. Specifically, we searched legal databases for court opinions that discussed the offense of "in-person voter fraud," "voter impersonation fraud," or "in-person voter impersonation fraud."[131] We reviewed these legal opinions and selected cases from the United States Supreme Court, United States Circuit Court of Appeals, and state supreme courts—which are the most authoritative sources of case law. We analyzed the following cases: *Crawford v. Marion County Election Bd.*, 553 U.S. 181 (2008); *Democratic Nat'l Comm. v. Republican Nat'l Comm.*, 673 F.3d 192 (3d Cir. 2012); *ACLU of New Mexico v. Santillanes*, 546 F.3d 1313 (10th Cir. 2008); *In re Request for Advisory Opinion Regarding Constitutionality of 2005 PA 71, 740 N.W.2d 444* (Mich. 2007); and *Weinschenk v. State*, 203 S.W.3d 201 (Mo. 2006).[132] In reviewing these decisions, we found that the type of conduct described as constituting in-person voter fraud and not constituting in-person voter fraud was generally consistent among the courts. Activities that the courts characterized as comprising in-person voter fraud included, for example, any fraud addressed by a photo ID requirement, a voter showing up at the polls and claiming to be someone he or she is not, a voter who votes in the place of a dead registered voter (so-called ghost-voting), and attempting to vote using a false identity, among others. As part of our analysis, we also reviewed activities the courts have characterized as not constituting in-person voter fraud to guide our analysis, which include, among others, absentee ballot fraud, felons and other disqualified individuals voting in their own names, voter registration fraud, and fraud or misconduct by election officials. We shared this definition of in-person voter fraud with relevant federal agency officials and solicited and integrated their feedback, as appropriate.

Literature Review

We conducted a review of academic literature, organizational studies, peer-reviewed journals, books, and other regularly cited research published from January 2004 through April 2014 to identify studies that attempted to estimate in-person voter fraud, using a documented methodology.[133] We conducted this review using search terms such as "voter impersonation" and "voter fraud," among others, in various databases, including Academic OneFile, Article First, Dissertation Abstracts, Online, ECO, JSTOR, NTIS, ProQuest, PolicyFile, PsycInfo, Social SciSearch, and Worldcat. We identified and reviewed more than 300 studies to determine whether they (1) contained data related to in-person voter fraud and (2) included a description of the methodology used for collecting the data related to in-person voter fraud.[134] We identified six studies that met these criteria. Two GAO analysts and, as applicable, a GAO statistician reviewed each of the six studies and determined that the design, implementation, and analyses of the studies were sufficiently sound to support the studies' results and conclusions based on generally accepted social science principles. We found that these studies used various sources and methodologies in their effort to provide estimates on in-person voter fraud.

Available Federal Information

To determine the extent to which federal information allows for identifying the number of in-person voter fraud investigations, prosecutions, and convictions, we identified federal databases that contain information on the incidence of reported federal crimes. The databases include the following:

- Executive Office for U.S. Attorneys' (EOUSA) Legal Information Office Network System (LIONS), which tracks investigations and prosecutions by U.S. Attorneys' Offices.
- Criminal Division's Automated Case Tracking System II (ACTS II), which is an automated activity-tracking system for all cases and matters that are the responsibility of DOJ's Criminal Division litigating attorneys.[135]
- Federal Judicial Center's Integrated Database (IDB), which contains federal court case data that are routinely reported by the courts to the Administrative Office of the U.S. Courts.
- United States Sentencing Commission's Oracle database, which includes data on individual offenders extracted and analyzed from sentencing documents submitted by federal courts to the Commission.

None of the four databases includes data on unreported incidents of in- person voter fraud or allegations for which there is no associated investigation or case. For each of these databases, we reviewed codebooks and other database documentation and interviewed relevant agency officials to ascertain (1) how data potentially related to in-person voter fraud are collected and managed using these databases and (2) whether in-person voter fraud cases can be identified directly from the databases. On the basis of interviews with agency officials and the review of relevant court cases we conducted to develop a definition of in-person voter fraud, we compiled a list of 14 possible statutory provisions under which our definition of in-person voter fraud could be prosecuted (see table 8).[136]

Table 8. Possible Statutory Provisions under Which In-Person Voter Fraud Could be Prosecuted

Statute	Description
18 U.S.C. § 2	Makes punishable as a principal one who aids and abets another in commission of substantive offense
18 U.S.C. § 241	Conspiracy to deprive a person of civil rights
18 U.S.C. § 242	Deprivation of civil rights
18 U.S.C. § 371	Conspiracy to commit any offense against the United States or to defraud the United States
18 U.S.C. § 609	Use of military authority to influence the vote of a member of armed forces
18 U.S.C. § 611	Voting by aliens
18 U.S.C. § 911	False claim of U.S. citizenship
18 U.S.C. § 1015(f)	False statement or claim of citizenship in order to register or to vote
18 U.S.C. § 1341	Use of the United States mails, or a private or commercial interstate carrier, to further a scheme or artifice to defraud
18 U.S.C. § 1342	Use of any fictitious name or address for the purpose of carrying out any scheme mentioned in 18 U.S.C. § 1341
18 U.S.C. § 1343	Use of wire, radio, or television, to further a scheme or artifice to defraud
42 U.S.C. § 1973i(c)	Payments for registering to vote or voting, fraudulent registrations, and conspiracies to encourage illegal voting
42 U.S.C. § 1973i(e)	Voting more than once
42 U.S.C. § 1973gg-10(2)	Fraudulent registration or voting

Source: GAO analysis of information provided by federal agency officials. | GAO-14-634.

Available State Information

To identify any challenges associated with using available information at the state level to estimate the incidence of in-person voter fraud, we interviewed election officials in 46 states and the District of Columbia.[137] Because of differences in election administration across states, these officials were located in various state offices, including state secretary of state or commonwealth offices, boards of elections, and lieutenant governors' offices. Upon the recommendation of the election officials we spoke with, in 8 of the 46 states, we also contacted officials from additional state agencies, such as the state attorney general or judicial branch. We corroborated the information we gathered through these interviews by reviewing the documentation the states provided to us related to the incidence of election fraud and state statutes related to election fraud and in-person voter fraud.

As a result of these interviews and our review of documentation the officials provided, we determined that 27 states had some information readily available at the state level related to election fraud. To determine the extent to which the incidence of in-person voter fraud could be estimated from the provided documentation, we reviewed the format and content of the documentation provided, as well as testimonial evidence from the original interviews and subsequent correspondence with state officials. This review allowed us to better understand the way in which the information was collected and compiled, and to identify any potential limitations associated with the provided information. We also reviewed how responsibility for addressing election fraud was distributed among various state and local agencies, in an effort to determine whether the information provided by the state represented a complete account of the in-person voter fraud allegations, investigations, prosecutions, or convictions that occurred within the state.

Demographic Characteristics of Select Voters

To assess demographic differences in voting patterns and methods of voter registration, we analyzed data from the Voting and Registration Supplement to the U.S. Census Bureau's Current Population Survey (CPS). The supplement collects data from a representative national sample of adults on the timing and method of voting and the method of registration in November of every presidential and congressional election year, in conjunction with the monthly CPS survey that also collects demographic information such as race, ethnicity, age, labor force participation, and income.

To examine the reliability of CPS data, we reviewed technical documentation and conducted electronic data reliability testing. We also examined our data to ensure logical consistency and that there were not excessive missing data on our variables of interest. We found the data to be sufficiently reliable for the purposes of our review.

To conduct our analysis of demographic characteristics of early and absentee voters, we merged separate variables on timing of voting (before Election Day and on Election Day) and method of voting (in person versus by mail) into one four-category variable, as shown below.

- in person on Election Day,
- in person before Election Day,
- by mail on Election Day, and
- by mail before Election Day.

CPS data do not identify whether early or absentee voting was through an absentee process requiring a reason, through no-excuse absentee voting, in person at a polling place, or by some other means.

In an effort to analyze the demographic characteristics of voters who register through nongovernmental organizations, or third parties, we collapsed information from the method of registration variable to highlight major categories such as registration at a government office versus by mail or online, as shown below:

- government office (including a department of motor vehicle office, public assistance agency, or polling place); by mail or online;
- through a registration drive or at a school, hospital, or campus; or
- other method/don't know.

While our data distinguish respondents who registered at a government office/DMV/public assistance agency from those who registered at another site, we cannot verify that respondents who reported having registered at (for example) schools or through a registration drive were actually registered by third parties or the nature of any third party involved. Additionally, because the question concerns the last time an individual registered, respondents may have difficulty recalling the method of registration if it did not occur recently.

We collapsed data from our demographic variables of interest to highlight specific comparisons, and analyzed cross tabulations of the proportion of individuals in each demographic category that voted or registered by a different method. We examined the following demographic variables:

- race,
- education,
- age,
- income,
- employment status,
- residential mobility,[138] and
- sex.

We were unable to analyze some variables that research has suggested are associated with the propensity to vote early or be registered by a third party (such as political interest or party affiliation) because the CPS does not collect these data. Finally, because CPS data are based on a complex sample design, we applied generalized variance equations from the CPS technical documentation to generate standard errors for our estimates.

APPENDIX III: BIBLIOGRAPHY OF IDENTIFICATION (ID) OWNERSHIP, VOTER TURNOUT AND IN-PERSON VOTER FRAUD STUDIES REVIEWED FOR THIS REPORT

Studies GAO Reviewed That Estimate ID Ownership

Ansolabehere, Stephen. "Report on Racial Differences in Matching Voter Registration Lists to Driver's License and License to Carry Databases in the State of Texas." Paper submitted June 30, 2012, *Texas v. Holder*, No. 12- 0128 (D.D.C).

Barreto, Matt A; Gabriel R. Sanchez. "Rates of Possession of Accepted Photo Identification, among Different Subgroups in the Eligible Voter Population, Milwaukee County, Wisconsin." Expert report submitted on behalf of plaintiffs April 23, 2012, in *Frank v. Walker*, No. 11-01128 (E.D. Wis.).

Barreto, Matt A; Stephen A. Nuño, and Gabriel R. Sanchez. "The Disproportionate Impact of Voter-ID Requirements on the Electorate— New Evidence from Indiana." *PS: Political Science & Politics* (January 2009): 111-116.

Barreto, Matt A; Stephen A. Nuño, Gabriel R. Sanchez. "Voter ID Requirements and the Disenfranchisement of Latino, Black, and Asian Voters." Paper presented at the 2007 American Political Science Association Annual Conference, Chicago, Illinois, September 1, 2007.

Barreto, Matt A; Gabriel R. Sanchez, and Hannah Walker. "Rates of Possession of Valid Photo Identification, and Public Knowledge of the Voter ID Law in Pennsylvania." Paper submitted July 16, 2012, in *Applewhite v. Commonwealth*, No. 330 MD 2012 (Pa. Commw. Ct.)

Beatty, Leland. Declaration submitted April 23, 2012, in *League of United Latin American Citizens v. Deininger*, No. 12-00185 (E.D. Wis.).

Bullock, Charles III; Hood III. MV. "Worth a Thousand Words?: An Analysis of Georgia's Voter Identification Statute." Paper presented at the Annual Meeting of the Southwestern Political Science Association, Albuquerque, New Mexico, March 2007.

Hood III, MV. "Declaration of M.V. Hood III." Paper submitted May 31, 2012, in *League of United Latin American Citizens v. Deininger*, No. 12-00185 (E.D. Wis.)

McDonald, Michael P. "May I See Your ID, Please? Measuring the Number of Eligible Voters with Photo Identification." Paper presented at the California Institute of Technology and Massachusetts Institute of Technology Voter Identification and Registration Conference, Cambridge, Massachusetts, October 2006.

North Carolina State Board of Elections. *April 2013 State Board of Elections-Department of Motor Vehicles ID Analysis*, a report prepared in response to legislative and media inquiries. April 2013.

Sanchez, Gabriel R. "The Disproportionate Impact of Photo-ID Laws on the Minority Electorate." In Latino Decisions, accessed April 15, 2014, http://www.latinodecisions.com/blog/2011/05/24/the-disproportionate- impact-of-stringent-voter-id-laws.

Stewart III, Charles. "Declaration of Charles Stewart III, PhD." Paper submitted June 26, 2012, in *South Carolina v. Holder*, 12 -203 (D.D.C.)

Stewart III, Charles. "Voter ID: Who Has Them? Who Shows Them?" *Oklahoma Law Review*, vol. 66, no. 1 (2013): 21-52.

Studies GAO Reviewed That Estimate Effects of Voter ID Requirements on Voter Turnout

Alvarez, R. Michael; Delia Bailey; Jonathan N. Katz. "An Empirical Bayes Approach to Estimating Ordinal Treatment Effects." *PS: Political Science & Politics*, vol. 19 (2011): 20-31.[139]

Ansolabehere, Stephen. "Effects of Identification Requirements on Voting: Evidence from the Experiences of Voters on Election Day." *PS: Political Science & Politics*, January 2009, 127-130.

Bullock III, Charles S; Hood III. MV. "Worth a Thousand Words? An Analysis of Georgia's Voter Identification Statute." *American Politics Research*, vol. 36, no. 4 (2008): 555-579.

Cobb, Rachel V; James Greiner, D; Kevin M. Quinn. "Can Voter ID Laws Be Administered in a Race-Neutral Manner? Evidence from the City of Boston in 2008." *Quarterly Journal of Political Science*, vol. 7 (2012): 1-33.

De Alth, Shelley. "ID at the Polls: Assessing the Impact of Recent State Voter ID Laws on Voter Turnout." *Harvard Law and Policy Review*, vol. 3 (2009): 185-202.

Dropp, Kyle A. *Voter Identification Laws and Voter Turnout* (May 2013), forthcoming.

Erikson, Robert S; Lorraine C. Minnite. "Modeling Problems in the Voter Identification—Voter Turnout Debate." *Election Law Journal*, vol. 8, no. 2 (2009): 85-101.

Gomez, Brad T. "Uneven Hurdles: The Effect of Voter Identification Requirements on Voter Turnout." Paper presented at the Annual Meeting of the Midwest Political Science Association, Chicago, Illinois, April 2007.

Lott, John R. *Evidence of Voter Fraud and the Impact that Regulations to Reduce Fraud have on Voter Participation Rate* (August 2006), forthcoming.

Milyo, Jeffrey. *The Effects of Photographic Identification on Voter Turnout in Indiana: A County-Level Analysis* (Columbia, Missouri: Institute of Public Policy, University of Missouri, 2007).

Muhlhausen, David B; Keri Weber Sikich. *New Analysis Shows Voter Identification Laws Do Not Reduce Turnout* (Washington, D.C.: the Heritage Foundation, 2007).

Mycoff, Jason D; Michael W. Wagner; David, C. Wilson. "The Effect of Voter Identification Laws on Aggregate and Individual Level Turnout." Paper presented at the 2007 American Political Science Association Annual Conference, Chicago, Illinois, August 2007.

Mycoff, Jason D; Michael W. Wagner; David, C. Wilson. "The Empirical Effects of Voter-ID Laws: Present or Absent." PS: Political Science & Politics, January 2009: 121-126.

Pitts, Michael J. "Photo ID, Provisional Balloting, and Indiana's 2012 Primary Election." *University of Richmond Law Review*, vol. 47, no.3 (2013): 939-957.

Vercellotti, Timothy; David Andersen. "Protecting the Franchise, or Restricting It? The Effects of Voter Identification Requirements on Turnout." Paper presented at the 2006 American Political Science Association Annual Conference, Philadelphia, Pennsylvania, August 31- September 3, 2006.

Vercellotti, Timothy; David Andersen. "Voter-Identification Requirements and the Learning Curve." *PS: Political Science & Politics* (January 2009): 117-120.

Studies GAO Reviewed That Attempted to Identify Instances of In-Person Voter Fraud

Ahlquist, John S; Kenneth R. Mayer; Simon Jackman. "Alien Abduction and Voter Impersonation in the 2012 U.S. General Election: Evidence from a Survey List Experiment," October 30, 2013, forthcoming. *Election Law Journal*.

Christensen, Ray; Thomas J. Schultz. "Identifying Election Fraud Using Orphan and Low Propensity Voters," *American Politics Research*, vol. 42 (2), 2014.

Corbin Carson, "Exhaustive Database of Voter Fraud Cases Turns Up Scant Evidence That It Happens" News21, Aug. 12, 2012, accessed July 24, 2014, http://votingrights.news21.com/article/election-fraud.

Hood III, MV; William, Gillespie. "They Just Do Not Vote Like They Used To: A Methodology to Empirically Assess Election Fraud," *Social Science Quarterly*, vol. 93 (1), 2012.
Levitt, Justin. "Election Deform: The Pursuit of Unwarranted Election Regulation," *Election Law Journal*, vol. 11 (1), 2012.
Minnite, Lorraine C. *The Myth of Voter Fraud*. Ithaca: Cornell University Press, 2010.

APPENDIX IV: DRIVER'S LICENSE AND NONDRIVER STATE ID COSTS IN SELECTED STATES, AS OF JULY 2014

Information in this appendix is also presented in figure 4 of the report. Table 9 describes, for each selected state, the (1) driver's license cost; (2) non-driver ID cost; and (3) whether or not an ID for voting can be obtained free of charge.

Table 9. Driver's License and Nondriver Identification (ID) Costs in Selected States

State	Driver's license cost	Nondriver ID cost[a]	Free ID for voting
Alabama	$28.50 ($23.50 + $5 test fee)	$23.50	Yes
Arkansas	$25 ($20 + $5 test fee)	$5	Yes
Florida	$48	$25	No[b]
Georgia	5-year: $20 8-year: $32	5-year: $20 8-year: $32	Yes
Indiana	4-year: $14.50, 5-year: $16, 6-year: $17.50 For certain drivers over 75: 3-year: $11 For drivers over 85: 2-year: $7	$11.50 Over 18: Free	Yes
Kansas	$29 ($18 + $8 photo fee + $3 exam fee) Over 65: $23 ($12 + $8 photo fee + $3 exam fee)	$22 Disabled/over 65: $18	Yes
	Under 21: $31 ($20 + $8 photo fee + $3 exam fee)		
Mississippi	4-year: $24 8-year: $51	$17	Yes
North Carolina	$32	$10	Yes
North Dakota	$25 ($15 + $5 written test fee + $5 road test fee)	$8	Yes
Oklahoma	$37.50 ($33.50 + $4 application fee) Over 62: $21.25 Over age 65: Free	$20	Yes
Pennsylvania	$34.50 Over 65: $24	$27.50	Yes[c]
Rhode Island	$58.50 ($32 + $26.50 road test fee)	$26.50 Over 59: no fee	Yes

Table 9. (Continued)

State	Driver's license cost	Nondriver ID cost[a]	Free ID for voting
South Carolina	5-year: $14.50 ($12.50 + $2 knowledge test fee) 10-year: $27 ($25 + $2 knowledge test fee)	Free	Yes
Tennessee	$19.50 ($17.50 + $2 application fee)	$9.50 ($7.50 + $2 application fee)	Yes
Texas	$25 Over 85: $9	$16 Over 60: $6	Yes
Virginia	$32	$10	Yes
Wisconsin	$43 ($28 + $15 skills exam fee)	$28	Yes

Source: GAO analysis of state information and data. | GAO-14-634.

Notes:

[a] The "Non-Driver ID Cost" category does not include non-driver ID issued for voting purposes.

[b] Florida allows as acceptable identification photo ID that may be nongovernment issued.

[c] Pennsylvania's voter ID was permanently enjoined on January 14, 2014, by the Pennsylvania Commonwealth Court. *Applewhite v. Commonwealth*, 2014 WL 184988 (Pa. Commw. Ct. Jan. 17, 2014). This injunction extended to issuance of free voter ID by the Pennsylvania Department of Transportation and Department of State.

Appendix V: Voter Turnout Analysis Design

We conducted an evaluation of how, if at all, changes in requirements for all eligible voters to present identification at the polls on Election Day— referred to in this appendix as voter ID laws—in selected states affected voter turnout. For our evaluation, we conducted a quasi-experimental analysis that compared changes in voter turnout between two states that implemented changes to voter ID requirements with changes in four states that did not implement changes to voter ID requirements between the 2008 and 2012 general elections. As part of our analysis, we took steps to control for factors other than changes in ID requirements that could affect voter turnout in either group of states. This appendix summarizes the logic of a quasi-experimental design and our approach to selecting states for analysis. Appendix VI discusses the methods of analysis, data, and detailed results.

Quasi-Experimental Analysis of Voter Identification Laws and Turnout

A quasi-experiment is a type of policy evaluation that compares how an outcome changes over time in a "treatment" group that adopted a new policy, as compared with a "comparison" group that did not make the change.[140] As with controlled experiments, researchers analyze separate groups before and after one of them changed a policy. Unlike in controlled experiments, the assignment to groups is not randomized, and the analyst cannot fully control the experiences of either group before or after treatment.

We used a quasi-experimental analysis to assess the effect, if any, of changes in selected state voter ID laws on voter turnout. We used this approach to account for the variation across states in the use of voter ID laws and the staggered adoption of such laws over time, which makes a quasi-experimental analysis possible. In this case, the treatment and comparison groups include all registered or eligible voters in states that did and did not change state ID laws in a certain time period (depending on the data source). Within each group, by comparing turnout before and after voter ID laws changed in the treatment group, we can estimate how turnout changed, if at all, and then calculate how any change varied between groups, known as a difference-in-difference. If turnout changed by a greater or lesser amount in the treatment states than in the comparison states, evidence would then suggest that changes in state voter ID laws in the treatment states affected voter turnout. In contrast, if turnout changes were similar in the treatment and comparison states, then the evidence would suggest that changes in state voter ID laws in the treatment states did not affect voter turnout.

Quasi-experiments have a number of strengths for estimating the effects of election administration practices.[141] The longitudinal nature of the analysis holds constant any differences between the treatment and comparison groups that do not change by large amounts over short periods of time. In our analysis, these could include differences across citizens in age, education, income, race, political interest, residential mobility, state political culture, and partisanship, which may affect turnout and the propensity for a state to adopt voter ID laws. Political science research has consistently shown that individual differences across citizens—and implicitly across the jurisdictions in which they live—largely explain the decision to vote.[142] For this reason, a quasi-experimental design is well suited to estimating the effect of legal reforms designed to change the voting process, because it holds constant many of the confounding variables that prior research has shown are most likely to affect individuals' decision to vote.

A valid quasi-experimental analysis depends on the careful selection of treatment and comparison states, in order to control for other factors that may change over time in each group.[143] For example, if a treatment state changed another election law or practice during the time period of analysis, or saw more robust voter mobilization from political campaigns, isolating the effect of ID laws, if any, becomes more difficult, since other factors could have contributed to change in turnout. If turnout changed by a smaller or larger amount in the treatment state than in the comparison state, either the new voter ID law or the other legal or administrative changes may have contributed to the change in turnout. Controlling for other changes over time allows us to better isolate the effects of the change in voter ID law, if an effect were to exist.

To carry out our quasi-experimental analysis, we identified treatment and comparison states for which we could hold constant other factors that vary over time, either through the selection of the states or statistical methods. Our selection of states controlled for the presence of competitive races for statewide or federal offices, controversial ballot questions, and the voter mobilization activities of political campaigns. The next section discusses our efforts to identify potential states for analysis, based on the presence of these factors.

Treatment State Selection

In our October 2012 report, we described state voter ID laws that were in effect for the 2012 general election and substantive changes to these laws since 2002.[144] We used that report, combined with supplemental research on the effective date of the laws, to identify candidate treatment states for analysis.

To select our treatment states from the 50 states and the District of Columbia we applied the following criteria:

1. A voter ID requirement was adopted or substantively modified after 2002 and implemented as of the November 2012 general election.
2. Voter ID requirements required the voter present a photo ID (government or non-government issued); a non-photo, government- issued ID; or a nonphoto, non-government issued ID, with the requirement that voters without acceptable ID at the polling place on Election Day to return within a specified amount of time with acceptable ID in order for their provisional ballot to be counted.[145]
3. The states had presidential general elections where the margin of victory did not substantially change from 2008 to 2012 and all other statewide elections, such as U.S. Senate races, were non-competitive in both the 2008 and 2012 general elections.
4. The states did not experience contemporaneous changes to other laws between the 2008 and 2012 general elections that may have significantly affected voter turnout on Election Day.

Fourteen states met the first and second criteria above. After identifying these states, we selected for further consideration the 4 states, of these 14, that implemented government-issued, photo ID requirements that also required voters to follow up with election officials if acceptable ID was not presented at the polls on Election Day—Georgia, Indiana, Kansas, and Tennessee.[146]

Voter ID policies in these states are preferable for statistical analysis, since previous studies have speculated that photo ID requirements could affect turnout more strongly than other requirements and it is easier to detect larger effects than smaller ones, if they exist. For example, a previous evaluation of voter ID laws found that only photo ID policies affected turnout, as compared with other ID policies, such as requiring a non-photo ID.[147]

In addition, analyzing policies that allow the fewest forms of ID provides an upper limit on the effects of identification laws in general, and focuses on the type of ID law that that many legislatures have approved since 2008. Thirteen of the 17 states that adopted requirements for photo and generally government-issued ID since the passage of HAVA adopted their policies after 2008.

We conducted a legal analysis for Georgia, Indiana, Kansas, and Tennessee to determine if election laws and procedures changed contemporaneously with the changes to these states' ID laws. We found that legal changes in Georgia were sufficient to eliminate it from consideration as a treatment state, but that there were no significant changes in the remaining 3 states to eliminate them from contention on that basis.

Specifically, in Georgia, no-excuse absentee voting was enacted in 2005, and expanded early voting hours were enacted in 2008. The first federal general election for which the state's ID requirement went into effect was the November 2008 general election. Thus, the change in ID requirements between the relevant midterm or presidential election occurred at the same time as other important changes in voting procedures. The simultaneity of these changes makes it difficult to isolate the effect of one law from the effect of another.

To determine whether competitive election environments were present in the remaining potential treatment states—Indiana, Kansas, and Tennessee—we conducted two evaluations. First, we evaluated the change in competitiveness of the presidential race between the 2008 and 2012 general elections. We eliminated Indiana based on this analysis, but retained Kansas and Tennessee.

The competitiveness of the race for President in Indiana changed substantially between the 2004 and 2008 general elections—from a margin of victory of 21 percent in 2004 to 1 percent in 2008.[148] Such a large change in competitiveness suggests that voters may have been subjected to more intense efforts by the campaigns and interest groups to affect turnout. This imbalance in voter mobilization efforts—which academic research has shown to be effective in some conditions—is an important potential factor that could affect turnout.[149] In contrast, the competitiveness of the presidential race in Kansas and Tennessee did not change significantly between the 2008 and 2012 general elections.[150]

Second, we collected data on the competitiveness of statewide and federal elections in Kansas and Tennessee in order to ensure that changes over time in voter mobilization efforts by campaigns were not likely to affect voter turnout in 2008 or 2012. We considered a race competitive if the margin of victory was less than 20 percentage points. Our analysis indicated that Kansas and Tennessee had generally noncompetitive election environments in both the 2008 and 2012 general elections. Neither Kansas nor Tennessee had statewide electoral races with margins of victory of less than 20 percentage points in either 2008 or 2012, with the exception of the 2008 presidential race in Kansas, which had a 15 percent margin of victory.

Both states elect statewide officers, such as governors, in federal midterm election years. None of the nine races for the U.S. House of Representatives in Tennessee was competitive in 2008, and one was competitive in 2012. Two of the four races in Kansas for the U.S. House of Representatives were competitive in 2008, and one of the same districts was competitive in 2012. No highly competitive or consequential ballot questions appeared in Kansas in either 2008 or 2012, and statewide ballot questions were not on the general election ballot in Tennessee in either year.[151]

In summary, the types of the voter ID laws that Kansas and Tennessee adopted, combined with minimal contemporaneous changes in other aspects of election administration, the offices and questions on the ballot, and the competitiveness of those races, made these states the strongest treatment states for analysis.[152] The characteristics of the 14 states we considered as potential treatment states are listed in table 10.

Table 10. Potential Treatment States

State	Federal midterm or presidential election when voter identification (ID) change was first in effect	Type of ID requirement[a]	Process if voter does not have acceptable ID	State requires both government issued photo ID and voter follow-up if ID is not provided at the poll on Election Day?	Contemporaneous changes to election laws?[b]
Georgia	2008 presidential election	Photo only; government issued only	Provisional ballot + follow-up	Yes	Yes
Indiana	2006 midterm election	Photo only; government issued only	Provisional ballot + follow-up	Yes	No
Kansas	2012 presidential election	Photo only; government issued only	Provisional ballot + follow-up	Yes	No
Tennessee	2012 presidential election	Photo only; government issued only	Provisional ballot + follow-up	Yes	No
South Dakota	2004 presidential election	Photo only; government issued only	Voter can verify own identity	No	X
Idaho	2010 midterm election	Photo only; government issued only	Voter can verify own identity	No	X
Michigan	2008 presidential election	Photo only; government issued only	Voter can verify own identity	No	X
New Hampshire	2012 presidential election	Photo only; can be nongovernment	Voter can verify own identity; can be verified by elections official	No	X
Oklahoma	2012 presidential election	Can be nonphoto; government issued only	Provisional ballot + do nothing	No	X
Florida	Many changes over time	Photo only; can be nongovernment	Provisional ballot; do nothing	No	X
Rhode Island	2012 presidential election	Can be nonphoto; government issued only	Provisional ballot + do nothing	No	X
Alabama	2008 presidential election	Can be nonphoto; nongovernment	Provisional ballot + follow-up; can be verified by elections official	No	X
Arizona	2006 midterm election	Can be nonphoto; nongovernment.	Provisional ballot + follow-up	No	X
Virginia	2012 presidential election	Can be nonphoto; nongovernment	Provisional ballot + follow-up	No	X

Source: GAO analysis of state election laws. | GAO-14-634.

Notes: Requirements are as of the 2012 general election. X indicates that analysis was not conducted because the state was eliminated based on criteria in a previous column.

[a] Refers to type of documents accepted and acceptable issuing entity. States requiring government-issued ID include those where there is an exception for a school ID.

[b] We reviewed election laws for changes that may significantly affect voter turnout, including changes in no-excuse absentee voting, early voting, Election Day registration, felon disenfranchisement, and third-party registration identifying states for further consideration as potential treatment states where such changes were unlikely to affect turnout significantly.

Comparison State Selection

To select comparison states, we applied four primary criteria to the universe of 35 states that either had no ID requirement or had an ID requirement that allowed voters to show a nonphoto, nongovernment ID as of the November 2012 general election.[153] This process ensured that various confounding variables were held constant at the state level for the treatment and comparison states. In effect, we applied "exact" matching methods to balance state-level covariates. The criteria were as follows:

1. States did not implement changes to voter ID laws between the 2008 and 2012 general elections, when Kansas and Tennessee implemented their amended ID requirements.
2. The election cycles for statewide elected offices were similar to those of Kansas and Tennessee.
3. The states did not have competitive general elections for federal and statewide elected offices and statewide ballot questions in 2008 and 2012.
4. The states did not experience contemporaneous changes to other laws between the 2008 and 2012 general elections that may have significantly affected voter turnout on Election Day.

To apply the first criterion, we reviewed state voter ID requirements to identify states that did and did not implement changes to voter ID requirements between the 2008 and 2012 general elections. If a state implemented changes to its ID requirements, we did not further consider it for selection.

To apply the second criterion, we matched the election schedules for U.S. Senate and governor's offices—years in which the elections for these offices are held—in the treatment and potential comparison states. Matching election cycles controls for the presence of statewide political campaigns, which typically run programs to encourage turnout. These voter mobilization efforts could coincide with changes to ID laws and bias our impact estimates. In instances where the cycles did not precisely match, we matched either the U.S. Senate cycle or the governors' race cycle (rather than both). We considered states that met any of these cycle match requirements and excluded all others.

To apply the third criterion, we reviewed the competitiveness of general elections in 2008 and 2012, using the margins of victory in state-wide elections for federal, gubernatorial, and statewide political offices and for statewide ballot questions. We sought to make the pattern in electoral competition similar in the treatment and comparison states, particularly in those cases where the election cycles did not precisely match.

To apply the fourth criterion, we reviewed election laws for changes that may significantly affect voter turnout, including changes in no-excuse absentee voting, early voting, Election Day registration, felon disenfranchisement, and third-party registration, identifying states where such changes did not occur or were unlikely to affect turnout significantly.

In addition to these four criteria, we considered other factors that could affect turnout, such as geographic proximity to Kansas and Tennessee, similarity in voter turnout histories between comparators and the treatment states, and unique events, such as the effect of Hurricane Sandy striking the East Coast 8 days before Election Day in 2012.[154] The quality of state voter registration data was also an important consideration when selecting comparison states, as our estimates of turnout percentages require accurate state records of registered voters at the time of the 2008 and 2012 general elections.[155] Table 11 lists the 35 states considered as comparators and the rationale for exclusion or inclusion, based on the four main criteria. Table notes indicate when additional factors, such as those listed above, were considered. As indicated in the table, Alabama, Arkansas, Delaware, and Maine met all of our criteria and were not eliminated from consideration because of other factors.

Table 11. Comparison State Selection Results

Potential comparison states[a]	Passed criteria? Yes = passed criterion; no =did not meet criterion			
	1 Voter identification (ID) requirements substantively unchanged?	2 Election cycles similar?	3 Noncompetitive elections?	4 No other legal changes that could significantly affect turnout?
Alabama	Yes	Yes	Yes	Yes
Alaska	Yes	Yes	No	X
Arizona	Yes	Yes	No	X
Arkansas	Yes	Yes	Yes	Yes
California	Yes	Yes	No	X
Colorado	No	X	X	X
Connecticut	Yes	Yes	No	X
Delaware	Yes	Yes	Yes	Yes
District of Columbia	Yes	Yes	c	X
Hawaii	Yes	Yes	No	X
Illinois	Yes	Yes	Yes	No
Iowa	Yes	Yes	Yes	No
Kentucky	Yes	Yes	No	X
Maine	Yes	Yes	Yes	Yes
Maryland	Yes	Yes	No	X
Massachusetts	Yes	Yes	No	X
Minnesota	Yes	Yes	No	X
Mississippi	Yes	Yes	c	X
Missouri	Yes	No	X	X
Montana	Yes	Yes	No	X
Nebraska	Yes	Yes	No	X
Nevada	Yes	Yes	No	X
New Jersey	Yes	Yes	No	X
New Mexico	No	X	X	X
New York	Yes	Yes	Yes	c
North Carolina	Yes	Yes	No[c]	X
North Dakota	Yes	No	X	X

Potential comparison states[a]	Passed criteria? Yes = passed criterion; no =did not meet criterion			
	1 Voter identification (ID) requirements substantively unchanged?	2 Election cycles similar?	3 Noncompetitive elections?	4 No other legal changes that could significantly affect turnout?
Ohio	Yes	Yes	No	X
Texas	Yes	Yes	No[c]	X
Utah	No	X	X	X
Vermont	Yes	No	X	X
Virginia	No	X	X	X
West Virginia	Yes	Yes	No	X
Wisconsin	Yes	Yes	No	X
Wyoming	Yes	Yes	Yes	c

Source: GAO analysis of state statutes, statutory changes, and election results provided by the U.S. House of Representatives Clerk's office and election results produced by state election officials. | GAO-14-634.

Notes: An X indicates that an analysis was not completed because the state was eliminated based on criteria in a previous column.

[a] The universe of potential comparison states included states that allowed non-photo, non-government issued IDs or had no voter ID requirement as of the November 2012 election.

[b] Criteria for selection are as follows: (1) Criterion 1: Voter ID requirements remained the same between the 2008 and 2012 general elections? (2) Criterion 2: State U.S. Senate and governors' election cycles match with Kansas or Tennessee? If no, does at least one cycle (governors' race or U.S. Senate) match Kansas or Tennessee cycles? (3) Criterion 3: Margins of victory for U.S. Senate, and governors' races more than 20 percent in both 2008 and 2012; margin of victory for presidential race changed less than 10 percentage points between 2008 and 2012 elections; ballot questions either noncompetitive, or similarly competitive questions present in both elections? (4) Criterion 4: No contemporaneous legal changes in the state that may have significantly affected voter turnout between the 2008 and 2012 general elections?

[c] Criterion not fully evaluated for this state because a separate factor eliminated the state, precluding such analysis. Factors for each state are listed below:

District of Columbia. Historical voter turnout pattern was highly dissimilar (ranked 47th of 50 states in historical turnout similarity with both Kansas and Tennessee in general elections from 1984 through 2012).

Mississippi. Voter registration data and history data were not sufficiently reliable for the purposes of our analysis.

New York. Hurricane Sandy hit southern New York shortly before the November 2012 election, making comparison of voter turnout in 2008 and 2012 problematic.

North Carolina. The U.S. Senate race in North Carolina was competitive in 2008, with an 8 percent margin of victory, while no U.S. Senate race was held in 2012.

Texas. The U.S. Senate races in Texas were competitive in both 2008 (margin of victory of 12 percent) and 2012 (margin of victory of 16 percent).

Wyoming. Voter registration and history data were not sufficiently reliable for the purposes of our analysis.

As shown in table 12, we selected Alabama, Arkansas, Delaware, and Maine as our comparison group of states because these 4 states most closely matched Kansas and Tennessee on our selection criteria. For example, changes to voter ID requirements were implemented in Kansas and Tennessee but not in the comparison states; the election cycles are similar; when races were held, they were noncompetitive; and none of the states had other legal changes that would significantly affect turnout. In addition, Alabama and Arkansas are geographically close to Kansas and Tennessee, which takes advantage of any geographic similarities, such as common weather conditions and regional political trends.[156] Consistent with a strong counterfactual, historical year-to-year change in turnout in the comparison states from 1984 through 2012 is similar to historical changes in turnout in Kansas and Tennessee, as shown in figure 21.

Historical turnout similarity between our treatment and comparison states is depicted in Figure 21. The general turnout increases and decreases trends among treatment and comparison states generally track one another.

For the 4 comparison state candidates that were the best choices based on the criteria applied above—Alabama, Arkansas, Delaware, and Maine—we also examined ballot questions in the 2008 and 2012 general elections. We collected data on the margin of victory for all statewide ballot questions in each state, and systematically searched news media and other electronic information databases to ensure that there were no particularly salient or competitive ballot questions that might affect voter turnout inconsistently across both elections (i.e., increase turnout in 1 year but not the next, or vice versa). A summary of our ballot question findings for the 4 states is presented below. We concluded that ballot questions in the selected comparison states would not have significantly affected turnout between the 2008 and 2012 general elections in the comparison states.

- **Alabama**. Eleven questions were on the 2012 general election ballot, three of which were competitive (having MOVs of less than 20 percent). Six questions were on the ballot in the 2008 general election, five of which were competitive. The presence of several competitive ballot questions in both 2008 and 2012 created a similar potential for voter mobilization and engagement in both years, such that the presence of ballot questions was unlikely to have affected turnout more in one election than the other. Competitive ballot questions in the 2012 general election considered the following policy issues: prohibiting requirements to participate in any health care system (MOV=18 percent); continue legislature's authority to tax corporations (MOV=16 percent); and repealing obsolete bank regulation language in the Alabama Constitution (MOV=8 percent). In the 2008 general election, competitive ballot questions were: 4 questions that were statewide but specific to individual city taxation issues (MOVs ranged from 1 percent to 16 percent) and one question to establish a statewide rainy day fund (MOV=14 percent).
- **Arkansas**. Three ballot questions were on the 2012 general election ballot, each of which was competitive. Five questions were on the 2008 general election ballot, one of which was competitive. Voter turnout was not likely to have been affected to a greater degree in 2012 or 2008 by the questions because each election had one competitive, salient ballot question race, with the remaining questions either noncompetitive or not on salient topics. The competitive and salient question was related to medical marijuana in 2012 (MOV=3 percent) and to limiting adoptions to

married cohabitants in 2008 (MOV=14 percent). The remaining competitive, but not salient, questions in 2012 were related to highway funding (MOV=16 percent) and a bond question (MOV=13 percent).

- **Delaware**. No ballot questions were present on the 2012 or 2008 general election ballots in Delaware.
- **Maine**. Five ballot questions were on the 2012 general election ballot, two of which were competitive. Three questions were on the 2008 general election ballot, two of which were competitive. The presence of competitive and salient initiatives in both years indicates that voter turnout was not likely affected to a greater degree in one of the elections versus the other. The competitive ballot questions in 2012 were a same-sex marriage initiative (MOV=5 percent) and a higher education bond proposal (MOV=2 percent), while in 2008 a casino question (MOV=8 percent) and a drinking water bond (MOV=1 percent) were on the ballot.

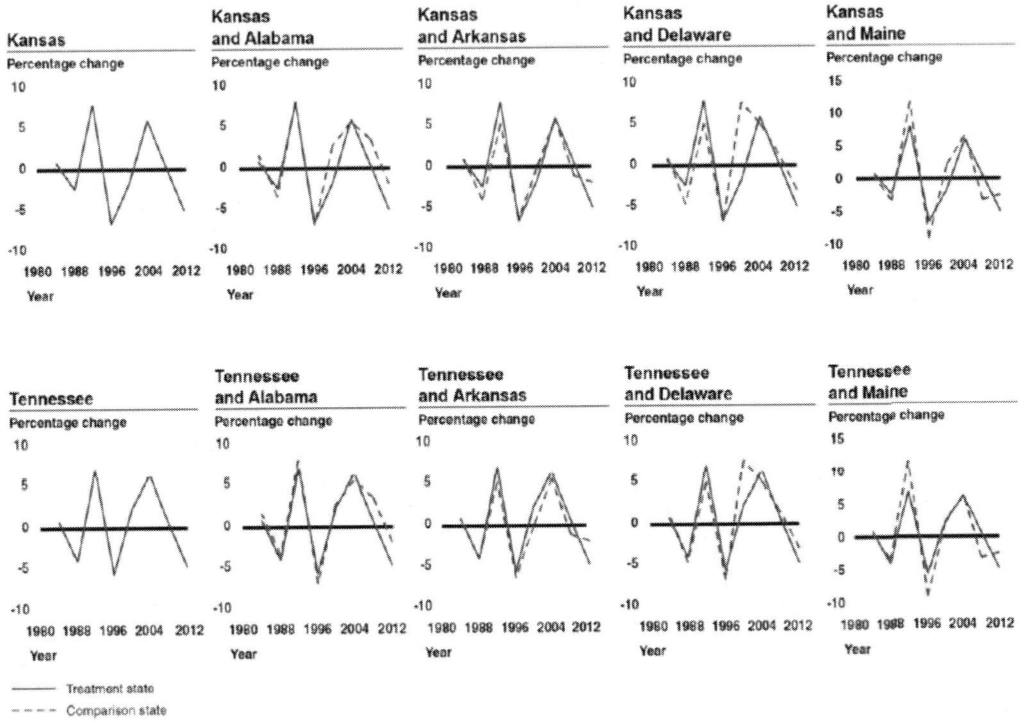

Source: GAO analysis of historical turnout data from the United States Elections Project. | GAO-14-634.

Figure 21. Yearly Change in Turnout in Treatment and Comparison States, 1984 to 2012 General Elections.

Table 12. Characteristics of Treatment and Comparison States

State	Substantive change in identification (ID) requirements between the 2008 and 2012 general elections	Change in presidential election margin of victory (MOV), 2008 to 2012	Had 2008 U.S. Senate election, and MOV	Had 2012 U.S. Senate election, and MOV	Had 2008 Governor's election, and MOV	Had 2012 Governor's election, and MOV	Had 2012/ 2008 other statewide office elections	Legal changes between the 2008 and 2012 general elections that could significantly affect turnout	Historical turnout similarity to Kansas and Tennessee (ranking, of the 50 states In general elections, 1984 through 2012)[a]	Geo- graphically proximate to Kansas or Tennessee
Kansas	Yes	+7 percentage points	Yes MOV=24%	No	No	No	No	No	X	X
Tennessee	Yes	+5 percentage points	Yes MOV=34%	Yes MOV=34%	No	No	No	No	X	X
Alabama	No	+1 percentage point	Yes MOV=27%	No	No	No	No	No	Kansas-10th Tennessee-5th	Yes
Arkansas	No	+4 percentage points	Yes MOV=59%	No	No	No	No	No	Kansas-2nd Tennessee-6th	Yes
Delaware	No	-6 percentage points	Yes MOV=29%	Yes MOV=37%	Yes MOV=35%	Yes MOV=41%	Yes[b]	No	Kansas-44th Tennessee-22nd	No
Maine	No	-2 percentage points	Yes MOV=23%	Yes MOV=23%	No	No	No	No	Kansas-23rd Tennessee-30th	No

Source: GAO analysis of state statutes, statutory changes, and election results provided by the U.S. House of Representatives Clerk's Office and election results produced by state election officials. | GAO-14-634.

[a] We measured historical turnout similarity by calculating a multivariate Euclidean distance between turnout in Kansas and Tennessee, respectively, and each of the remaining states. We used turnout data for the eight presidential general elections from 1980 through 2008, defined as a state's ratio of votes cast for President to its voting-eligible population, as compiled by Michael MacDonald at the United States Elections Project, George Mason University. We differenced the turnout data between elections to ensure that the distance measures reflected change over time, rather than cross-sectional variation. Since our difference-in-difference analysis holds constant fixed differences across states, differenced turnout is the relevant lagged outcome measure for matching treatment and comparison states.

[b] Delaware's other statewide office elections in 2012 and 2008 were generally noncompetitive: Lieutenant Governor MOVs of 23 percent (2012) and 24 percent (2008) and Insurance Commissioner MOVs of 24 percent (2012) and 16 percent (2008).

Table 13. Competitiveness of U.S. House of Representatives Races in Alabama, Arkansas, Delaware, and Maine (2012 and 2008 General Elections)

State	U.S. congressional district	2012 margin of victory	2008 margin of victory
Alabama	1	96%	97%
	2	27%	1%
	3	28%	8%
	4	48%	50%
	5	30%	4%
	6	43%	96%
	7	52%	97%
Arkansas	1	17%	100%
	2	16%	53%
	3	60%	57%
	4	23%	72%
Delaware	At large	31%	23%
Maine	1	28%	10%
	2	16%	35%

Source: GAO analysis of election results provided by the U.S. House of Representatives Clerk's Office. | GAO-14-634.

In addition to the presence and competitiveness of ballot questions, we reviewed margins of victory for U.S. House of Representatives races in the 2012 and 2008 general elections for Alabama, Arkansas, Delaware, and Maine. As shown in table 13, Alabama had no competitive districts in 2012, but three of seven competitive districts in 2008. In Arkansas, two of four districts were competitive in 2012 but none were competitive in 2008. Delaware's at-large U.S. House district was not competitive in either year, and Maine had one of its two districts competitive in each year. To control for the general change in competition between 2012 and 2008 in Alabama and Arkansas when analyzing changes in voter turnout, we conducted the analysis for the full states but also conducted a separate analysis of registrants living in non-competitive districts. Specifically, we excluded from our analysis registrants living in districts where U.S. House of Representative races were competitive in 1 year but not the other. These analyses are discussed in more detail in appendix VI.

Appendix VI: Voter Turnout Analysis Methods, Data Sources, and Additional Results

To evaluate the extent to which changes in voter ID laws affected turnout in Kansas and Tennessee, if at all, we applied several forms of "difference-in-difference" methods to three different sources of data. Any application of these methods must make certain assumptions to make valid causal inferences with real-world data. In this appendix, we identify these assumptions and justify them for our specific policy evaluation. We describe the methods of data collection and analysis we used to estimate the causal effects of interest. Finally, we present detailed estimates of policy impact for each source of data we analyzed and for subgroups of voters and alternative comparison groups. We show that the results presented in the body of this report generally are not affected greatly by the different data sources or methods we chose to use, or by the different assumptions we made, except when using Maine in the comparison group.[157]

Parameters of Interest

We use the Rubin Causal Model to specify the statistical parameters to be estimated using observed data.[158] Registered voters, $i \in \{1, 2, \ldots, N\}$, in the analysis states for time periods $T \in \{0, 1\}$ make up the population of interest, where T = 0 denotes the 2008 general election and T = 1 denotes the 2012 general election. The treatment, $D \in \{0, 1\}$, equals 1 if a registrant was required to show government-issued, photo ID before voting, according to the laws adopted by Kansas or Tennessee in this time period, and equals 0 otherwise.

Each registrant has potential turnout decisions, Y_{DT}, that could be observed for any combination of the time periods and treatment conditions. Thus, in principle, four potential outcomes are possible for each registrant, $\{Y_{00}, Y_{10}, Y_{01}, Y_{11}\}$, with the observed outcome at T equal to $Y._T = D * Y_{1T} + (1 - D) * Y_{0T}$. However, in this application, no registrant could have been exposed to the treatment at $T = 0$, so $Y._0 = Y_{00}$ *and* $Y._1 = D * Y_{11} + (1 - D) * Y_{01}$.

We seek to estimate two parameters: (1) the average treatment effect for the treated (ATT) at $T = 1$ conditional on an exogenous vector of covariates, $X = x$, including both controls and subpopulations of interest, and (2) the ATT at $T = 1$ for the entire population:

$$\theta_x = E(Y_{11} - Y_{01} | D = 1, X = x) \tag{1}$$

$$\begin{aligned} \theta &= E_x(E(Y_{11} - Y_{01} | D = 1, X = x)) \\ &= E(Y_{11} - Y_{01} | D = 1) \end{aligned} \tag{2}$$

The last line shows the unconditional ATT, which, by the law of iterated expectations, equals the conditional ATT integrated over the distribution of X for the treatment states at $T = 1$.[159]

Difference-in-difference Estimators and Their Assumptions

We estimate ATT and ATT_x using difference-in-difference methods:

$$\begin{aligned} \delta_x = {} & [E(Y._1 | D = 1, X = x) - E(Y.0 | D = 1, X = x)] - \\ & [E(Y._1 | D = 0, X = x) - E(Y.0 | D = 0, X = x)] \end{aligned} \tag{3}$$

$$\begin{aligned} \delta &= E_x(\delta_x) \\ &= [E(Y._1 | D = 1) - E(Y.0 | D = 1)] - \\ &\quad [E(Y._1 | D = 0) - E(Y.0 | D = 0)] \end{aligned} \tag{4}$$

Replacing $E(Y_{DT} \mid D = d, X = x)$ with the equivalent sample proportions produces unbiased and consistent estimates of δ and δ_x. These estimates equal θ and θ_x under several assumptions,[160] which we apply to the adoption of voter ID laws in Kansas and Tennessee below.

Common counterfactual trend: $E(Y_{01} - Y_{00} \mid D = 1, X = x) = E(Y_{01} - Y_{00} \mid D = 0, X = x)$

Difference-in-difference methods require that the potential outcomes for registrants who were and were not actually required to show voter ID would have changed by the same amount over time (on average), if Kansas and Tennessee did not change their requirements (withheld treatment). This is the critical identifying assumption for difference-in- difference estimates. Voters in the treatment and comparison states may have different expected potential outcomes in either time period, so long as this difference is constant over time: $E(Y_{00} \mid D = 1, X = x) - E(Y_{00} \mid D = 0, X = x) = E(Y_{01} \mid D = 1, X = x) - E(Y_{01} \mid D = 0, X = x)$. This is equivalent to allowing an unobserved state “fixed effect” or a voter fixed effect when difference-in-difference designs are carried out using regression models fit to panel data.

Controlling for state and voter fixed effects is particularly important for evaluating the effects of electoral administration practices, as previous studies have argued.[161] Political science researchers have found that long- term differences across voters, such as education and political interest, explain much more of the variation in turnout than factors that vary over time, such as campaign mobilization efforts and administrative reforms to make voting easier.[162] In addition, states vary widely in political and election administration practices, demographics, and political culture. This variation is associated with consistent, long-term differences in turnout at the state level. By holding constant these stable but influential variables across voters and states, difference-in-difference methods account for a large number of potential confounds, such as age, race, and pre- treatment laws, practices, and political culture, which might otherwise explain differences in turnout across voters at any one time. Moreover, difference-in-difference methods control for common trends between elections that affect turnout in both the treatment and comparison states, such as novel political issues and foreign or economic crises that vary over time at the national level. By accounting for these confounds by design, difference-in-difference methods allow us to focus on controlling for the smaller number of factors that varied over time within the treatment states, but not the comparison states, between the 2008 and 2012 general elections, in order to isolate the causal effects of changes in ID laws on turnout, if any.

Since the voters subject to ID laws in 2012 cannot be observed in the counterfactual scenario in which they were never required to present ID, $E(Y_{01} \mid D = 1, X = x)$ is not identified, and the common trend or equivalent stable bias assumptions cannot be tested empirically. Instead, we support these assumptions through our selection of comparison states and our use of covariates in statistical analysis.

We selected comparison states to ensure that the distributions of several time-varying covariates at the state level were as similar as possible in the treatment and comparison states (see appendix V). Our selection of states to balance these specific covariates is similar to using exact matching methods at the state level.[163] We matched on covariates that political science research has identified to be correlated with turnout and that can vary substantially over time. The covariates matched by design included:

- electoral competition (margin of victory) in campaigns for Presidential, statewide, and U.S. House offices;[164]
- presence of elections to statewide offices (federal or state);[165]
- changes to other election administration laws, including no excuse absentee voting, early voting, Election Day registration, felon disenfranchisement, and third party registration;[166]
- geographic proximity and shared borders with the treatment states, which implicitly controls for weather conditions on election day and exposure opportunities to broadcast news media and campaign advertising that cross state borders;[167] and
- the number, visibility, and competitiveness of statewide ballot questions.[168]

While we could not achieve exact balance on all of these covariates, we found that choosing Alabama, Arkansas, Delaware, and Maine as comparison states would hold constant these covariates most effectively. Because the covariates of interest changed in similar ways over time in these states and in the treatment states, the common counterfactual trend (stable bias) assumption becomes more credible. Nevertheless, the treatment and comparison states do not match exactly, which introduces the potential for bias. Appendix V discusses the primary ways in which the treatment and comparison states differ, and this appendix discusses our strategy for mitigating bias that may result.

In some versions of our analysis, we use statistical models to control for additional covariates beyond those controlled by design at the state level, in order to further support the common counterfactual trend assumption. Depending on the data available, our covariates include race, age, sex, family income, marital status, education, length of registration (proxy for residential mobility), labor force participation, and party registration. Although difference-in-difference methods control for the main effects of time-invariant covariates (e.g., race), including covariates in statistical analysis can improve the precision of the estimates and, more important, control for interactions with time. Trends in potential outcomes may not be parallel within demographic or political groups if political campaigns or interest groups disproportionately encouraged turnout among some groups in one year but not another, even though our design ensures that overall levels of competition were similar at the state level. Controlling for interactions between these covariates and time further supports the assumption that outcomes would have been parallel if the treatment were absent.

Although the common counterfactual trend assumption is a critical difference-in-difference identification assumption, several others are also necessary, which we discuss below.

Stable Unit Treatment Value

The stable unit treatment value assumption requires that changes in voter ID laws in Kansas or Tennessee, respectively, must not have affected turnout decisions in the other treatment state or in the comparison states. This could occur if registrants in comparison states adjacent to the treatment states mistakenly believed they were subject to the ID laws, perhaps due to misinformation from residents of the treatment states or news media sources that serve both sides of a state border, such as in Kansas City, Kansas, or Memphis, Tennessee. If this were true, the assumption that $Y_{.1} = D * Y_{11} + (1 - D) * Y_{01}$ would be false, because a voter's observed outcome would not depend solely on his or her own treatment status.

Our selection of comparison states makes this assumption both more and less plausible. It is possible that registrants in areas of Arkansas and Alabama near the borders of Kansas and Tennessee, respectively, could incorrectly conclude that ID laws across the border applied to them. Alternatively, if ID laws affected turnout by preventing registrants of ID states from voting due to their lack of proper documentation, registrants in the comparison states could not be affected by definition (assuming perfect policy implementation).[169] In this scenario, the stable unit treatment value assumption would be more reasonable, particularly in the interior parts of Alabama and Arkansas and in Delaware and Maine, where the lack of shared borders reduces the chance of cross-over. Our use of Delaware and Maine as comparison states checks the sensitivity of our estimates to this assumption.

Common support of the covariates: $0 < Pr(D = 1 \mid X = x) < 1$ *for all* x

Since the expectations in equations 3 and 4 above are conditional on D and X, observations on X must exist for all four combinations of D and T in order to estimate δ_x. This "covariate overlap" exists when the fraction of treated voters at $X = x$ is greater than 0 and less than 1. By matching comparison and treatment states on the variables described in Appendix V, we satisfied the common support assumption for state-level covariates through design. In addition, matching avoids the risk of extrapolation bias when using regression adjustments for state-level variables.[170] A limited pool of potential comparison states exists with identical observed changes to critical covariates between 2008 and 2012, because only 14 states since 2002 have adopted or implemented substantively modified requirements for photo and/or government-issued ID or requirements for registrants without these ID to follow-up. Sparse data increases the chance of violating the common support assumption, such that no comparison state can be observed for a given treatment state with an identical set of covariates and the causal parameter of interest cannot be identified. Our covariates of interest at the voter level are demographic variables, such as age and race. Each type of voter should exist in the treatment and comparison states in large samples, so the overlap assumption should be satisfied. We tested this assumption by comparing the empirical distribution of covariates in the treatment and comparison states, and redefined the populations for which estimates apply when common support is not achieved for the original populations of interest.

Covariates Are Exogenous

Our covariates must be independent of the potential outcomes and the use of ID laws. The presence of an ID law is unlikely to affect the fixed or long-term social and political characteristics that we plan to control for. For example, age, race, or education are clearly not causally related (subsequent) to whether a registrant lives in a treatment state. These are biological or social characteristics that election administration practices cannot plausibly influence. Similarly, covariates such as party registration and length of residence are unlikely to be causally related to changes in ID laws and voting decisions between two consecutive Presidential elections. ID laws are only a minor consideration among many others when forming political beliefs and deciding where to live.

No pre-treatment effect: $E(Y_{10} - Y_{00} \mid D = 1, X = x) = 0$ *for all x.*

Voter ID laws must not have influenced potential outcomes for the treated before they were enacted. This assumption is almost certainly true in our application. The ID laws in Kansas and Tennessee were not in effect for the 2008 election, so they could not have been legally applied by jurisdictions and formally affected the ability to vote. Moreover, voters probably could not have anticipated the laws' passage, and in any case, would have no reason to make turnout decisions in 2008 based on expected ID laws in 2012, given that the 2012 candidates were unknown.

Implementation Methods

Implementing difference-in-difference methods involves estimating the conditional expectations in equations 3 and 4 above. In principle, the data used for estimation could consist of aggregate counts or frequencies across subgroups of a population, which could be combined into an estimate for the entire population or a specific type of registrant by averaging the estimates across the subgroups. Specifically, one could estimate the conditional expectations in equations 3 and 4 nonparametrically by computing the sample analogues at $X = x$ and then integrating these estimates over the post-treatment sample distribution of x for the treatment states. This approach would produce average difference-in-difference estimates either for the entire population or subpopulations of voters having certain values of x. The identification assumptions and standard statistical results ensure that the equivalent conditional sample means equal the average treatment effect for the treated in large samples.[171]

Nevertheless, when the dimension of X is large, it can become convenient to assume a parametric model for the conditional expectations. This allows us to construct difference-in-difference estimates with a linear regression model:

$$E(Y_{it} \mid D_{it}, T_t, X_{it}) = \beta_0 + \beta_1 D_{it} + \beta_2 T_t + \delta\, D_{it} * T_t + \boldsymbol{X}_{it}\boldsymbol{\alpha} \tag{5}$$

where $\boldsymbol{X}_{it}$ is a vector of covariates and all other variables and parameters are as defined previously.[172] The estimated effect of changes in voter ID laws is given by δ, the additional amount by which turnout changes in the treatment states relative to the comparison states. Note that this model could be estimated using either repeated observations on the same registrants (panel data) or pooled, repeated cross-sections from the population of interest. Covariates can be measured at either time, so long as they are exogenous in both.

We estimated the effect of the changes in voter ID laws in Kansas and Tennessee using multiple sources of data on voter turnout: official vote totals, voter registration and history databases, and post-election surveys. Because the level of analysis and availability of covariates varied across sources, we used various combinations of the parametric and nonparametric methods above to estimate the effects of interest, as well as various approaches to estimating the uncertainty of these estimates.

The literature in statistics and economics is currently conflicted about how to assess the uncertainty of difference-in-difference estimates. On one extreme, finite population sampling theory might view official data on turnout decisions, either in the form of aggregate totals or voter-level data in registration and history databases, as having zero sampling error.[173] Voting decisions and other characteristics are observed for the entire population of registrants (assuming zero measurement error), so difference-in-difference estimates could be viewed as comparisons of population proportions that have no uncertainty.[174] These population parameters identify ATT if the assumptions above hold. On the other extreme, researchers have argued that difference-in-difference methods suffer from a potential clustering problem.[175] These authors imply that since we observe data on the same states and, in the case of panel data, voters over time, clustered data generation processes can cause the decision to vote to be correlated within states, even conditional on fixed effects for states and time periods. For example, changes in turnout may be correlated over time around long-term state means, due to contemporaneous changes in campaign mobilization efforts, the presence of more or less salient races, and Election Day weather conditions for registrants in the same state.

We view our data as the product of a partially random process. A population of registrants decides whether to vote in a given time period, given fixed registrant and environmental variables, such as education, campaign mobilization, and ID requirements. This decision is a binary random variable with a conditional expectation $E(Y_i \mid X_i, T) = Pr(Y_i = 1 \mid X_i, T)$. We view data on turnout from official records or surveys, measured at either the registrant or aggregate levels, as numerous draws from this conditional distribution, which may be non-independent within states, counties, or other politically meaningful groups, depending on the extent to which contextual variables such as campaign mobilization and changes to state election administration practices are controlled.

Our selection of treatment and comparison states should hold constant many sources of clustered turnout decisions. By matching states on election schedules and electoral competition, we hold constant the campaign mobilization efforts that might cause turnout to be correlated among voters in the same states. Geographic matching approximately holds constant Election Day weather conditions. The lack of contemporaneous changes to other state election laws holds constant administrative shocks (changes to jurisdictions' practices over time). Because these factors are implicitly controlled, we do not believe that clustered sampling processes should substantially inflate standard error estimates when viewing the number of registrants as the sample size. In addition, our short panel of two time periods reduces the impact of serial correlation, according to previous research of clustering in the context of difference-in-difference methods.[176]

Despite this substantial control for contextual variables, we made adjustments for possible within-state and within-county clustering in several versions of our analysis below. Several of the methods proposed to adjust for clustered sampling processes produce correct variance estimates only when the number of clusters and/or number of units within each cluster becomes large.[177] Accordingly, we used several methods of variance estimation that the literature has shown to work more effectively in situations with a small number of time periods and clusters.

Specifically, we estimated δ using linear probability regression models fit to registrant-level data from the Current Population Survey and state voter registration and history files (enhanced by the commercial firm, Catalist, LLC). In these analyses, we used "cluster-robust" variance estimators, which allow for observations to be arbitrarily correlated within groups but independent across groups, conditional on the covariates and design variables.[178] Versions of this analysis used state and state-county clusters, since the decision to vote is most plausibly correlated within counties in an analysis that holds constant several state-level factors associated with turnout. However, turnout decisions also may be correlated within counties in the same state, if any meaningful covariates at the state level are unobserved. We estimated 95 percent confidence intervals as $\hat{\delta} \pm t_{n_c-1,.025} * \sqrt{\mathrm{Var}(\hat{\delta})}$, where the degrees of freedom is a function of the number of clusters, n_c. Although in theory cluster-robust methods estimate variances correctly only when n_c is large, Monte Carlo simulations have found that the method performs well in finite samples with two time periods and six clusters—a structure similar to that of our data.[179] Because sample sizes are large and all covariates are categorical, the cluster-robust covariance matrix estimators adjust for the heteroskedasticity implied by linear probability regression models fit to registrant-level data, such as equation 5 above, and model estimates of turnout are bounded on [0,1].[180] Moreover, a generalized linear model with a specification equivalent to equation 5 above does not allow for time- invariant differences between groups (common trend), unlike linear models.[181] Despite the validity of linear probability models in these conditions and the limitations of generalized linear models, we replicated 4 versions of our results within a maximum absolute difference of 0.4 percentage points using identically specified logit models.[182]

For analyses of aggregate turnout data, we assumed that turnout decisions occur independently within each state and time period, and estimated the variance of δ using the normal approximation for differences in proportions across large, independent samples. Since δ is a sum of independent proportions, the variance of its estimator using sample proportions, $\bar{y}_{DT}$ is equal to the sum of the variances across time periods and treatment conditions:

$$\mathrm{Var}(\hat{\delta}) = \mathrm{Var}((\bar{y}_{11} - \bar{y}_{10}) - (\bar{y}_{01} - \bar{y}_{00})) \qquad (6)$$

$$= \sum_D \sum_T \frac{\bar{y}_{DT}\,(1 - \bar{y}_{DT})}{n_{DT}}$$

We calculate $\mathrm{Var}(\hat{\delta}_x)$ similarly for subpopulations, replacing $\bar{y}_{DT}$ and n_{DT} with equivalent sub-sample quantities. We estimate 95 percent margins of error using the normal approximation, $\hat{\delta} \pm z_{.025} * \sqrt{\mathrm{Var}(\hat{\delta})}$.

Data and Results

Multiple versions of our analysis, spanning three data sources and various analytical methods, found decreases in turnout in Kansas and Tennessee beyond decreases in turnout in our comparison states, and our analysis suggests that these differences are attributable to changes in voter ID laws in those states because we held constant other factors that could have affected turnout.[183] Below, we discuss the three sets of data we analyzed, the particular version of difference-in-difference methods we applied, and detailed estimates of policy impact under various assumptions. For each of the data sources, we reviewed documentation describing steps taken by the data managers to ensure data reliability and tested the data for anomalies that could indicate reliability concerns. We found that each of the three sets of data was sufficiently reliable for the purposes of our review.

Official Vote Totals

Our data on official vote totals come from United States Elections Project at George Mason University.[184] The project collected data on the total ballots and votes counted for the highest office in our six analysis states in the 2008 and 2012 general elections, as part of a larger effort to accurately estimate turnout among people eligible to vote. To calculate turnout rates, the project collected data on the total number of people in each state who were at least 18 years old and who were likely to be eligible to vote, after subtracting totals of people known to be ineligible, such as non-citizens and convicted felons in some states. Thus, the data available for analysis consisted of aggregate voting-eligible and voting- age turnout rates for the treatment and comparison states in 2008 and 2012, along with the number of voters from whom the rates were calculated.

Certified vote totals have several benefits, compared to other sources of turnout data available. Vote and ballot totals reflect the results of state vote certification processes to determine election outcomes. These totals do not reflect the errors of recall and self-reporting that can affect election surveys, which ask voters whether or not they voted. In addition, vote and ballot totals do not reflect data entry errors that can occur when election administrators fail to update a registrant's turnout history in official records, or update these records incorrectly.[185] Lastly, vote and ballot totals include only those ballots or votes that election officials ultimately counted toward deciding the election outcomes. Voter ID laws may affect turnout by requiring registrants without proper ID to cast provisional ballots, which election officials may or may not count pursuant to state law. Because vote and ballot totals only include provisional ballots that were counted, they provide a unique measure of turnout as the votes actually counted, rather than just attempted.

We estimated difference-in-differences by using aggregate data in which we substituted the turnout rates for each group of states and time period in equation (3). For each treatment state, we calculated separate estimates for each comparison state individually, and created alternative comparison groups by pooling the data for various combinations of states. Because the difference-in-difference is a difference of proportions using data on up to several million registrants, we used standard Normal approximations for calculating the sampling error of proportions and their 95 percent confidence intervals, assuming independent observations within states in an alternative version of our analysis below.

Table 14 provides estimates of eligible-voter turnout in Kansas and Tennessee, respectively, using various combinations of the comparison states, along with the change in turnout between the 2008 and 2012 general elections. Turnout in both Kansas and Tennessee declined by about 5 percentage points in this period, compared to declines of 1.9 to 3.0 percentage points in the comparison states. As shown in table 15, these turnout estimates imply difference-in-difference impact estimates of –2.1 to –3.2 percentage points in Kansas and –1.8 to –2.9 percentage points in Tennessee. The relatively small variation in the effect estimates suggests that our results are robust across multiple alternative choices of comparison groups.

Table 14. Eligible Voter Turnout Estimates by State and Year, Using Official Vote Totals

State	2008 (%)	2012 (%)	Difference (%)
Kansas	62.1	57.0	-5.1
Tennessee	57.0	52.2	-4.8
Alabama	60.8	58.9	-1.9
Arkansas	52.5	50.5	-1.9
Delaware	65.7	62.7	-3.0
Maine	70.6	68.1	-2.5
Alabama, Arkansas pooled	57.7	55.8	-1.9
Delaware, Maine pooled	68.7	66.0	-2.7
All comparison states pooled	60.2	58.1	-2.1

Source: GAO analysis of United States Elections Project data. | GAO-14-634.

Table 15. Effects of Changes in Voter ID Requirements on 2012 Eligible Voter Turnout in Kansas and Tennessee, Using Official Vote Totals

Comparison state	Treatment state	
	Impact estimate, % (margin of error) — Kansas	Impact estimate, % (margin of error) — Tennessee
Alabama	-3.2 (0.12)	-2.9 (0.10)
Arkansas	-3.1 (0.14)	-2.9 (0.12)
Delaware	-2.1 (0.19)	-1.8 (0.18)
Maine	-2.5 (0.16)	-2.3 (0.14)
Alabama, Arkansas pooled	-3.1 (0.12)	-2.9 (0.10)
Delaware, Maine pooled	-2.3 (0.16)	-2.1 (0.14)
All comparison states pooled	-3.0 (0.12)	-2.7 (0.09)

Source: GAO analysis of United States Elections Project data. | GAO-14-634.

Note: Entries are difference-in-difference estimates scaled in percentage points, with 95 percent margins of error in parentheses (e.g., +/- 0.12 percentage points).

Voter Registration and History Databases

Official vote totals do not allow for separate impact estimates among various subgroups of registrants, because they do not disaggregate the data according to subgroup membership. To address this limitation, we conducted parallel analyses of voter registration and history databases to check the robustness of our estimates using a different version of official data, to estimate effects within subgroups of registrants, and to control for additional variables at the voter level. We purchased access to a version of voter registration and history databases maintained by state election officials from Catalist, LLC. Catalist provides data on characteristics of registrants and their turnout decisions in the 2008 and 2012 general elections derived from official state data and commercial sources. Catalist extensively cleans the official data to more accurately measure voter eligibility. The firm collects data from all 50 state governments and the District of Columbia several times per year and tracks changes in the files over time. This allows the company to identify voters who move across states lines, which avoids counting voters as eligible in multiple states. In addition, Catalist matches the official data to the National Change of Address Registry from the U.S. Postal Service, in order to further identify registrants who have moved, and to the Death Master File from the Social Security Administration, in order to identify registrants who have died. Finally, Catalist applies a large number of electronic reliability tests to the data, clarifies potential errors with state officials, collapses duplicate records from the source data, and documents unresolved problems with the source data.[186]

Catalist's data on registrants' race are particularly important for our analysis. Some states, including Alabama and Tennessee, have measured registrants' self-reported race in their voter registration and history databases. These data are included in official versions of voter registration and history databases, and are preserved in the versions of these databases we purchased from Catalist. Other states, including Arkansas, Delaware, Kansas, and Maine, have not collected self-reported racial data on almost all registrants as part of their databases. For these registrants, Catalist estimates race using an algorithm supplied by a commercial firm, CPM Ethnics.

To assess the reliability of these racial estimates, we received a custom validation from Catalist, which compared the estimated race of registrants in North Carolina to the actual race that registrants self-reported to state election officials. This analysis found that approximately 70 to 90 percent of registrants, depending on racial group, coded by Catalist as "likely" or "highly likely" to self-identify with a certain racial group did, in fact, identify with that group in official records. Academic research has found similar levels of reliability. One peer-reviewed study matched racial estimates from Catalist's voter files to a nationwide survey, in which respondents were allowed to identify with various racial groups. For at least 93 percent of survey respondents, Catalist's estimates matched the race that respondents identified for themselves.[187] This evidence allowed us to conclude that Catalist's estimates of race were sufficiently reliable for the purpose of estimating impact estimates for various racial subgroups. However, we assess the sensitivity of our results to potential racial misclassification by estimating effects separately for Alabama and Tennessee, where 98.8 and 63.4 percent of the racial data, respectively, are provided by registrants directly. In addition, several versions of the analysis include only registrants with self-reported race and/or age in these states.

Several political scientists have used Catalist data to study voter turnout, including to estimate the effects of changes in voter ID laws. One study extensively evaluated the reliability of Catalist data, in part through comparisons to official records, and found a high degree of correspondence between the official and Catalist versions. This study was submitted as evidence by the Department of Justice in its case against Texas before a 3-judge panel of the U.S. District Court for the District of Columbia in June 2012.[188] Other studies using Catalist data have been published in *Political Analysis* and the *Quarterly Journal of Political Science*, which are both peer-reviewed scientific journals.[189] Nevertheless, we supplemented our analysis of Catalist's data with analyses of the two alternative sources of data described in this appendix to mitigate the risk of relying on one source of data.

A final strength of Catalist data is that the company's version of the official voter databases allows us to identify people who were registered in the past. Catalist archives state voter files over time and applies identifiers for people who have been dropped from registration lists due to death, moving, or other eligibility changes. Archiving allowed us to analyze a consistent set of voters. Specifically, we selected registrants in the Catalist database as of April 2014 who were registered on or before Election Day 2008 and whose current registration was "active" (73.6 percent of the analysis sample), "inactive" (8.1 percent) or "dropped" (18.3 percent). Active and inactive registrants are defined by each state. Active registrants are generally people who have voted or interacted with election administrators recently, while inactive registrants are generally people who do not meet the definition of "active" and are in the process of potentially being dropped as registered voters, possibly due to death or moving out of state. By selecting voters who were registered on or before the 2008 election, including people who were dropped from the file between 2008 and April 2014, we defined a consistent panel of voters for analysis over time who could have participated in both elections of interest.

We did not attempt to use specific criteria to identify eligible voters in 2008 and 2012, such as adjusting registration dates or voter history, because the error in these methods would vary across years and states and potentially bias difference-in-difference estimates that heavily rely on over-time variation. Time-varying measurement error is a particularly important source of bias for difference-in-difference analysis, because it is not controlled by design.

We assessed the sensitivity of our results to this method of constructing an analysis population by excluding "dropped" voters from one set of estimates. Our primary strategy of identifying registered voters included people who were registered in 2008 but dropped from official versions of state voter files by 2012, and therefore were not eligible to vote in 2012. Our sensitivity check considers how excluding these people affects our results—essentially the opposing bias of our primary strategy. However, federal law prevents states from dropping inactive registrants until after two federal elections have occurred (4 years). Since our analysis of voter databases in April 2014 occurred a maximum of six years after the elections of interest, the voters registered to vote in the files we analyzed likely closely approximate the registered voter populations as of Election Day 2008 and 2012.

We could not analyze the complete Catalist files at the registrant level, due to the terms of our subscription to the data. As a result, we estimated the parameters in equation 3 and 4 above using aggregate data on the full population of registrants, in order to maximize the amount of data available for analysis. Because this approach limited our ability to analyze a large number of covariates and subpopulations, we also analyzed a sample of registrant-level data, which we describe below.

For our analysis of aggregate Catalist data, we calculated turnout rates for G subsets of registrants formed by the cross-classification of race, age, and year of registration (a proxy for residential mobility). For each covariate cell, $g \in \{1, 2, \ldots, G\}$, we estimated turnout separately for the treatment and comparison states ($D \in \{0, 1\}$) in 2008 and 2012 ($T \in \{0, 1\}$). We combined these saturated conditional turnout estimates (or estimates across mutually exclusive and exhaustive subgroups) to estimate difference-in-difference parameters for the population of registrants as

$$\hat{\delta}_a = [(\bar{y}_{.1} \mid D = 1, X = g) - (\bar{y}_{.0} \mid D = 1, X = g)] - [(\bar{y}_{.1} \mid D = 0, X = g) - (\bar{y}_{.0} \mid D = 0, X = g)] \quad (7)$$

$$\hat{\delta} = \sum_g \hat{\delta}_g \hat{p}_{11}(g) \quad (8)$$

$$= [(\bar{y}_{.1} \mid D = 1) - (\bar{y}_{.0} \mid D = 1)] -$$

$$[(\bar{y}_{.1} \mid D = 0) - (\bar{y}_{.0} \mid D = 0)]$$

where $\hat{p}_{11}(g)$ is the empirical probability mass function (sample distribution) of g for the 2012 treatment state sample. We constructed estimates for subpopulations of registrants using similar calculations, except that we averaged the subgroup estimates over the marginal distribution of g conditional on membership in the subpopulation. Operationally, this approach amounted to calculating weighted averages of subgroup-specific estimates, with the weights given by the sample proportion of the subgroup cells. Per the results above, estimates derived from aggregate data can be interpreted as difference-in-differences and as having held constant the covariates used to form the covariate cells (age, race, and registration year) and their interactions with time.[190] Conditioning on the covariate cells makes our approach equivalent to applying matching estimators with exact adjustment cells equal to the cross-classified covariates above.[191]

In table 16 below, we show difference-in-difference estimates for various combinations of the comparison states and subpopulations of registered voters. The top rows provide the effect when excluding registrants from analysis if they were listed as dropped from the state's voter file as of April 2014 (but were registered on or before Election Day 2008). The middle rows include these registrants. The bottom rows limit the analysis to voters registered in counties that were not in several Congressional districts that we identified as potentially having experienced more or less electoral competition between 2008 and 2012 (see appendix V), which further controls for campaign competition. These counties overlapped districts with a margin of victory of less than 20 percentage points in either 2008 or 2012.

Across all of versions of the analysis that do not use Maine as a comparison, the effect of changes in voter ID requirements on registered voter turnout ranged from –0.6 to –3.9 percentage points in Kansas and from –1.1 to –3.2 percentage points in Tennessee. The consistency of our estimates across various comparison states and subpopulations suggests that our results are robust to various threats to validity at the state level, such as changes in campaign competition, voter mobilization efforts, and weather conditions on Election Day.

Estimates using Maine as the comparison group are consistently larger than in other versions of the analysis, though in the same direction. The larger effects with respect to Maine could reflect the presence of a salient ballot proposition in 2012 on same-sex marriage. If this proposition caused turnout in 2012 to be higher than it would have been in Kansas and Tennessee, impact estimates would be biased downward, given that turnout declined in Kansas and Tennessee. In addition, the completeness of Maine's voter history database improved between 2008 and 2012, with the votes recorded in the database accounting for 90.3 percent of the certified vote in 2008 but 98.6 percent in 2012. This change in measurement error over time could have caused similar bias in our impact estimates, because it would not have been controlled by design and would have uniquely affected a comparison state but not the treatment states. For these reasons, estimates using Maine as a comparison state may be somewhat inflated in size across all data sources.

Table 16. Effects of Changes in Voter ID Requirements on 2012 Registered Voter Turnout in Kansas and Tennessee, Using Voter Registration and History Databases

	Impact estimate, % (margin of error) - Kansas	Impact estimate, % (margin of error) - Tennessee
Excluding registrants dropped from voter file		
All comparison states	-2.2 (0.12)	-3.2 (0.09)
Alabama	-0.6 (0.13)	-1.9 (0.11)
Arkansas	-2.2 (0.15)	-3.2 (0.13)
Delaware	-1.5 (0.21)	-2.2 (0.19)
Maine	-5.2 (0.18)	-5.9 (0.16)
Alabama, Arkansas pooled	-1.1 (0.12)	-2.4 (0.10)
Delaware, Maine pooled	-4.1 (0.15)	-4.6 (0.13)
Including registrants dropped from voter file		
All comparison states	-3.5 (0.12)	-2.9 (0.09)
Alabama	-1.8 (0.13)	-1.6 (0.11)
Arkansas	-3.8 (0.15)	-3.1 (0.13)
Delaware	-1.9 (0.20)	-1.1 (0.19)
Maine	-6.8 (0.17)	-6.0 (0.16)
Alabama, Arkansas pooled	-2.6 (0.12)	-2.2 (0.10)
Delaware, Maine pooled	-5.1 (0.15)	-4.1 (0.13)
Excluding registrants in Congressional districts with change in competition		
All comparison states	-2.9 (0.18)	-1.7 (0.11)
Alabama	-2.1 (0.20)	-1.3 (0.13)
Arkansas	-3.9 (0.22)	-2.7 (0.17)
Delaware	-3.1 (0.24)	-1.3 (0.19)
Alabama, Arkansas pooled	-2.8 (0.19)	-1.8 (0.12)

Source: GAO analysis of state voter registration and history databases (commercially enhanced). | GAO-14-634.

Note: Entries are difference-in-difference estimates scaled in percentage points, with 95 percent margins of error in parentheses (e.g., +/- 0.12 percentage points). Some competition existed in 2008 or 2012 in each of Maine's two districts, so no estimates appear for comparison groups that include Maine.

We estimated effects among three subpopulations of registrants, according to the race, length of registration, and age.[192] The effects varied across these subpopulations, with larger effects among African-American registrants, younger registrants, and recent registrants.

When estimating effects separately by race, we found that turnout among African-American registrants declined more than turnout among White registrants in Kansas and Tennessee between the 2008 and 2012 general elections, and our analysis suggests that this difference is attributable to changes in those states' voter ID laws (see table 17). The effect among African-Americans was -7.0 percentage points in Kansas and -4.1 percentage points in Tennessee, using all comparison states, compared to -3.2 percentage points among Whites in Kansas and -2.6 percentage points in Tennessee.[193]

Expressed as a ratio, African- American registrants were affected 2.2 and 1.6 times more strongly in Kansas and Tennessee, respectively, than White registrants. We found similar results when comparing African-American registrants to Asian- American and Hispanic registrants, respectively.

The effects among Asian-American, White, and Hispanic registrants were similar to each other, particularly when considering the effects' margins of error. In addition, we found similar results using Alabama, Arkansas, and Delaware separately as comparison groups, and using the pooled Alabama and Arkansas comparison group. However, we found African-American registrants were less strongly affected relative to other groups using Maine as a comparison group. Several confounding factors specific to Maine, as discussed above and in appendix V, may explain this difference. Using Delaware as the comparison group, the effects among both African-American and Hispanic registrants were larger than among Whites.

To assess the potential effect of imputed racial data on our results, as discussed above, we conducted a version of our analysis using only registrant-reported racial data from Tennessee and Alabama, the only states in our design with such data available. Using these data, we estimated effects of -4.2 percentage points (+/- 0.3) among African- American registrants, compared to -0.7 (+/- 0.1) percentage points among White registrants. The limited number of Asian-American and Hispanic registrants in these states prevented us from estimating separate effects for these groups using registrant-reported data.

Table 17. Effects of Changes in Voter ID Laws on 2012 Registered Voter Turnout in Kansas and Tennessee, by Racial and Ethnic Subgroups, Using Voter Registration and History Databases

	Impact estimate, %(margin of error) -Kansas	Impact estimate, %(margin of error) -Tennessee
All comparison states		
Asian-American	-2.3 (1.4)	-1.3 (1.3)
African-American	-7.0 (0.5)	-4.1 (0.2)
White	-3.3 (0.1)	-2.6 (0.1)
Hispanic	-2.2 (0.9)	-2.6 (1.1)
Other/unknown	-6.6 (1.6)	-1.4 (1.7)
Alabama		
Asian-American	0.1 (1.7)	1.1 (1.6)
African-American	-7.3 (0.5)	-4.6 (0.2)
White	-1.6 (0.2)	-1.0 (0.1)
Hispanic	0.9 (1.4)	0.8 (1.5)
Other/unknown	-3.1 (2.0)	3.5 (2.1)
Arkansas		
Asian-American	-4.8 (2.0)	-3.5 (1.9)
African-American	-7.6 (0.5)	-4.1 (0.3)
White	-3.6 (0.2)	-2.8 (0.1)
Hispanic	-4.1 (1.2)	-5.0 (1.4)
Other/unknown	-5.6 (2.2)	-1.2 (2.3)

	Impact estimate, %(margin of error) -Kansas	Impact estimate, %(margin of error) -Tennessee
Delaware		
Asian-American	-3.6 (2.0)	-2.5 (1.9)
African-American	-5.2 (0.6)	-2.1 (0.4)
White	-1.5 (0.2)	-0.9 (0.2)
Hispanic	-3.5 (1.2)	-3.9 (1.4)
Other/unknown	-6.9 (2.6)	-3.1 (2.7)
Maine		
Asian-American	-3.9 (2.3)	-2.9 (2.3)
African-American	-5.9 (1.5)	-3.9 (1.4)
White	-7.0 (0.2)	-6.5 (0.2)
Hispanic	-2.3 (2.2)	-2.5 (2.2)
Other/unknown	-9.6 (2.6)	-3.4 (2.7)
Alabama, Arkansas pooled		
Asian-American	-1.5 (1.5)	-0.4 (1.4)
African-American	-7.3 (0.5)	-4.4 (0.2)
White	-2.3 (0.1)	-1.7 (0.1)
Hispanic	-1.7 (1.0)	-2.3 (1.2)
Other/unknown	-4.7 (1.7)	0.2 (1.9)
Delaware, Maine pooled		
Asian-American	-3.8 (1.7)	-2.7 (1.7)
African-American	-5.2 (0.6)	-2.1 (0.4)
White	-5.1 (0.2)	-4.5 (0.1)
Hispanic	-2.9 (1.1)	-3.2 (1.3)
Other/unknown	-8.9 (2.0)	-3.4 (2.2)

Source: GAO analysis of voter registration and history databases (commercially enhanced). | GAO-14-634.

Note: Entries are difference-in-difference estimates scaled in percentage points, with 95 percent margins of error in parentheses (e.g., +/- 1.3 percentage points). Estimates include registrants who were dropped from the voter files prior to April 2014.

The effect of changes in voter ID laws in both Kansas and Tennessee declined as the length of registration increased (see table 18). Between the 2008 and 2012 general elections, compared to the comparison states pooled, turnout declined by 7.5 percentage points more in Kansas and 5.5 percentage points more in Tennessee for people registered to vote within the past year; turnout declined by 2.3 percentage points more in Kansas and 1.4 percentage points more in Tennessee for people registered to vote for at least 20 years. We found similar patterns using the other comparison states except those involving Maine, with the interaction being particularly strong using Alabama and Delaware.

Lastly, we found that in both Kansas and Tennessee, as registrants' age increased, the effects of changes in voter ID laws had decreasing effects on turnout (see Table 19). Pooling all comparison groups, turnout among 18 year-old registrants as of November 2008, declined by 9.0 percentage points in Kansas and 4.1 percentage points in Tennessee between the 2008 and 2012 general elections, compared to reductions of 1.9 percentage points and 2.8

percentage points among registrants between the ages of 44 and 53. The same decline among registrants between the ages of 19 and 23 was 5.5 percentage points in Kansas and 4.0 percentage points in Tennessee. Our analysis suggests that these differences were attributable to changes in voter ID laws in Kansas and Tennessee. This interaction persisted when using each comparison group or state except those including Maine.

Table 18. Effects of Changes in Voter ID Laws on 2012 Registered Voter Turnout in Kansas and Tennessee, by Length of Registration, Using Voter Registration and History Databases

	Impact estimate, %(margin of error) -Kansas	Impact estimate, %(margin of error) -Tennessee
All comparison states		
Registered for 0-1 year	-7.5 (0.3)	-5.5 (0.3)
Registered for 1-2 years	-4.2 (0.7)	-4.9 (0.5)
Registered for 3-4 years	-4.6 (0.4)	-4.3 (0.3)
Registered for 5-9 years	-3.3 (0.2)	-3.3 (0.2)
Registered for 10-19 years	-2.1 (0.2)	-1.6 (0.2)
Registered for 20+ years	-2.3 (0.3)	-1.4 (0.2)
Alabama		
Registered for 0-1 year	-5.0 (0.4)	-3.5 (0.3)
Registered for 1-2 years	-2.1 (0.8)	-3.4 (0.6)
Registered for 3-4 years	-2.2 (0.5)	-2.4 (0.4)
Registered for 5-9 years	-1.3 (0.3)	-1.7 (0.2)
Registered for 10-19 years	-1.1 (0.3)	-0.8 (0.2)
Registered for 20+ years	-1.6 (0.3)	-0.8 (0.2)
Arkansas		
Registered for 0-1 year	-13.4 (0.4)	-11.1 (0.4)
Registered for 1-2 years	-5.1 (0.8)	-5.8 (0.7)
Registered for 3-4 years	-4.3 (0.6)	-4.3 (0.5)
Registered for 5-9 years	-2.8 (0.3)	-2.9 (0.3)
Registered for 10-19 years	-1.8 (0.3)	-1.4 (0.2)
Registered for 20+ years	-1.4 (0.3)	-0.3 (0.3)
Delaware		
Registered for 0-1 year	-8.8 (0.7)	-6.3 (0.6)
Registered for 1-2 years	-0.5 (1.0)	-1.0 (0.9)
Registered for 3-4 years	-0.9 (0.7)	-0.6 (0.7)
Registered for 5-9 years	-1.0 (0.4)	-1.1 (0.4)
Registered for 10-19 years	-0.7 (0.4)	0 (0.3)
Registered for 20+ years	-1.0 (0.4)	-0.2 (0.3)
Maine		
Registered for 0-1 year	-4.0 (0.5)	-0.7 (0.5)
Registered for 1-2 years	-9.2 (1.0)	-8.8 (0.9)
Registered for 3-4 years	-8.2 (0.6)	-7.2 (0.5)

	Impact estimate, %(margin of error) -Kansas	Impact estimate, %(margin of error) -Tennessee
Registered for 5-9 years	-7.0 (0.3)	-7.0 (0.3)
Registered for 10-19 years	-6.4 (0.4)	-5.9 (0.3)
Registered for 20+ years	-7.9 (0.4)	-6.4 (0.4)
Alabama, Arkansas pooled		
Registered for 0-1 year	-7.9 (0.3)	-5.9 (0.3)
Registered for 1-2 years	-3.5 (0.7)	-4.6 (0.5)
Registered for 3-4 years	-3.1 (0.5)	-3.2 (0.4)
Registered for 5-9 years	-1.9 (0.2)	-2.2 (0.2)
Registered for 10-19 year	-1.4 (0.2)	-1.0 (0.2)
Registered for 20+ years	-1.5 (0.3)	-0.8 (0.2)
Delaware, Maine pooled		
Registered for 0-1 year	-6.3 (0.5)	-4.1 (0.4)
Registered for 1-2 years	-5.4 (0.8)	-5.3 (0.7)
Registered for 3-4 years	-6.4 (0.5)	-5.6 (0.4)
Registered for 5-9 years	-5.5 (0.3)	-5.2 (0.2)
Registered for 10-19 years	-4.0 (0.3)	-2.9 (0.3)
Registered for 20+ years	-4.6 (0.3)	-3.3 (0.3)

Source: GAO analysis of voter registration and history databases (commercially enhanced). | GAO-14-634.

Note: Entries are difference-in-difference estimates scaled in percentage points, with 95% margins of error in parentheses (e.g., +/- 0.3 percentage points). Estimates include registrants who have been dropped from the voter files prior to April 2014.

Table 19. Effects of Changes in Voter ID Laws on 2012 Registered Voter Turnout in Kansas and Tennessee, by Age in 2008, Using Voter Registration and History Databases

	Impact estimate, % (margin of error) -Kansas	Impact estimate, % (margin of error) -Tennessee
All comparison states		
18	-9.0 (0.9)	-4.1 (0.7)
19-23	-5.5 (0.5)	-4.0 (0.4)
24-33	-2.7 (0.3)	-5.1 (0.2)
34-43	-2.7 (0.3)	-3.7 (0.2)
44-53	-1.9 (0.2)	-2.8 (0.2)
54-63	-1.3 (0.2)	-2.0 (0.2)
64-73	-0.8 (0.3)	-1.6 (0.3)
74+	-0.1 (0.4)	-1.7 (0.4)
Alabama		
18	-6.6 (1.0)	-2.3 (0.8)
19-23	-4.1 (0.6)	-3.2 (0.4)
24-33	-0.8 (0.4)	-3.9 (0.3)

Table 19. (Continued)

	Impact estimate, % (margin of error) -Kansas	Impact estimate, % (margin of error) -Tennessee
34-43	-1.0 (0.3)	-2.5 (0.3)
44-53	-0.3 (0.3)	-1.6 (0.2)
54-63	0.2 (0.3)	-0.8 (0.2)
64-73	0.7 (0.3)	-0.4 (0.3)
74+	1.1 (0.5)	-0.4 (0.5)
Arkansas		
18	-16.2 (1.1)	-10.8 (0.9)
19-23	-9.4 (0.7)	-6.9 (0.6)
24-33	-3.3 (0.4)	-5.0 (0.4)
34-43	-2.4 (0.4)	-3.4 (0.3)
44-53	-1.6 (0.3)	-2.5 (0.3)
54-63	-1.1 (0.3)	-1.8 (0.3)
64-73	-0.1 (0.4)	-1.3 (0.3)
74+	2.5 (0.5)	0.6 (0.5)
Delaware		
18	-12.6 (1.6)	-6.4 (1.5)
19-23	-6.3 (0.9)	-4.1 (0.8)
24-33	-0.8 (0.6)	-2.9 (0.5)
34-43	-1.0 (0.5)	-1.9 (0.5)
44-53	-0.5 (0.4)	-1.5 (0.4)
54-63	-0.8 (0.4)	-1.3 (0.4)
64-73	-1.5 (0.5)	-2.2 (0.5)
74+	-2.0 (0.8)	-3.4 (0.8)
Maine		
18	-3.6 (1.5)	3.3 (1.3)
19-23	-3.3 (0.8)	-1.5 (0.7)
24-33	-6.0 (0.5)	-8.1 (0.5)
34-43	-6.3 (0.4)	-7.4 (0.4)
44-53	-5.4 (0.4)	-5.7 (0.3)
54-63	-4.8 (0.3)	-5.8 (0.3)
64-73	-4.7 (0.4)	-5.7 (0.4)
74+	-4.8 (0.6)	-5.9 (0.6)
Alabama, Arkansas pooled		
18	-9.5 (0.9)	-4.7 (0.7)
19-23	-5.8 (0.5)	-4.4 (0.4)
24-33	-1.7 (0.4)	-4.4 (0.3)
34-43	-1.5 (0.3)	-2.8 (0.2)
44-53	-0.7 (0.3)	-1.9 (0.2)
54-63	-0.3 (0.2)	-1.2 (0.2)
64-73	0.4 (0.3)	-0.6 (0.3)

	Impact estimate, % (margin of error) -Kansas	Impact estimate, % (margin of error) -Tennessee
74+	1.5 (0.4)	-0.1 (0.4)
Delaware, Maine pooled		
18	-7.1 (1.2)	-2.0 (1.1)
19-23	-4.6 (0.7)	-3.2 (0.5)
24-33	-4.4 (0.4)	-6.2 (0.4)
34-43	-4.7 (0.4)	-5.0 (0.3)
44-53	-3.9 (0.3)	-4.3 (0.3)
54-63	-3.4 (0.3)	-3.8 (0.3)
64-73	-3.4 (0.4)	-4.2 (0.3)
74+	-3.8 (0.6)	-5.3 (0.5)

Source: GAO analysis of voter registration and history databases (commercially enhanced). | GAO-14-634.

Note: Entries are difference-in-difference estimates scaled in percentage points, with 95% margins of error in parentheses (e.g., +/- 0.7 percentage points). Estimates exclude registrants who have been dropped from the voter file prior to April 2014.

Voter Registration and History Databases – Registrant-Level Analysis

We replicated the results of our aggregate analysis of voter registration and history databases by analyzing a probability sample of records from these files at the registrant level.[194] These data allowed us to check the consistency of our results across levels of analysis and statistical methods. In addition, the sample allowed us to more easily adjust for the possibility of correlated residual variation among registrants living in the same states, as we discuss above. Due to smaller sample sizes, we did not attempt to estimate effects separately among subpopulations.

The sample consisted of 60,000 records per state, producing a total sample size of 360,000. We selected registrants using an unequal probability stratified sample design. We defined the strata as the cross- classification of state, race, age, and the year of registration. Within each state, we allocated sample to strata proportionally with respect to their distribution in the population. Because the population size varied across states, this allocation produced unequal selection probabilities across states. As a result, we constructed sampling weights equal to the inverse of the sampling probabilities, and applied these weights in all analyses. We assessed the reliability of the data by comparing the distributions of key variables, such as the strata, race, and age, in the sample and in the population, and found no substantial differences.

To replicate our aggregate results, we estimated the difference-in- difference parameter using linear probability regression models fit to the registrant-level sample. Specifically, we estimated three versions of equation 5 above:

$$\mathrm{E}(Y_{it} \mid D_{it}, T_t, X_{it}) = \beta_0 + \beta_1 D_{it} + \beta_2 T_t + \delta\, D_{it} * T_t \qquad \text{(Model 1)}$$

$$\mathrm{E}(Y_{it} \mid D_{it}, T_t, X_{it}) = \beta_0 + \beta_1 D_{it} + \beta_2 T_t + \delta\, D_{it} * T_t + \boldsymbol{X}_{it}\boldsymbol{\alpha} \qquad \text{(Model 2)}$$

$$\mathrm{E}(Y_{it} \mid D_{it}, T_t, X^{i}_{t}) = \beta_0 + \beta_1 D_{it} + \beta_2 T_t + \delta\, D_{it} * T_t + \boldsymbol{X}_{it}\boldsymbol{\alpha} + T_t * \boldsymbol{X}_{it}\boldsymbol{\alpha} \qquad \text{(Model 3)}$$

The covariates in X_{it} included age, length of registration, party registration, race, and sex. The specification consisted of a series of indicators for each level of each variable, in order to allow flexibly non- linear relationships with turnout. We coded Y_{it} as 1 if the registrant reported voting in year t and 0 otherwise. In model three, we specified interactions between time and the covariates, in order to allow for unique trends (but not unique effect estimates) within different subgroups of registrants. We estimated the parameters' standard errors using heteroskedasticity-robust or, when we analyzed at least three states, cluster-robust methods assuming state and state-county clusters. These methods adjust for the hereroskedasticity implied by a linear probability model, given that Y_{it} is binary. In addition, the methods adjust for potentially non-independent observations within states, due to unobserved contextual covariates (such as local campaign mobilization). Since turnout may be correlated among registrants living in the same counties, due to a shared set of electoral offices and ballot questions (for example), we also applied adjustments using state-county clusters. Estimates of $\Pr(Y_{it}=1| D_{it}, T_t, X_{it})$ are guaranteed to lie in the unit interval, because all of the covariates are discrete.

We estimated the models among the three subpopulations of registrants we analyzed using aggregate data. First, we excluded registrants living in U.S. House districts that we found to experience some change in electoral competition between 2008 and 2012. Second, we excluded registrants who were registered in the analysis states on or before Election Day 2008 but had since been dropped from the files. Third, we excluded registrants with imputed racial and/or age data. When these data are missing from official versions of state voter registration and history files, Catalist imputes them using proprietary methods (as discussed above) or matches data from commercial sources. We excluded these data from one version of our analysis, in order to control for the possibility that measurement or imputation error affected our results. Excluding imputed data also provides more accurate parameter variance estimates, since these data have additional imputation error that is not propagated when analyzing the estimates as if they were ordinary observations.[195]

Table 20 reports difference-in-difference impact estimates using these various approaches (estimates of δ in models 1 through 3). Although our estimates using aggregate and micro data are not exactly equivalent, they support broadly similar conclusions about the effects of changes in ID laws in Kansas and Tennessee on turnout. We estimate that reductions in turnout by 3.6 percentage points in Kansas and 3.1 percentage points in Tennessee are attributable to ID law changes in those states, using all comparison states, adjusting for clustered sampling within states, including registrants dropped from the files, and applying the more demanding control specification of model 3. By comparison, our aggregate, nonparametric analysis produced estimates of -3.5 and -2.9 percentage points for Kansas and Tennessee, respectively (see table 16). Our regression impact estimates are not highly sensitive to the choice of comparison state, except that the estimates are somewhat higher using comparison groups consisting of Maine alone or pooling Maine and Delaware. Similarly, most of the impact estimates remain in the range of -2 to -5 percentage points, regardless of whether we exclude registrants who were dropped from the voter files, had imputed race and/or age data, or lived in U.S. House districts that experienced some change in competition. In sum, our analysis of the Catalist voter registration and history files produces similar conclusions using either the aggregate methods described above or the regression methods described here.

Our estimates using micro data have more uncertainty than our estimates using complete voter files—an expected consequence of probability sampling. Without adjusting for residual correlations within states, the 95 percent margins of error in table 20 can be about 7 to 8 times larger than the margins of error for the aggregate analysis reported in table 16.

Adjusting for clustered sampling within states increases the margins of error within the micro analysis by a factor of approximately 2 to 3 times. Nevertheless, most of the micro estimates support the conclusion that decreases in turnout in Kansas and Tennessee beyond decreases in turnout in the comparison states were attributable to changes in the two states' voter ID requirements, with effects remaining significantly negative at the $\alpha = 0.05$ level when using the full sample and all comparison states.

While these impact estimates are still sizable and negative, they are not significant when using the pooled Delaware and Maine comparison group and in several other specifications, such as those excluding registrants living in House districts with some change in electoral competition. However, the generally similar point estimates in the aggregate and micro analysis, along with the fact that the micro estimates derive from a probability sample, suggests that fitting the same models to the complete registrant-level data likely would produce significantly negative results.

For example, consider the estimates in tables 16 and 20 for registrants living in non-competitive House districts in Kansas, using all comparison states. Comparing these results suggests that the aggregate effect estimate of -2.9 percentage points would be negative and marginally significant at $0.10 > \alpha > 0.05$, assuming the clustered margin of error of +/- 3.0 percentage points from table 20.

Table 20. Effects of Changes in Voter ID Requirements on 2012 Registered Voter Turnout in Kansas and Tennessee, Using Registrant-Level Sample from Voter Registration and History Databases

Comparison State	Model	Special adjustment	Impact estimate, % (margin of error) - Kansas	Impact estimate, % (margin of error) - Tennessee
Alabama	1	None	-2.3 (0.8)	-1.4 (0.8)
Alabama	2	None	-2.3 (0.7)	-1.4 (0.8)
Alabama	3	None	-2.1 (0.8)	-1.8 (0.8)
Arkansas	1	None	-4.2 (0.8)	-3.4 (0.8)
Arkansas	2	None	-4.2 (0.7)	-3.4 (0.8)
Arkansas	3	None	-4.4 (0.8)	-3.7 (0.8)
Delaware	1	None	-3.8 (0.8)	-2.9 (0.8)
Delaware	2	None	-3.8 (0.8)	-2.9 (0.8)
Delaware	3	None	-3.2 (0.8)	-2.5 (0.8)
Maine	1	None	-7.3 (0.8)	-6.5 (0.8)
Maine	2	None	-7.3 (0.8)	-6.5 (0.8)
Maine	3	None	-6.5 (0.8)	-6.3 (0.8)

Table 20. (Continued)

Comparison State	Model	Special adjustment	Impact estimate, % (margin of error) - Kansas	Impact estimate, % (margin of error) - Tennessee
Alabama, Arkansas pooled	1	State clusters	-3.0 (3.4)	-2.1 (3.4)
Alabama, Arkansas pooled	2	State clusters	-3.0 (3.4)	-2.1 (3.4)
Alabama, Arkansas pooled	3	State clusters	-2.9 (4.1)	-2.5 (3.3)
Delaware, Maine pooled	1	State clusters	-6.0 (6.2)	-5.2 (6.2)
Delaware, Maine pooled	2	State clusters	-6.0 (6.2)	-5.2 (6.2)
Delaware, Maine pooled	3	State clusters	-5.4 (5.3)	-4.9 (6.1)
All comparison states pooled	1	State clusters	-3.7 (2.8)	-2.9 (2.8)
All comparison states pooled	2	State clusters	-3.7 (2.8)	-2.9 (2.8)
All comparison states pooled	3	State clusters	-3.6 (2.8)	-3.1 (2.4)
All comparison states pooled	1	State-county clusters	-3.6 (0.9)	-2.9 (1.4)
All comparison states pooled	2	State-county clusters	-3.6 (0.9)	-2.9 (1.4)
All comparison states pooled	3	State-county clusters	-3.6 (0.8)	-3.1 (1.3)
All comparison states pooled	1	State clusters, no competitive House	-4.4 (1.9)	-2.0 (1.9)
All comparison states pooled	2	State clusters, no competitive House	-4.4 (1.9)	-2.0 (1.9)
All comparison states pooled	3	State clusters, no competitive House	-3.6 (3.0)	-2.1 (1.7)
All comparison states pooled	1	State clusters, no dropped registrants	-2.5 (2.9)	-3.1 (2.9)
All comparison states pooled	2	State clusters, no dropped registrants	-2.5 (2.9)	-3.1 (2.9)
All comparison states pooled	3	State clusters, no dropped registrants	-2.5 (3.1)	-3.2 (2.6)
All comparison states pooled	1	State clusters, no imputed race and/or age	-3.4 (2.4)	NA
All comparison states pooled	2	State clusters, no imputed race and/or age	-3.4 (2.4)	NA
All comparison states pooled	3	State clusters, no imputed race and/or age	-3.5 (2.6)	NA

Comparison State	Model	Special adjustment	Impact estimate, % (margin of error) - Kansas	Impact estimate, % (margin of error) - Tennessee
Alabama	1	No imputed race and/or age	NA	-1.9 (0.9)
Alabama	2	No imputed race and/or age	NA	-1.9 (0.9)
Alabama	3	No imputed race and/or age	NA	-2.7 (0.9)

Source: GAO analysis of state voter registration and history databases (commercially enhanced) | GAO-14-634.

Note: Entries are difference-in-difference estimates scaled in percentage points, with 95% margins of error in parentheses (e.g., +/- 0.8 percentage points).

Current Population Survey

The Current Population Survey (CPS) Voting and Registration Supplement served as our final source of data. Within several weeks after the 2008 and 2012 federal general elections, the U.S. Census Bureau asked a nationwide sample of adults a battery of questions about their registered voter status and whether they voted in the election. The CPS serves as a check on official data sources, because it measures turnout using the responses of survey respondents. Although self-reported turnout is often biased upward, compared to official turnout rates,[196] the CPS provides an opportunity to assess the sensitivity of our impact estimates to a different source of measurement error. In addition, the CPS provides a different set of covariates than are available in the Catalist version of voter registration and history databases.

We pooled the 2008 and 2012 CPS data in order to estimate the effect of changes in voter ID laws, if any, for the population of registered voters in Kansas and Tennessee. We limited the sample to adult respondents reporting that they were citizens of the United States and registered to vote, and weighted all estimates using the person-level weights provided by the CPS. Due to sample size limitations, we could not estimate separate impact estimates for subpopulations using the CPS.

We fit the same type of linear probability regression models to the CPS data as we fit to the sample of Catalist voter registration and history data, except that the data consisted of repeated cross-sections:

$$E(Y_{it} \mid D_{it}, T_t, X_{it}) = \beta_0 + \beta_1 D_{it} + \beta_2 T_t + \delta\, D_{it} * T_t \qquad \text{(Model 1)}$$

$$E(Y_{it} \mid D_{it}, T_t, X_{it}) = \beta_0 + \beta_1 D_{it} + \beta_2 T_t + \delta\, D_{it} * T_t + \boldsymbol{X}_{it}\boldsymbol{\alpha} \qquad \text{(Model 2)}$$

$$E(Y_{it} \mid D_{it}, T_t, X_{it}) = \beta_0 + \beta_1 D_{it} + \beta_2 T_t + \delta\, D_{it} * T_t + \boldsymbol{X}_{it}\boldsymbol{\alpha} + T_t * \boldsymbol{X}_{it}\boldsymbol{\alpha} \qquad \text{(Model 3)}$$

The covariates in $\boldsymbol{X}_{it}$ included age, education, employment status, family income, marital status, race, residential mobility, and sex. The specification consisted of a series of indicators for each level of each variable, in order to allow flexibly non-linear relationships with turnout. We coded Y_{it} as 1 if the respondent reported voting in year t and 0 otherwise, treating "don't know" responses as missing data. In model 3, we specified interactions between time and the covariates, in order to allow for unique trends (but not unique effects) within different subgroups of registrants. We estimated the parameters' standard errors using heteroskedasticity- robust or cluster-robust methods, assuming state or state-county clusters, when we analyzed at least three states.

We estimated the models above using various combinations of comparison states. As with our analysis of official turnout data, this approach tests the robustness of our results to plausible alternative choices of comparison states and to specific imbalances in state-level factors we discuss in appendix V, such as ballot questions and campaign competition. However, we included an additional control group in our analysis of CPS data: registrants living in all states other than the treatment states (Kansas and Tennessee) and our standard comparison states (Alabama, Arkansas, Delaware, and Maine). This alternative control group assesses whether our results hold, even using all other possible comparison states that we did not choose for analysis in appendix V. In addition, the larger number of states included in the analysis (45) increases the number of observed clusters and better satisfies the asymptotic assumptions of cluster-robust variance estimation methods.

The CPS data support similar conclusions about the effect of changes in voter ID laws on turnout as made from the official data (see table 21). Across all of the assumptions we made when analyzing the CPS data, the estimated effect of changes in Kansas's ID law ranged from -1.2 percentage points to -5.6 percentage points, with the exception of fitting model 3 to respondents living in Alabama. The same effect estimates for Tennessee ranged from -1.4 to -5.0 percentage points (again excluding model 3 for Alabama). Estimates using a single comparison state had relatively large margins of error, in part due to these groups' smaller populations and sample sizes. When pooling data across respondents in all comparison states, however, our estimates are distinguishable from zero at $\alpha = 0.05$. Moreover, the point estimates are consistent with those we made using much larger quantities of official data, suggesting that declines in turnouts between the 2008 and 2012 general elections in Kansas and Tennessee are attributable to changes in those states' voter ID laws.

Table 21. Effects of ID Requirements on 2012 Registered Voter Turnout in Kansas and Tennessee, Using Current Population Survey

Comparison state	Model	Impact estimate, % (margin of error) - Kansas	Impact estimate, % (margin of error) - Tennessee
Alabama	1	-2.3 (4.6)	-1.7 (5.0)
Alabama	2	-2.0 (4.7)	-1.4 (5.0)
Alabama	3	0.4 (5.0)	-0.6 (5.1)
Arkansas	1	-3.5 (5.0)	-2.8 (5.3)
Arkansas	2	-3.7 (5.0)	-3.6 (5.3)
Arkansas	3	-3.3 (5.1)	-3.8 (5.4)
Delaware	1	-5.6 (3.8)	-5.0 (4.2)
Delaware	2	-5.3 (3.9)	-4.1 (4.3)

Comparison state	Model	Impact estimate, % (margin of error) - Kansas	Impact estimate, % (margin of error) - Tennessee
Delaware	3	-5.3 (4.1)	-4.6 (4.3)
Maine	1	-4.7 (3.7)	-4.1 (4.1)
Maine	2	-3.6 (3.6)	-3.1 (4.1)
Maine	3	-2.3 (3.8)	-3.2 (4.4)
Alabama, Arkansas pooled	1	-2.7 (2.0)	-2.1 (2.0)
Alabama, Arkansas pooled	2	-2.5 (3.0)	-2.2 (3.8)
Alabama, Arkansas pooled	3	-1.2 (7.8)	-1.7 (6.4)
Delaware, Maine pooled	1	-5.1 (1.6)	-4.4 (1.6)
Delaware, Maine pooled	2	-4.3 (3.3)	-3.4 (2.2)
Delaware, Maine pooled	3	-3.5 (5.4)	-3.6 (3.1)
All comparison states pooled	1	-3.2 (1.7)	-2.6 (1.7)
All comparison states pooled	2	-2.9 (1.9)	-2.5 (2.0)
All comparison states pooled	3	-1.9 (3.5)	-2.2 (2.8)
Nationwide, excluding comparison states	1	-2.7 (0.6)	-2.1 (0.6)
Nationwide, excluding comparison states	2	-2.8 (0.6)	-2.3 (0.6)
Nationwide, excluding comparison states	3	-2.7 (0.8)	-2.2 (0.7)

Source: GAO analysis of 2008 and 2012 Current Population Survey, Voting and Registration Supplement. | GAO-14-634.

Note: Entries are difference-in-difference estimates scaled in percentage points, with 95% margins of error in parentheses (e.g., +/- 4.6 percentage points).

Comparing results across models and the use of a nationwide comparison group further supports the validity of our design. The lack of substantial variation between model 1, which estimates only the raw difference-in-difference, and models 2 and 3, which condition on demographic covariates and their interactions with time, is consistent with a strong design. If unobserved campaign or ballot question mobilization changed between elections, and these efforts disproportionately affected turnout among certain demographic groups of registrants, we would expect controls for the interaction between time and the covariates to affect the impact estimates. The stability of the estimates makes this scenario less likely. Similarly, the consistency in the estimates between our comparison groups and a nationwide alternative suggests that our specific choice of analysis states does not strongly affect the results.

APPENDIX VII: ADDITIONAL PROVISIONAL BALLOT ANALYSIS

We analyzed data from the EAVS to determine how provisional ballot rates changed over time in our treatment states (Kansas and Tennessee) and comparison states (Alabama, Arkansas, Delaware, and Maine) using data obtained about all jurisdictions in those states (e.g., to include all jurisdictions from which data were obtained in the EAVS in either 2008 or 2012). We conducted this additional analysis to determine if missing data affected the results of the analysis we discussed earlier in the report regarding changes in provisional ballot rates over time in which we excluded jurisdictions that did not report data for both the 2008 and 2012 EAVS. In our second analysis, as shown in tables 22 and 23, we obtained results similar to those in our first analysis, indicating that our exclusion of jurisdictions with missing data did not affect our conclusion that provisional ballot usage increased in Kansas and Tennessee from the 2008 to the 2012 general election relative to ballot usage in comparison states.

These results include data provided by local election jurisdictions in selected states to the EAVS in either 2008, 2012, or in both years. All jurisdictions in Delaware, Kansas, and Tennessee provided data to the EAVS in each year, but data were missing for some jurisdictions in either year in the other states. Between 0.2 and 28.9 percent of the jurisdictions in Alabama, Arkansas, and Maine did not provide data to the EAVS for 1 or both years (see notes for table 22).

Table 22. Change in Provisional Ballot Usage between 2008 and 2012 General Elections, in Treatment and Comparison States

State	Percentage of total ballots that were provisional in 2008	Percentage of total ballots that were provisional in 2012	Change inprovisional ballot usage between 2008 and 2012 general elections[a]
Kansas	3.18	3.48	0.30
Tennessee	0.17	0.29	0.12
Alabama	0.34[b]	0.32[c]	-0.02
Arkansas	0.20[d]	0.24[e]	0.04
Delaware	0.09	0.11	0.01
Maine	0.04[f]	0.04[g]	0.00
Alabama/Arkansas pooled	0.29	0.29	0.01
Delaware/Maine pooled	0.06	0.07	0.01
All comparison states pooled	0.23	0.23	0.00

Source: GAO analysis of U.S. Election Assistance Commission's Election Administration and Voting Survey (EAVS) 2008 and 2012 data from selected states. | GAO-14-634.

[a] The change in provisional ballot usage between 2008 and 2012 may not equal the percent of total ballots that were provisional in 2012 minus the percent of total ballots that were provisional in 2008 due to rounding in subtraction.

[b] In 2008, 7.46 percent of jurisdictions in Alabama did not report data on the total number of provisional ballots cast.

[c] In 2012, 22.39 percent of jurisdictions in Alabama did not report data on the total number of provisional ballots cast.

[d] In 2008, 10.67 percent of jurisdictions in Arkansas did not report data on the total number of provisional ballots cast.

[e] In 2012, 2.67 percent of jurisdictions in Arkansas did not report data on the total number of provisional ballots cast.

[f] In 2008, 28.86 percent of jurisdictions in Maine did not report data on the total number of provisional ballots cast.

[g] In 2012, 0.20 percent of jurisdictions in Maine did not report data on the total number of provisional ballots cast.

Table 23. Comparison of Change in Provisional Ballot Usage between 2008 and 2012 General Elections in Treatment and Comparison State Groups

State	Kansas (%)	Tennessee (%)
Alabama/Arkansas pooled	0.29 (0.047)	0.11 (0.012)
Delaware/Maine pooled	0.29 (0.046)	0.11 (0.011)
All comparison states pooled	0.30 (0.046)	0.11 (0.010)

Source: GAO analysis of U.S. Election Assistance Commission's Election Administration and Voting Survey (EAVS) 2008 and 2012 data from selected states. | GAO-14-634.

Notes: Entries in parentheses are 95 percent margins of error (e.g., +/- 0.047 percentage points).

Analyzing provisional ballot rates using data provided by all jurisdictions responding to the EAVS in either 2008 or 2012 could, in principle, produce biased results, given that data were missing for some jurisdictions. However, we have no basis to conclude that the missing data in this situation cause substantial bias. With the exception of Alabama in 2012 and Maine in 2008, the rate of missing data was less than 11 percent. Since the potential bias caused by missing data is proportional to the amount of data that are missing, the relatively low rates of missing data in our analysis has a similarly low risk of introducing bias. This is true even if the jurisdictions that did not report data had substantially different provisional ballot rates than those that did.[197]

Consistent with this conclusion, our estimates of change over time are similar across states, regardless of their rates of missing data. The larger increase in provisional ballot rates among voters in Kansas and Tennessee, compared with the change among voters in the other states, is consistent with the results of our turnout analysis earlier in this report. Finally, we obtained similar results when we conducted the analysis using only jurisdictions that responded to the EAVS in both 2008 and 2012.

Together, this evidence suggests that the provisional ballot rate is not highly sensitive to which jurisdictions chose to report data in a particular year and supports our assumption that the missing data are not consequential.

Appendix VIII: Selected Federal Databases and the Types of Information They Contain

Table 24 provides a description of each of the four databases we identified that contain information on possible federal in-person voter fraud investigations, prosecutions, and convictions.

Table 24. Selected Federal Databases and the Types of Information They Contain

Name of database	Federal agency that manages the database	Description	Types of information included in the data (investigations, prosecutions, convictions)
Legal Information Office Network System (LIONS)	U.S. Department of Justice Executive Office for United States Attorneys	Used to compile, maintain, and track information relating to defendants, crimes, criminal charges, court events, and witnesses.	Investigations, prosecutions, convictions
Automated Case Tracking System II (ACTS II)	U.S. Department of Justice Criminal Division	Tracks all cases and matters that are the responsibility of the Criminal Division's litigating sections. It provides the Criminal Division's managers with reports and statistics for determining attorney workloads and productivity.	Investigations, prosecutions, convictions
Integrated Database	Federal Judicial Center	Contains federal court data such as statute violations at the time of case filing and case termination that are routinely reported to the Administrative Office of the U.S. Courts.	Prosecutions, convictions
Oracle database	United States Sentencing Commission	Contains data extracted and analyzed from sentencing documents submitted by federal courts to the United States Sentencing Commission.	Convictions

Source: GAO analysis of each database's associated codebooks and interviews with agency officials. | GAO-14-634.

End Notes

[1] This includes states in which ID requirements are not currently in effect because, for example, the law is legislated to go into effect at a later date or the law has been enjoined pursuant to litigation. Vote-by-mail states are not included.

[2] These include the National Voter Registration Act of 1993, the Help America Vote Act of 2002, and the Voting Rights Act of 1963, among others.

[3] Pub. L. No. 107-252, 116 Stat. 1666 (2002) (codified as amended at 42 U.S.C. §§ 15301-545).

[4] Under section 5 of the Voting Rights Act of 1965, as amended, 42 U.S.C. § 1973c, covered jurisdictions may not change their election practices or procedures until they obtain federal "preclearance" for the change. The jurisdictions targeted for "coverage" are those states or localities evidencing discriminatory voting practices, based upon a triggering formula, as defined in section 4 of the Voting Rights Act, 42 U.S.C. § 1973b. In June 2013, the Supreme Court ruled in *Shelby County v. Holder* that section 4 of the Voting Rights Act is unconstitutional. 133 S. Ct. 2612 (2013). The effect of this decision is that the jurisdictions identified by the

coverage formula in section 4(b) no longer need to seek preclearance for new voting changes (unless they are covered by a separate court order entered under section 3(c) of the Voting Rights Act).

[5] GAO, *Elections: State Laws Addressing Voter Registration and Voting on or before Election Day*, GAO-13-90R (Washington, D.C.: Oct. 4, 2012).

[6] States requiring government-issued ID include those where there is an exception for a school ID.

[7] Some states allow voters to provide a utility bill, a bank statement, or a pay-check, among other documents, as voter identification. It would be difficult to measure the cost to obtain these non-photo and non-government issued IDs, and the specifics of the cost would vary based on the voter and the type of document allowed to be presented.

[8] The 17 states in our scope are Alabama, Arkansas, Florida, Georgia, Indiana, Kansas, Mississippi, North Carolina, North Dakota, Oklahoma, Pennsylvania, Rhode Island, South Carolina, Tennessee, Texas, Virginia, and Wisconsin. These 17 states include those in which ID requirements are not currently in effect because, for example, the law is legislated to go into effect at a later date or the law has been enjoined pursuant to litigation. *See, e.g., Applewhite v. Commonwealth*, 2014 WL 184988 (Pa. Commw. Ct. Jan. 17, 2014); *Frank v. Walker*, 2014 WL 1775432 (E.D. Wis. Apr. 29, 2104). As of June 2014, litigation was pending in Arkansas, North Carolina, Oklahoma, Texas and Wisconsin.

[9] Significant changes in presidential election margins of victory suggests that voters may have been subjected to more intense efforts by campaigns and interest groups to affect turnout. This imbalance in voter mobilization efforts—which academic research has shown to be effective in some conditions—is an important potential factor that could affect turnout.

[10] The USEP's database provides voter turnout data for eligible voters by calculating the total number of people in each state who were at least 18 years old and who were likely to be eligible to vote, after subtracting totals of people known to be ineligible, such as non- citizens and convicted felons in some states. The official voter records enhanced by a vendor provide turnout information for registered voters. The vendor enhances the data by cleaning them to improve reliability (e.g., by removing duplicate entries, deceased registrants, and registrants who may have moved out of state) and by matching additional variables for analysis from commercial sources. The CPS, conducted by the U.S. Census Bureau, asks a nationwide sample of adults questions about their registered voter status and whether they voted in the most recent election.

[11] The Election Assistance Commission administers the biennial Election Administration and Voting Survey, which is an instrument used to collect state-by-state data on the administration of federal elections. The survey is divided into two parts. The first part captures quantitative data pertaining to the National Voter Registration Act, the Uniformed and Overseas Citizens Absentee Voting Act (UOCAVA), and other election administration issues such as the counting of provisional ballots and poll worker recruitment. The second part is the Statutory Overview, which asks state officials to respond to a series of open- ended questions about their states' election laws, definitions, and procedures.

[12] This included provisional ballots cast for ID reasons related to an ID requirement for all eligible voters, not ID requirements for first-time voters who register by mail pursuant to HAVA.

[13] This was necessary because there is no standard federal definition for in-person voter fraud.

[14] "Organizational studies" refers to those studies published by non-governmental organizations, such as the Heritage Foundation and the Brennan Center for Justice. Studies produced by state-level agencies are not included in the literature review, but are discussed in our report.

[15] We excluded studies that reported on previously compiled data or anecdotal reports of in-person voter fraud, including those reported in the media.

[16] According to DOJ officials, while EOUSA manages LIONS, district U.S. Attorney offices are responsible for maintaining the accuracy and integrity of the data.

[17] We also contacted election officials from the 4 remaining states, but they declined to be interviewed.

[18] As described by the Supreme Court, "the States have evolved comprehensive, and in many respects complex, election codes regulating in most substantial ways, with respect to both federal and state elections, the time, place, and manner of holding primary and general elections, the registration and qualifications of voters, and the selection and qualification of candidates." *Storer v. Brown*, 415 U.S. 724, 730 (1974).

[19] Congress' authority to regulate congressional elections derives primarily from Article I, Section 4, Clause 1 of the Constitution (known as the Elections Clause).

[20] Federal law does not generally address third-party voter registration organizations, but many states have enacted laws regulating how registration drives by third parties may be conducted, by whom, and other aspects of voter registration efforts by nongovernmental organizations.

[21] 42 U.S.C. § 1973gg.

[22] 42 U.S.C. § 1973gg-2. Certain states are exempt from the NVRA, including North Dakota—which has no voter registration requirement—and Idaho, Minnesota, New Hampshire, Wisconsin, and Wyoming—which have election-day registration. The NVRA does not apply to states where either (1) under law that is in effect continuously on and after August 1, 1994, there is no voter registration requirement for any voter in the state for a federal election or (2) under law that was is in effect continuously on and after, or enacted prior to,

August 1, 1994, all voters in the state may register to vote at the polling place at the time of voting in a general election for federal office. *Id.*

[23] 42 U.S.C. §§ 1973gg-4(a)(2), 1973gg-7(b).

[24] 42 U.S.C. § 15483.

[25] *Id.* The NVRA also allows states to require all first-time voters who register by mail to vote in person at the polling place, where the voter's identity can be confirmed. 42 U.S.C. § 1973gg-4(c).

[26] 42 U.S.C. § 15483.

[27] For example, Alaska law limits the types of acceptable forms of identification that first- time voters who register by mail may provide in order to register if they do not have a driver's license or do not provide the last four digits of their Social Security number. Alaska does not permit using a utility bill, bank statement, government check, paycheck, or other government document that shows the name and address of the voter. Instead, Alaska specifies that applicants may provide a state identification card, current and valid photo identification, birth certificate, passport, or hunting and fishing license.

[28] Absentee voting is a process that allows citizens to cast a vote when they are unable to vote at their precinct on Election Day and is generally conducted by mail. Early voting is any process by which a voter may cast a ballot in person, without providing an excuse, prior to Election Day, regardless of the name the state gives to that process. A state may provide for both in-person absentee voting and early voting. For example, in Alaska, which provides both, according to the Alaska Secretary of State's website, the difference between in-person absentee and early voting is that an early voter is already determined to be eligible to vote at the time of voting, and thus the voter's ballot is placed directly in the ballot box to be counted and tabulated along with those of other eligible voters on Election Day. With in-person absentee voting, the voter's eligibility is not verified at the time of voting, and thus the voter's ballot is placed inside an absentee voting envelope—pending subsequent verification—prior to being placed in the ballot box.

[29] Examples of excuses a voter may provide for not voting on Election Day include being sick, having a disability, being out of the country, or having religious commitments.

[30] GAO-13-90R.

[31] *Id.*

[32] GAO, *Elections: Views on Implementing Federal Elections on a Weekend*, GAO-12-69 (Washington, D.C.: Jan. 12, 2012).

[33] These requirements are in addition to identification requirements applicable to first-time voters who register by mail pursuant to HAVA. The states are Alabama, Alaska, Arizona, Arkansas, Connecticut, Delaware, Florida, Georgia, Hawaii, Idaho, Indiana, Kansas, Kentucky, Louisiana, Michigan, Mississippi, Missouri, Montana, New Hampshire, New Mexico, North Carolina, North Dakota, Ohio, Oklahoma, Pennsylvania, Rhode Island, South Carolina, South Dakota, Tennessee, Texas, Utah, Virginia, and Wisconsin. These states include those with laws that are either currently in effect or scheduled to go into effect prior to a future election pursuant to state legislation, including those laws that have been the subject of litigation. For example, the Federal District Court for the Eastern District of Wisconsin recently found Wisconsin's voter ID law unconstitutional, *Frank v. Walker*, 2014 WL 1775432 (E.D. Wis. Apr. 29, 2104), as did the Commonwealth Court in Pennsylvania with respect to that state's ID law, *Applewhite v. Commonwealth*, 2014 WL 184988 (Pa. Commw. Ct. Jan. 17, 2014). Many of these state voter identification laws have been the subject of controversy and litigation. The Supreme Court addressed the constitutionality of Indiana's voter identification law in 2008 in *Crawford v. Marion County Election Board,* 553 U.S. 181, and upheld the law. The lead opinion identified several purported state interests justifying Indiana's law, such as deterring and detecting voter fraud, justifying the burdens that the law imposed on voters and potential voters. The dissent, in contrast, found that given no evidence of in-person voter fraud in the state, Indiana had failed to justify the practical limitations on voting rights created by the law. As of June 2014, litigation was pending in Arkansas, North Carolina, Oklahoma, Texas and Wisconsin.

[34] The remaining three states, Colorado, Oregon and Washington, are vote-by–mail states and do not require voters to provide identification when casting a ballot by mail; although Colorado and Washington have identification requirements for voters who opt to vote in person. States may have additional verification requirements, such as signature matching at the polling place.

[35] These include state ID requirements for all eligible voters at the polls on Election Day. In addition to enacting new identification requirements and amending the type of document accepted and acceptable issuing authority, states also changed the processes for voters who do not present acceptable identification on Election Day, generally concurrent with these other changes.

[36] While the ID requirements generally apply to all voters, states may have exceptions for certain categories of voters. For example, in Kansas, voters with a permanent physical disability or those whose religious beliefs prohibit photographic identification are exempt from the photographic ID requirement. In Indiana, a voter who votes in person at a precinct polling place that is located at a state-licensed care facility where the voter resides is not required to provide proof of ID.

[37] Of the remaining 15 states, 1 state does not provide an alternative process if a voter does not have acceptable ID; 10 allow the voter to verify his or her identity and cast a regular ballot; and 4 allow for a voter's identity to be

verified by elections officials and vote a regular ballot; and, of those 4, 3 additionally allow for the voter to cast a provisional ballot.

[38] In Ohio, for example, if a voter does not provide acceptable identification the voter may cast a provisional ballot and either (1) write the voter's driver's license or state identification card number or the last four digits of the voter's social security number on the provisional ballot envelope; or (2) appear at the office of the board of elections not later than the seventh day after Election Day and provide the required identification.

[39] A nationwide survey of 2012 general election voters found that between 84 and 90 percent of voters reported they used a driver's license or state ID card when voting in states that require voters to show photo ID (Stewart, 2013). The survey also found that 64 percent of voters reported using a driver's license or state ID card when voting in states where acceptable ID includes nonphoto ID. We reviewed three additional studies related to ID ownership, but excluded them because we determined there was either insufficient information provided about the study's methodology or implementation, or the study was outside the scope of our work. Those studies were: Barreto, Matt A.; Stephen A. Nuno, and Gabriel R. Sanchez. "Voter ID Requirements and the Disenfranchisement of Latino, Black, and Asian Voters." Paper presented at the 2007 American Political Science Association Annual Conference, Chicago, IL, September 1, 2007; McDonald, Michael P. "May I See Your ID, Please? Measuring the Number of Eligible Voters with Photo Identification." Paper presented at the California Institute of Technology and Massachusetts Institute of Technology Voter Identification and Registration Conference, Cambridge, MA, October 2006; and Sanchez, Gabriel R. "The Disproportionate Impact of Photo-ID Laws on the Minority Electorate," 2011. In Latino Decisions, accessed April 15, 2014, http://www.latinodecisions.com/blog/2011/05/24/the-disproportionate-impact-of- stringent-voter-id-laws.

[40] We had two GAO social scientists review each of the 10 studies to determine whether the design, implementation, and analyses of the study were sufficiently sound to support the study's results and conclusions based on generally accepted social science principles.

[41] North Carolina State Board of Elections (April 2013). As of June 2014, North Carolina voters were not required to provide documentation at the polls in order to vote on Election Day. However, the state legislature passed a voter ID statute in August 2013 that is scheduled by legislation to go into effect in 2016.

[42] Barreto, Nuño, Sanchez (January 2009). Indiana voters must show a government- issued photo ID at the polls on Election Day. The ID requirement was implemented in 2005.

[43] Stephen Ansolabehere and Eitan Hersh, "Validation: What Big Data Reveal about Survey Misreporting and the Real Electorate," *Political Analysis* 20 (2012): 437-459.

[44] Stephen Ansolabehere and Eitan Hersh, "The Quality of State Voter Registration Records: A State-by-State Analysis." Working paper, Cal-Tech/MIT Voting Technology Project and the Institute for Quantitative Social Science, Harvard University, July 14, 2010.

[45] We selected states whose voter ID requirements fell into one of three categories (1) photo only, government issued; (2) photo only, can be nongovernment issued; (3) nonphoto, government issued. We also excluded states that allow all voters without ID to cast a regular ballot by affirming their own identity at the polling place, since there would be no cost to the voter in this situation. For example, in Tennessee, a voter who is indigent and unable to obtain proof of identification without payment of a fee or a voter who has a religious objection to being photographed may execute an affidavit of identity and then be permitted to vote. States requiring government-issued ID include those where there is an exception for a school ID.

[46] Additional ID documents that meet state voter ID requirements may include handgun permits, student ID, and tribal ID, among others. In some states, certain populations may be exempt from the requirement that acceptable identification contain a photograph of the voter; for example, in Pennsylvania, if the voter has a religious objection to being photographed, a valid-without-photo driver's license or a valid-without-photo identification card issued by the Department of Transportation may be used. Certain federal IDs are also allowed, but the cost of those IDs is standard across states. A U.S. passport can be obtained for $110 plus a $25 processing fee. A passport card, which may be used to enter the United States from Canada, Mexico, the Caribbean, and Bermuda at land border crossings or sea ports of entry, costs $30 to $55 plus a $25 processing fee. Members of the U.S. military can obtain a uniformed services ID card free of charge.

[47] Pennsylvania's voter ID was permanently enjoined on January 14, 2014, by the Pennsylvania Commonwealth Court. *Applewhite v. Commonwealth*, 2014 WL 184988 (Pa. Commw. Ct. Jan. 17, 2014). This injunction extended to issuance of free voter ID by the Pennsylvania Department of Transportation and Department of State.

[48] Rhode Island charges a $32 fee for an individual's first license and license renewals are $41.50.

[49] To fulfill the identity requirement, birth certificates are also available at no cost in Kansas to enable an individual to assert his or her identity to obtain an ID without incurring any direct costs. Kansas residency may be established using a utility bill, mail from a financial institution, a Kansas Voter Registration Card, educational institution transcript forms or grade cards for the current school year, a letter from a social welfare institution, or an identification certificate issued by the Kansas Department of Corrections to an offender, among others.

[50] According to the Alabama Secretary of State's legal counsel, a voter obtaining a free ID from the Alabama Secretary of State's office or a county board of registrar's office does not need to independently provide documentation showing he or she is registered to vote in the state and documentation showing his or her name

and address as reflected in the voter registration record because this information can be verified electronically in Alabama's voter registration system.

[51] As previously stated, the types of documents and combinations of documents that an individual could present to obtain a driver's license, nondriver state ID, or free ID vary by state. Given this variation, we focused on obtaining and presenting information on costs for a state birth certificate, which is a common type of document individuals could present among the 17 states we reviewed. Other types of documents that could be presented in certain states include a Social Security card or other federal forms of ID; these federal forms of ID may have costs, but those costs are standard across states, and are therefore not discussed in this review. In addition, other types of documents could be presented in certain states, but we excluded them from our review, as the costs and combinations of documents vary across the states.

[52] We reviewed six additional studies related to the effects of state voter ID requirements on voter turnout, but excluded them from our report because of limitations in the studies' scope or methods for estimating effects. Those studies were: Ansolabehere, Stephen. "Effects of Identification Requirements on Voting: Evidence from the Experiences of Voters on Election Day." *PS: Political Science & Politics*, January 2009: 127-130; Bullock III, Charles S and M.V. Hood III. "Worth a Thousand Words? An Analysis of Georgia's Voter Identification Statute." *American Politics Research*, vol. 36, no. 4 (2008): 555-579; Cobb, Rachel V., D. James Greiner, and Kevin M. Quinn. "Can Voter ID Laws Be Administered in a Race-Neutral Manner? Evidence from the City of Boston in 2008." *Quarterly Journal of Political Science*, vol. 7 (2012): 1-33; Gomez, Brad T. "Uneven Hurdles: The Effect of Voter Identification Requirements on Voter Turnout." Paper presented at the Annual Meeting of the Midwest Political Science Association, Chicago, IL, April 2007; Lott, John R. Evidence of Voter Fraud and the Impact that Regulations to Reduce Fraud have on Voter Participation Rate (August 2006), forthcoming; and Pitts, Michael J. "Photo ID, Provisional Balloting, and Indiana's 2012 Primary Election." *University of Richmond Law Review*, vol. 47, no.3 (2013): 939-957.

[53] The study that did not group states was focused on turnout effects in one state (Indiana). The remaining nationwide studies generally grouped states by type of ID requirement, such as by states that require voters to state their name, states that require voters to present ID or a voter registration card, and states that require photo ID. Also, ID requirements studied include those that do not require voters to present documentation at the polls. For example, voters may be required to provide a signature as a form of identification, which is verified by election officials as matching the voter's signature provided when the voter registered.

[54] Dropp (2013).

[55] Muhlhausen and Sikich (2007) reported results for racial sub-groups that they found to be statistically significant. However, we determined that the methods used to quantify the sub-group results they presented were not sufficiently reliable, and therefore have not included those in the report.

[56] The author did not describe which racial groups were included in the non-white category for analysis. Some states require registered voters to identify their race when registering to vote. For those states, the vendor reports what registered voters indicate as their race. For states that do not require self-reporting of race, the vendor classifies each voter's race based on other characteristics kept in official voter records and U.S. Census information.

[57] For each of these estimates, the researcher did not report standard errors, but asserts that the differences are significantly distinguishable from zero.

[58] The difference for Hispanics was distinguishable from zero at the 0.05 level of statistical significance, and each difference for African-American, Asian Americans, and whites was distinguishable from zero at the 0.01 level.

[59] We reviewed the published study (2011), as well as the working paper that led to the published study (2008).

[60] Milyo defines minority groups as non-white or Hispanic.

[61] In one of the 7 studies, the authors used both survey responses and official voter records (Mycoff, Wagner, and Wilson, 2007).

[62] Specifically, five studies used data from the Voting and Registration Supplement of the Current Population Survey (CPS), administered by the U.S. Census Bureau, one study used data from the American National Election Studies (ANES) survey (produced through a collaboration of Stanford University and the University of Michigan), and one study used data from the Cooperative Congressional Election Study (CCES) survey (produced by Harvard University). The U.S. Census Bureau conducts the CPS monthly to measure unemployment and other workforce data, but adds a battery of voter participation questions to the November survey in even-numbered years to coincide with the presidential and midterm congressional elections. Administered since 1948, the ANES survey is conducted just after biennial national elections. During presidential elections, the ANES is also conducted just before the election.

[63] Ansolabehere and Hersh, "Validation: What Big Data Reveal about Survey Misreporting and the Real Electorate,"437-459.

[64] Ansolabehere and Hersh, "The Quality of State Voter Registration Records: A State-by- State Analysis." Pew Center for the States, Election Initiatives. Inaccurate, Costly, and Inefficient: Evidence that America's Voter Registration System Needs and Upgrade. February 2012, http://www.pewstates.org/research/ reports/inaccurate-costly-and- inefficient-85899378437.

[65] The six states that implemented government-issued photo ID requirements after the 2006 general election and as of the 2012 general election are: Georgia (2008 presidential election), Idaho (2010 midterm election), Kansas (2012 presidential election), Michigan (2008 presidential election), Pennsylvania (2012 presidential election), and Tennessee (2012 presidential election). The remaining two states that implemented government- issued photo ID requirements as of the 2006 general election are: Indiana (2006 midterm election) and South Dakota (2004 presidential election). When requirements were implemented is not necessarily when legislated to go into effect, due to litigation.

[66] See, for example, Raymond E. Wolfinger, and Steven J. Rosenstone. *Who Votes?* New Haven, Connecticut: Yale University Press, 1980; Luke Keele and William Minozzi, "How Much is Minnesota Like Wisconsin? Assumptions and Counterfactuals in Causal Inference with Observational Data." *Political Analysis* (2013): 1-24; Robert S. Erikson and Lorrane C. Minnite. "Modeling Problems in the Voter Identification—Voter Turnout Debate." *Election Law Journal* (2009): 85-101.

[67] GAO, *Designing Evaluations*, GAO-12-208G (Washington, DC: Jan. 31, 2012); Debra J. Rog, "Constructing Natural 'Experiments'." In *Handbook of Practical Program Evaluation*, Joseph P. Wholey, Harry P. Hatry, and Kathryn E. Newcomer, eds. San Francisco: Jossey-Bass Publishers, 2010.

[68] Luke Keele and William Minozzi, "How Much is Minnesota Like Wisconsin? Assumptions and Counterfactuals in Causal Inference with Observational Data." Political Analysis (2013): 1-24; Michael J. Hanmer, *Discount Voting: Voting Registration Reforms and Their Effects*. New York: Cambridge University Press, 2009.

[69] Raymond E. Wolfinger, and Steven J. Rosenstone. *Who Votes?* New Haven, CT: Yale University Press, 1980. Steven J. Rosenstone and John Mark Hansen. *Mobilization, Participation, and Democracy in America*. New York: MacMillan, 1993.

[70] In 2004, Kansas amended its election laws to provide for ID requirements for all first- time voters. In 2011, Kansas added new photo ID requirements for all eligible voters, effective January 1, 2012. In 2003, Tennessee added a form of acceptable ID to its existing ID requirement, allowing voters to present a valid voter's registration certificate in addition to a Tennessee driver's license, Social Security card, a credit card bearing the voter's signature, or other document bearing the voter's signature. In 2011, Tennessee amended the voter ID requirement to require voters to present state or federal government-issued, photo ID, which was effective on January 1, 2012. In Tennessee, a voter who is indigent and unable to obtain proof of identification without payment of a fee or a voter who has a religious objection to being photographed may execute an affidavit of identity and may then be permitted to vote. More information about Kansas and Tennessee voter ID laws for all eligible voters to cast a ballot at the polls on Election Day and how those laws have changed since HAVA was enacted can be found in GAO-13-90R.

[71] We considered a change in the margin of victory of less than 10 percentage points to be a non-substantial change in the margin of victory for a presidential race. The margin of victory for the presidential general election changed by 7 percentage points in Kansas and 5 percentage points in Tennessee from 2008 to 2012. In addition, we considered an election noncompetitive if the margin of victory was greater than 20 percent.

[72] To calculate voter turnout in the 2008 and 2012 general elections, we divided the number of individuals who voted by the population of registered or eligible voters. Specifically, for our analysis of the enhanced state voter databases, we calculated turnout by dividing the number of individuals officially recorded as having voted by the number of voters listed as registered within state voter registration databases. For our analysis of the CPS, we divided the number of individuals who self-reported to have voted in the survey by the number of self-reported registered voters within each state. For the USEP data source, we divided the number of individuals officially reported to have voted by the voting-eligible population. The voting-eligible population is the voting age population adjusted for segments of the population that are not eligible to vote, such as non-citizens or ineligible felons.

[73] In its letter commenting on excerpts from our draft report, Kansas' Secretary of State's Office stated that photo ID laws are intended to reduce or eliminate fraudulent voting and that if lower overall turnout occurs after implementation of a photo ID law, some of the decrease may be attributable to the prevention of fraudulent votes.

[74] When selecting comparison states, Alabama and Arkansas were most comparable to Kansas and Tennessee, because of geographic proximity to Kansas and Tennessee and similarity in historical turnout patterns. See app. V for a more detailed explanation of our analysis of historical turnout patterns.

[75] The CPS estimates using Alabama or Arkansas as comparison states, respectively, are not distinguishable from zero at $\alpha = 0.05$. However, these results are consistent with those that we obtained from samples that pool data from a large number of registrants in multiple comparison states (see app. VI, tables 16, 20, and 21). The latter estimates are distinguishable from zero at conventional levels of significance.

[76] We found different effects among Hispanic registrants, as compared to White registrants, in alternative versions of our analysis that used various combinations of the comparison states (see app. VI, table 17). Unlike the effects among African-American registrants, these effects were not consistently higher or lower or statistically distinguishable from zero.

[77] In its letter commenting on excerpts from our draft report, Tennessee's Secretary of State's Office noted that most newly registered voters were sent a voter guide that explained the voter ID law and that voters registered for longer periods of time may not be as familiar with ID requirements.

[78] Election officials in both Kansas and Tennessee launched voter education campaigns prior to the 2012 election to inform voters of the new ID requirements.

[79] One study we reviewed examined the possibility of education campaign effects when analyzing the effect of ID laws, but did not produce conclusive findings (Dropp, 2013).

[80] Guido W. Imbens and Jeffrey W. Wooldridge, "Recent Developments in the Econometrics of Program Evaluation," *Journal of Economic Literature*, vol. 47, no. 1, 6-7.9.

[81] W. G. Cochran, 1965, "The Planning of Observational Studies of Human Populations," *Journal of the Royal Statistical Society, Series A*, 128 (2): 234-266.

[82] HAVA requires states to provide a provisional ballot process for voters in certain circumstances, including for first-time voters who register by mail but have not provided acceptable identification as required by HAVA, among other situations.

[83] Tennessee has two types of provisional ballots, according to officials in its Secretary of State's office. A voter who fails to provide required ID at the polling place receives an orange ballot, and a voter whose eligibility is uncertain for any other reason receives a green ballot, such as when the voter's name does not appear on the registration list at the polling place. Tennessee Secretary of State officials stated that orange provisional ballots are not to be issued to voters who lack HAVA-required identification (for example, a first- time voter who registered by mail who did not provide ID when registering). According to officials from the Tennessee Secretary of State's office, a green provisional ballot is to be issued in Tennessee for issues related to HAVA-required identification.

[84] "ID reasons" refers to ID requirements that apply to all eligible voters, not HAVA ID requirements.

[85] Other states differ in how officials determine whether a provisional ballot cast for ID reasons will be counted. For example, in Florida, those ballots will be counted if the voter's signature on the provisional ballot matches the signature in the registration record and the voter has voted in the proper precinct.

[86] The EAVS is an instrument used to collect state-by-state data on the administration of federal elections. According to EAC's survey methodology, states vary in their approaches to and completeness of their election data collection and their responses to the EAVS. Most states relied, at least to some degree, upon centralized voter-registration and voter history databases, which allow state election officials to respond to each survey question with information from the local level. Other states collected relatively few election data at the state level and instead relied on cooperation from local jurisdiction election offices to complete the survey. Some states were not able to provide data in all the categories requested in the survey and some did not provide data for all of their local jurisdictions. Kansas and Tennessee reported data to EAVS for all local jurisdictions for the 2012 general election.

[87] Alabama did not provide data on the total number of provisional ballots cast for 7.46 percent of jurisdictions in 2008 and 22.39 percent of jurisdictions in 2012. Arkansas did not provide data on the total number of provisional ballots cast for 10.67 percent of jurisdictions in 2008 and 2.67 percent of jurisdictions in 2012. Maine did not provide data on the total number of provisional ballots cast for 28.86 percent of jurisdictions in 2008 and 0.20 percent of jurisdictions in 2012.

[88] Alternatively, registrants could have chosen not to attempt to vote at all. A final possibility is that registrants attempted to vote, could not provide adequate ID, and chose not to cast a provisional ballot.

[89] For example, in its letter commenting on excerpts from the draft report, Tennessee's Secretary of State's Office stated that in June 2011 Tennessee's provisional statute was amended to allow any voter whose eligibility was challenged by an election official to cast a provisional ballot. With this amendment, according to the letter, Tennessee extensively trained its election officials regarding the usage of the provisional ballot throughout 2012 as well as the new photo ID requirements. Tennessee identified these as factors that contributed to increased usage of provisional ballots.

[90] For the purposes of this report, we have defined "in-person voter fraud" as involving a person who (1) attempts to vote or votes; (2) in person at the polling place; and (3) asserts an identity that is not the person's own, whether it be that of a fictional registered voter, dead registered voter, a false identity, or whether the voter uses a fraudulent identification. In-person voter fraud is also often referred to as "voter impersonation fraud."

[91] Like other crimes, instances of in-person voter fraud may occur that are never identified by or reported to officials. This is due, in part, to challenges associated with identifying this type of fraud, as both successful fraud and deterred fraud may go undetected. In addition, it has been suggested that without a personal identification requirement it is difficult to detect in-person voter fraud. *See, e.g., Crawford v. Marion Cnty. Election. Bd.,* 472 F.3d 949, 953 (7th Cir. 2007); *In re Request for Advisory Opinion Regarding Constitutionality of 2005 PA 71*, 740 N.W.2d 444, 457-58 (Mich. 2007). However, others have suggested that in-person voter fraud in particular may be more easily detectible. *See, e.g., Crawford v. Marion Cnty. Election Bd.*, 553 U.S. 181, 227 (2008) (Souter, J., dissenting) (stating that "there is reason to think that impersonation of voters is the most likely type of fraud to be discovered") (internal citations omitted).

[92] GAO, *Medicare: Progress Made to Deter Fraud, but More Could Be Done*, GAO-12-801T (Washington, D.C.: June 8, 2012).

[93] GAO-12-801T and GAO, *Identity Theft: Total Extent of Refund Fraud Using Stolen Identities is Unknown*, GAO-13-132T (Washington, D.C.: Nov. 29, 2012).

[94] GAO, *Identity Theft: Prevalence and Cost Appear to be Growing*, GAO-02-363 (Washington, D.C.: Mar. 1, 2002).

[95] We conducted a literature review to identify studies that attempted to identify instances of in-person voter fraud among the populations studied and sources used. We reviewed more than 300 studies and determined that five attempted to collect data on in-person voter fraud using a systematic methodology. The remaining studies either did not provide sufficient information about the methodology used for us to evaluate it, or relied on anecdotal examples of fraud as their basis for analysis. One study we reviewed but did not include among the five profiled here attempted to determine the extent to which reports submitted to the Supreme Court in defendants' and amicus briefs in *Crawford v. Marion County Election Board,* 553 U.S. 181, contained supporting evidence for allegations of in- person voter fraud but the description of the study's methodology did not provide sufficient information for us to evaluate the methods used. (Justin Levitt, "Election Deform: The Pursuit of Unwarranted Electoral Regulation," *Election Law Journal,* vol. 11 (1), 2012). For additional detail regarding our methodology, see app. II.

[96] The five studies include John S. Ahlquist, Kenneth R. Mayer, and Simon Jackman, "Alien Abduction and Voter Impersonation in the 2012 U.S. General Election: Evidence from a Survey List Experiment," October 30, 2013, forthcoming. *Election Law Journal*; Ray Christensen and Thomas J. Schultz, "Identifying Election Fraud Using Orphan and Low Propensity Voters," *American Politics Research*, vol. 42 (2), 2014; M.V. Hood III and William Gillespie, "They Just Do Not Vote Like They Used To: A Methodology to Empirically Assess Election Fraud," *Social Science Quarterly,* vol. 93 (1), 2012; Lorraine C. Minnite, *The Myth of Voter Fraud.* Ithaca: Cornell University Press, 2010; and Corbin Carson, "Exhaustive Database of Voter Fraud Cases Turns Up Scant Evidence That It Happens," News21, Aug. 12, 2012, http://votingrights.news21.com/article/election-fraud- explainer/, accessed July 24, 2014.

[97] These studies are: Minnite (2010) and News21 (2012).

[98] These studies are: Ahlquist, Mayer, and Jackman (2012); Christensen and Schultz (2013); and Hood III and Gillespie (2012).

[99] Flynn, Julie. *Investigation of Suspected Dual Voting in November 2008 and 2009 Elections,* a special report prepared for the Maine Secretary of State, January 2012; General Assembly of Maryland, Department of Legislative Reference, *Report of the Task Force to Review the State's Election Law* (Annapolis, MD: Dec. 31, 1995); South Carolina Law Enforcement Division, *Preliminary Inquiry—Alleged Dead Voter Fraud—2010 SC General Election* (Columbia, SC: May 11, 2012); State of Colorado, Secretary of State, *Non-Citizens on Colorado's Voting Roles: Problems and Solutions* (Denver, CO: Aug. 16, 2012); State of Utah, Office of the Legislative Auditor General, *Driver's Licenses Issued to Undocumented Aliens* (Salt Lake City, UT: Feb. 8, 2005).

[100] The report cited multiple instances where election officials allocated the vote of a father or son to their deceased relative of the same name.

[101] *Veasey v. Perry*, No. 13-193 (S.D. Tex. July 7, 2014), ECF No. 390-2.

[102] In its filing, for the purposes of its database review, DOJ defined "in-person voter impersonation" as the use of the name of another person to obtain and vote a ballot while physically present at the polls. For a description of each database and the types of information each contains, see appendix VIII.

[103] Federal jurisdiction over election fraud is established in elections when a federal candidate is on the ballot. In the absence of a federal candidate on the ballot, federal jurisdiction may be obtained where facts exist to support the application of federal criminal laws that potentially apply to both federal and non-federal elections. According to DOJ, these generally include election frauds that involve the necessary participation by public officers, voting by noncitizens, and fraudulently registered voters.

[104] We excluded the District of Columbia from this portion of our analysis because officials told us that election fraud cases are referred directly to the U.S. Attorney's Office for the District of Columbia.

[105] Corbin Carson, "Exhaustive Database of Voter Fraud Cases Turns Up Scant Evidence That It Happens" News21, Aug. 12, 2012, accessed July 24, 2014, http://votingrights.news21.com/article/election-fraud-explainer/.

[106] For a description of each database and the types of information each contains, see appendix VIII. We identified these databases through discussions with agency officials and our review of relevant literature.

[107] For example, 18 U.S.C § 911 sets forth the offense of falsely and willfully representing oneself to be a citizen of the United States, which may encompass conduct and actions beyond in-person voter fraud. Additionally, 42 U.S.C § 1973i(c) involves, among other things, knowingly or willfully giving false information as to name, address, or period of residence in the voting district for the purpose of establishing voter registration eligibility, which is a separate and distinct offense from in-person voter fraud. Agency officials stated that in-person voter fraud could be prosecuted under either of these statutes, depending on the facts and circumstances of the case.

[108] As mentioned above, jurisdiction for in-person voter fraud is shared by federal, state, and local authorities. DOJ officials said that determining the incidence of allegations of voter fraud would require contacting states, because most election administration is carried out at the state level and that states have first level jurisdiction. These officials told us that whether or not the federal agencies learn of an incident of voter fraud generally depends on two factors (1) which official first receives the allegation and (2) whether the state involves the federal government, among other things.

[109] In addition, as previously discussed, five states provided us with investigative studies that focused on specific types of election fraud.

[110] As of June 2014, neither Delaware nor Maine required all eligible voters to present either a government issued ID or a photo ID at the polls prior to voting.

[111] We identified as potential treatment states those that had implemented government issued photo ID requirements between the 2008 and 2012 general elections that also generally required voters to follow up with elections officials with acceptable ID in order to have their votes counted if they attempt to vote without acceptable ID.

[112] For example, we reviewed for all potential treatment states laws related to early voting and no-excuse absentee voting because the enactment of such laws may have a significant impact on voter turnout. Tennessee law, which provides for an early voting period, was amended in 2011 to shorten the early voting period by ending early voting 7 days, as opposed to 5 days, prior to the election for a presidential preference primary. Because this change only related to the presidential preference primary, we concluded it was not likely to substantially affect voter turnout for the 2008 or 2012 general elections. In addition to laws related to early and no-excuse absentee voting, we reviewed enacted election-related legislation for each treatment state for changes related to Election Day registration, felon disenfranchisement, and third-party registration, as well as for other legal changes that could significantly affect voter turnout, such as those related to voter mobilization or education efforts.

[113] For example, under Arkansas law, a designated bearer—a person identified and authorized by the applicant to obtain from the county clerk or to deliver to the county clerk the applicant's ballot—may obtain absentee ballots for not more than 2 voters; we identified amendments to this law in 2011 that required the county clerk to notify the prosecuting attorney if the county clerk knows or reasonably suspects that a designated bearer has more than 2 absentee ballots in his or her possession, and provided that the county clerk cannot accept any absentee ballots from a designated bearer who does not sign the voter register under oath (the requirement for a signature under oath by the designated bearer did not change). We determined that these changes were unlikely to substantially affect voter turnout because they enacted additional procedures for county clerks and did not impose any new requirements for voters or designated bearers.

[114] Stephen Ansolabehere and Eitan Hersh, 2012, "Validation: What Big Data Reveal About Survey Misreporting and the Real Electorate," Political Analysis 20: 437-459. Stephen Ansolabehere, Eitan Hersh, and Kenneth Shepsle, 2012, "Movers, Stayers, and Voter Registration," Quarterly Journal of Political Science 7 (4): 333-363.

[115] *Texas v. Holder*, No. 12-128 (D.D.C. June 30, 2012).

[116] Absentee voting is a process that allows citizens to cast a vote when they are unable to vote at their precinct on Election Day and is generally conducted by mail. Early voting is any process by which a voter may cast a ballot in person, without providing an excuse, prior to Election Day, regardless of the name the state gives to that process. A state may provide for both in-person absentee voting and early voting. For example, in Alaska, which provides both, according to the Secretary of State's website, the difference between in- person absentee and early voting is that an early voter is already determined to be eligible to vote at the time of voting, and thus the voter's ballot is placed directly in the ballot box to be counted and tabulated along with those of other eligible voters on Election Day. With in-person absentee voting, the voter's eligibility is not verified at the time of voting, and thus the voter's ballot is placed inside an absentee voting envelope—pending subsequent verification—prior to being placed in the ballot box.

[117] Examples of excuses a voter may provide for not voting on Election Day include being sick, having a disability, being out of the country, or having religious commitments.

[118] This is defined as the length of time the voter has lived in the community in which he or she voted.

[119] Federal law does not generally address third-party voter registration organizations.

[120] This is defined as the length of time the voter has lived in the community in which he or she voted.

[121] While our data distinguish respondents who registered at a government office/DMV/public assistance agency/polling place from those who registered at another site, we cannot verify that respondents who reported having registered at (for example) schools or through a registration drive were actually registered by third parties or the nature of any third party involved.

[122] We excluded three additional studies because, after review, we determined there was either insufficient information provided about a study's methodology or implementation or the study was outside the scope of our work. Those studies were: Barreto, Nuño, and Sanchez (2007), McDonald (2006), and Sanchez (2011).

[123] States requiring government-issued ID include those where there is an exception for a school ID.

[124] Some states allow voters to provide a utility bill, a bank statement, or a paycheck, among others, as voter identification. It would be difficult to measure the cost to obtain these nonphoto and nongovernment IDs and the specifics of the cost would vary greatly based on the voter.

[125] The states in scope are Alabama, Arkansas, Florida, Georgia, Indiana, Kansas, Mississippi, North Carolina, North Dakota, Oklahoma, Pennsylvania, Rhode Island, South Carolina, Tennessee, Texas, Virginia, and Wisconsin. These 17 states include those in which ID requirements are not currently in effect because, for example, the law is legislated to go into effect at a later date or the law has been enjoined pursuant to litigation. *See, e.g., Applewhite v. Commonwealth*, 2014 WL 184988 (Pa. Commw. Ct. Jan. 17, 2014); *Frank v. Walker*, 2014 WL 1775432 (E.D. Wis. Apr. 29, 2104). As of June 2014, litigation was pending in Arkansas, North Carolina, Oklahoma, Texas and Wisconsin.

[126] Alabama, Arkansas, Kansas, North Dakota, Rhode Island, South Carolina, and Wisconsin require a test or exam fee when applying for a driver's license. Kansas also charges a "photo fee" when applying for a driver's license or state ID. Oklahoma charges an application fee in addition to a license fee when applying to obtain a driver's license and Tennessee charges an application fee when applying for either a driver's license or a state ID card.

[127] We reviewed six additional studies related to the effects of state voter ID requirements on voter turnout, but excluded them from our report due to limitations in the studies' scope or methods for estimating effects. Those studies were: Ansolabehere (2009), Bullock III and Hood III (2008), Cobb et. al. (2012), Gomez (2008), Lott (2006), and Pitts (2013).

[128] Social science research standards are discussed in the scientific literature. For example, see Thomas D. Cook, and Donald T. Campbell, *Quasi-experimentation: Design and Analysis Issues for Field Settings* (Boston: Houghton Mifflin, 1990); William R. Shadish, Thomas D. Cook, and Donald T. Campbell, *Experimental and Quasi-Experimental Designs for Generalized Causal Inference* (Boston: Houghton Mifflin, 2002); and GAO, *Designing Evaluations: 2012 Revision*, GAO-12-208G (Washington, D.C.: January 2012).

[129] EAC administers the biennial EAVS, an instrument used to collect state-by-state data on the administration of federal elections. The survey is divided into two parts. The first part captures quantitative data pertaining to the National Voter Registration Act (NVRA), the Uniformed and Overseas Citizens Absentee Voting Act (UOCAVA), and other election administration issues such as the counting of provisional ballots and poll worker recruitment. The second part is the Statutory Overview, which asks state officials to respond to a series of open-ended questions about their states' election laws, definitions, and procedures. According to EAC's survey documentation for the 2012 EAVS, states varied in their approaches to data collection, the completeness of their election data, and their response rate to questions on the EAVS. Most states relied, at least to some degree, upon centralized voter-registration databases and voter history databases, which allowed state election officials to respond to each survey question with information from the local level. Other states collected relatively little election data at the state level and instead relied on cooperation from local jurisdiction election offices to complete the survey. In 2012, some states were not able to provide data in all the categories requested in the survey and some did not have data for all of their local jurisdictions. We confirmed data from the EAVS on the total number of provisional ballots cast in Kansas and Tennessee for the 2012 general election with Kansas and Tennessee election officials.

[130] During the course of our review, in July 2014, DOJ developed a definition of "in-person voter impersonation" for purposes of litigation.

[131] Courts have used the terms "voter impersonation fraud," "in-person voter fraud," or "in- person voter impersonation fraud" to describe the same conduct. While the terms appear somewhat distinct, they are generally used interchangeably.

[132] These cases were identified in May 2013 in order to inform the design and conduct of our work.

[133] "Organizational studies" refers to those studies published by nongovernmental organizations, such as the Heritage Foundation and the Brennan Center for Justice. Studies produced by state-level agencies are not included in the literature review, but are discussed below.

[134] We excluded studies that reported on previously compiled data or anecdotal reports of in-person voter fraud, including those reported in the media.

[135] Investigations on which DOJ staff have worked for 30 minutes or more are referred to as matters.

[136] Officials with whom we met stated that certain statutes are more likely to be used with respect to the prosecution of in-person voter fraud, but that it is possible that any of these provisions could be used, depending on the facts and circumstances of the case. We relied on agency officials' identification of statutes under which this conduct could be prosecuted.

[137] We also contacted election officials from the 4 remaining states, but they declined to be interviewed.

[138] This is defined as the length of time the respondent has lived at his or her current address.

[139] We also reviewed the working paper that led to this published study: Alvarez, R. Michael; Delia Bailey and Jonathan N. Katz. *The Effect of Voter Identification Laws on Turnout, Social Science Working Paper 1267R.* California Institute of Technology: Pasadena, California (2008).

[140] See GAO-12-208G.

[141] GAO, *Campaign Finance Reform: Experiences of Two States That Offered Full Public Funding for Political Candidates,* GAO-10-390 (Washington, D.C.: May 28, 2010) used a similar approach to estimate the effect of campaign finance laws in Arizona and Maine on the competitiveness of elections. Previous studies of voter ID laws using a quasi- experimental design include Alvarez (2008), Dropp (2013), and Milyo (2007). Keele and Minozzi (2013) identified quasi-experiments as one of several methods of causal inference for election administration practices.

[142] Wolfinger, and Rosenstone. *Who Votes?;* Rosenstone, and Hansen. *Mobilization, Participation, and Democracy in America.*

[143] William R. Shadish, Thomas D. Cook, and Donald T. Campbell, *Experimental and Quasi- Experimental Designs for Generalized Causal Inference* (Boston: Houghton Mifflin Company, 2002), 159.

[144] GAO-13-90R. Substantive changes were identified as of the time the Help America Vote Act (HAVA) was enacted.

[145] Ohio and Utah were excluded based on this criterion because these states generally counted provisional ballots if the voter's identify could be verified through other means and only required voters in certain circumstances to return with acceptable ID. As part of the identification requirements states have established for voting at the polls on Election Day, states have also adopted processes for voters who do not provide the requisite documentation at the polls to vote and have their ballots counted. There is variety in these processes, with some states allowing voters to resolve the deficiency on Election Day, for example by signing an affidavit attesting to their identity and providing identifying information such as their address and date of birth, while others require the voter to return to a local election office with acceptable documentation within a specified number of days after the election. Under the Help America Vote Act (HAVA), states are required to permit individuals, under certain circumstances, to cast a provisional ballot in federal elections. For example, if a voter does not have the requisite identification at the polls, HAVA requires that the voter be allowed to cast a provisional ballot. Under HAVA, election officials receiving provisional voter information are to determine whether such individuals are eligible to vote under state law. If an individual is determined to be eligible, HAVA specifies that such individual's provisional ballot be counted as a vote in that election in accordance with state law.

[146] We ruled out Alabama, Arizona, and Virginia as potential treatment states for analysis, even though they generally require voters to follow up with the relevant election authority to provide acceptable identification within a specified time period after the election in order for the provisional ballots to be counted. Although the ID laws in those states generally require additional action on the part of voters to have their ballots counted, these states allow a larger number of types of ID to be used, including nongovernment issued nonphoto IDs. In contrast, Georgia, Indiana, Kansas, and Tennessee allowed fewer types of ID and also generally required voters without ID to follow-up with election officials and provide acceptable identification in order for their ballots to be counted.

[147] Alvarez, Bailey, and Katz, (2010). These researchers defined the spectrum of voter ID requirements as ranging from voters stating their name to photo ID requirements.

[148] Margins of victory for the presidential races in Indiana were calculated based on official vote total records published for the 2008 and 2012 general elections by the Clerk of the U.S. House of Representatives.

[149] Donald P. Green, and Alan S. Gerber. *Get Out the Vote! How to Increase Voter Turnout.* Washington, DC: Brookings Institution Press, 2004.

[150] The margin of victory for the presidential race in Kansas changed from 15 percent in 2008 to 22 percent in 2012; in Tennessee it changed from 15 percent in 2008 to 20 percent in 2012.

[151] One ballot question appeared on the ballot in Kansas's 2012 general election and no ballot questions were present on the ballot for the 2008 general election. The ballot question in 2012 sought to provide the Kansas legislature constitutional authority to adjust watercraft property tax rates. In addition to the factors we considered, local ballot questions may affect turnout in particular jurisdictions or precincts; we did not consider the extent of local ballot questions in our analysis.

[152] In addition, the quality of state voter registration data was also an important consideration when confirming Kansas and Tennessee as treatment states, as our estimates of turnout percentages require accurate state records of registered voters at the time of the 2008 and 2012 general elections. The vendor that provided enhanced state registration records which we used for our analysis also provided documentation of data quality for voter registration and history records across states. We used this information to ensure that such data for Kansas and Tennessee were sufficiently reliable for our analysis.

[153] Washington and Oregon were not included among potential comparators because both states use vote-by-mail election systems. Pennsylvania and South Carolina were not included among our universes of potential treatment or comparison states. Both states enacted substantive changes to their ID requirements between 2002 and October 1, 2012 but the requirements in both states were subject to litigation and not fully implemented as of the 2012 general election. Pennsylvania and South Carolina were also not included in our universe of comparison states because the laws that were in effect in those states fell outside the criterion for the types of laws we allowed for potential comparison states—no ID requirement or one that allowed nonphoto, nongovernment IDs. Pennsylvania required a photo ID (voters were allowed to cast a regular ballot if they did

not present ID) and South Carolina required a government issued ID. Louisiana was not included among our potential treatment states because the state's ID requirements were generally consistent since HAVA was enacted, and it was not included among our potential comparison states because it required photo ID.

[154] Geographic proximity to Kansas and Tennessee allows for potential similarities in political culture, weather patterns, and media campaigns, all of which can affect turnout. We measured historical turnout similarity by calculating the Euclidean distance between turnout in Kansas and Tennessee, respectively, and each of the remaining states. We used turnout data for the eight presidential general elections from 1980 through 2008, defined as a state's ratio of votes cast for President to its voting-eligible population, as compiled by the United States Elections Project at George Mason University.

[155] The vendor that provided enhanced state registration records which we used for our analysis also provided documentation of data quality for voter registration and history records across states. We used this information to inform our selection of comparison states.

[156] State border regions may experience similar factors that can affect turnout, such as campaign media markets that overlap in border areas and weather patterns similar in portions of the states on Election Day. Brad T. Gomez, Thomas G. Hansford and George A. Krause, 2007, "The Republicans Should Pray for Rain: Weather, Turnout, and Voting in U.S. Presidential Elections." *The Journal of Politics* 69 (3): 649-663. Paul Freedman, Michael Franz, and Kenneth Goldstein, 2004, "Campaign Advertising and Democratic Citizenship." *American Journal of Political Science* 48 (4): 723-741.

[157] When evaluating the robustness of our results, we removed Maine from the comparison group in some of the analyses because of an imbalance in the competitiveness of elections between the 2008 and 2012 general elections in that state.

[158] Donald B. Rubin, 1974, "Estimating Causal Effects of Treatments in Randomized and Nonrandomized Studies," *Journal of Educational Psychology* 66 (5): 688-701.

[159] Joshua D. Angrist and Jorn-Steffen Pischke, *Mostly Harmless Econometrics* (Princeton, NJ: Princeton University Press, 2009), 56-57, 71. Jeffrey M. Wooldridge, *Econometric Analysis of Panel and Cross-Section Data*, Cambridge, MA: MIT Press, 2003, 609. Michael Lechner, "The Estimation of Causal Effects by Difference-in-Difference Methods." *Foundations and Trends in Econometrics* 4 (2010): 183. G.W. Imbens and Jeffrey M. Wooldridge, "Recent Development in the Econometrics of Program Evaluation. *Journal of Economic Literature 47* (2009)*:* 27.

[160] For discussions of these assumptions, see Michael Lechner, "The Estimation of Causal Effects by Difference-in-Difference Methods." *Foundations and Trends in Econometrics* 4 (2010): 174-203.

[161] Luke Keele and William Minozzi, "How Much is Minnesota Like Wisconsin? Assumptions and Counterfactuals in Causal Inference with Observational Data." *Political Analysis* (2013): 1-24. Michael J. Hanmer, *Discount Voting: Voting Registration Reforms and Their Effects*. New York: Cambridge University Press, 2009.

[162] Raymond E. Wolfinger, and Steven J. Rosenstone. *Who Votes?* New Haven, CT: Yale University Press, 1980. Steven J. Rosenstone and John Mark Hansen. *Mobilization, Participation, and Democracy in America*. New York, NY: MacMillan Publishing, 1993.

[163] Exact matching methods produce two groups of units for analysis with identical values of covariates. In contrast, other matching methods produce two groups that have approximately the same distributions of the covariates.

[164] Gary W. Cox and Michael C. Munger. 1989. "Closeness, Expenditures, and Turnout in the 1982 U.S. House Elections." *American Political Science Review* 83 (1): 217–31. Michael P. McDonald and Caroline J. Tolbert, 2012, "Perceptions vs. Actual Exposure to Electoral Competition and Effects on Political Participation." *Public Opinion Quarterly* 76 (3): 538-554.

[165] Mark A. Smith, 2001, "The Contingent Effects of Ballot Initiatives and Candidate Races on Turnout." *American Journal of Political Science* 45 (3): 700-706.

[166] Paul Gronke, et al., 2008, "Convenience Voting," *Annual Review Of Political Science* 11:437-455. Raymond E Wolfinger, Benjamin Highton, and Megan Mullin, 2005, "How Postregistration Laws Affect the Turnout of Citizens Registered to Vote." *State Politics and Policy Quarterly* 5 (1): 1-23. Barry C. Burden, et al., 2012, "Election Laws, Mobilization, and Turnout: the Unanticipated Consequences of Election Reform," *American Journal of Political Science* 58 (1): 95-109.

[167] Brad T. Gomez, Thomas G. Hansford and George A. Krause, 2007, "The Republicans Should Pray for Rain: Weather, Turnout, and Voting in U.S. Presidential Elections." *The Journal of Politics* 69 (3): 649-663. Paul Freedman, Michael Franz, and Kenneth Goldstein, 2004, "Campaign Advertising and Democratic Citizenship." *American Journal of Political Science* 48 (4): 723-741.

[168] Caroline J. Tolbert, John A. Grummel, and Daniel A. Smith, 2001, "The Effects of Ballot Initiatives on Voter Turnout in the American States." *American Politics Research* 29 (6):625-648. Matthew Childers and Mike Binder, 2012, "Engaged by the Initiative? How the Use of Citizen Initiatives Increases Voter Turnout." *Political Research Quarterly* 65 (1): 93-103.

[169] At least two other mechanisms might produce spillover. First, registrants in the comparison states who had misinformation could have chosen not to vote, regardless of whether the policy legally affected them. Second, more registrants in comparison states could choose to vote if ID policies improved their confidence in the

integrity of elections. Our use of Delaware and Maine as comparison states mitigates these risks, as well, due to the lack of shared regional sources of information.

170 William G. Cochran and Donald B. Rubin, 1973, "Controlling Bias in Observational Studies: a Review," *Sankhya: The Indian Journal of Statistics, Series A* 35 (4): 417-466. Daniel E. Ho, et al., 2007, "Matching as Nonparametric Preprocessing for Reducing Model Dependence in Parametric Causal Inference," *Political Analysis* 15: 199-206.

171 Joshua D. Angrist and Jorn-Steffen Pischke, *Mostly Harmless Econometrics* (Princeton, NJ: Princeton University Press, 2009), 56-57, 71. Jeffrey M. Wooldridge, *Econometric Analysis of Panel and Cross-Section Data*, Cambridge, MA: MIT Press, 2003, 609. Michael Lechner, "The Estimation of Causal Effects by Difference-in-Difference Methods." *Foundations and Trends in Econometrics* 4 (2010): 183. G.W. Imbens and Jeffrey M. Wooldridge, "Recent Development in the Econometrics of Program Evaluation. *Journal of Economic Literature 47* (2009)*:* 26-27.

172 We implicitly assume that *Yit* is the result of a partially random process, such that $Yit \mid Dit, Tt, Xit = \beta 0 + \beta 1 Dit + \beta 2 Tt + \delta\, Dit * Tt + Xit\, \alpha + \varepsilon it$.

173 William G. Cochran, *Sampling Techniques*, John Wiley and Sons: New York, 1977.

174 For an alternative view on the precision of DID estimates, incorporating uncertainty with respect to the choice of comparison groups, see Alberto Abadie, Alexis Diamond, and Jens Hainmueller, 2010, "Synthetic Control Methods for Comparative Case Studies: Estimating the Effect of California's Tobacco Control Program." *Journal of the American Statistical Association* 105 (490): 493-505.

175 Marianne Bertrand, Ester Duflo, and Sendhil Mullainathan, 2004, "How Much Should We Trust Difference-in-Difference Estimates?" *The Quarterly Journal of Economics* 119 (1):249-275. Stephen G. Donald and Kevin Lang, 2007, "Inference with Difference-in- Differences and Other Panel Data." *The Review of Economics and Statistics* 89 (2): 221-233. Robert S. Erikson and Lorraine C. Minnite, 2009, "Modeling Problems in the Voter Identification-Voter Turnout Debate." *Election Law Journal* 8 (2): 85-101.

176 Marianne Bertrand, Ester Duflo, and Sendhil Mullainathan, 2004, "How Much Should We Trust Difference-in-Difference Estimates?" *The Quarterly Journal of Economics* 119 (1):261-262.

177 Jeffrey M. Wooldridge, 2003, "Cluster-Sample Methods in Applied Econometrics," *The American Economic Review* 93 (2): 134. Marianne Bertrand, Ester Duflo, and Sendhil Mullainathan, 2004, "How Much Should We Trust Difference-in-Difference Estimates?" *The Quarterly Journal of Economics* 119 (1): 261-262.

178 Manuel Arellano, 1987, "Computing Robust Standard Errors for Within-Groups Estimators," *Oxford Bulletin of Economics and Statistics* 49 (4): 431-434.

179 Marianne Bertrand, Ester Duflo, and Sendhil Mullainathan, 2004, "How Much Should We Trust Difference-in-Difference Estimates?" *The Quarterly Journal of Economics* 119 (1):265, 270-271.

180 Jeffrey M. Wooldridge, *Econometric Analysis of Cross-Section and Panel Data*, Cambridge, MA: MIT Press, 2002, 454-457.

181 Michael Lechner, "The Estimation of Causal Effects by Difference-in-Difference Methods." *Foundations and Trends in Econometrics* 4 (2010): 196-200.

182 The specific estimates replicated were rows 20 and 21 of table 20.

183 This range excludes results for some comparison groups that included Maine.

184 We obtained these data from the project's website (elections.gmu.edu/voter_turnout.htm) on May 30, 2013.

185 Stephen Ansolabehere and Eitan Hersh, 2012, "Validation: What Big Data Reveal About Survey Misreporting and the Real Electorate." *Political Analysis* 20: 437-459.

186 We considered other commercial vendors of voter file data, but selected Catalist due to the company's archiving of voter files over time, the use of their data in peer-reviewed publications, and validation of their estimated racial data by Catalist and third parties.

187 Stephen Ansolabehere and Eitan Hersh, "Validation: What Big Data Reveal About Survey Misreporting and the Real Electorate," *Political Analysis* 20 (2012): 453-454.

188 *Texas v. Holder*, No. 12-128 (D.D.C. June 30, 2012).

189 Stephen Ansolabehere and Eitan Hersh, 2012, "Validation: What Big Data Reveal About Survey Misreporting and the Real Electorate," *Political Analysis* 20: 437-459. Stephen Ansolabehere, Eitan Hersh, and Kenneth Shepsle, 2012, "Movers, Stayers, and Voter Registration," *Quarterly Journal of Political Science* 7 (4): 333-363.

190 Also see Jeffrey M. Wooldridge, *Econometric Analysis of Cross-Section and Panel Data*, Cambridge, MA: MIT Press, 2002, 609. Michael Lechner, "The Estimation of Causal Effects by Difference-in-Difference Methods." *Foundations and Trends in Econometrics* 4 (2010): 183. G. W. Imbens and Jeffrey M. Wooldridge, "Recent Development in Econometrics for Program Evaluation. *Journal of Economic Literature 47* (2009)*:* 26-27.

191 Joshua D. Angrist and Jorn-Steffen Pischke, *Mostly Harmless Econometrics* (Princeton, NJ: Princeton University Press, 2009), 70-71.

192 Some states require registered voters to identify their race when registering to vote. For those states, the vendor reports what registered voters indicate as their race. For states that do not require self-reporting of race, the vendor classifies each voter's race based on other characteristics kept in official voter records and U.S. Census information. We recoded the racial category names used by the vendor (Asian, Black, Caucasian, Hispanic)

into the following category names (Asian-American, African-American, White, and Hispanic). The vendor provided us with voter ages as of 2014. For the purposes of our analysis, we adjusted the ages of these voters to be measured as of the 2008 general election.

[193] These differences are distinguishable from zero at $\alpha = 0.05$.

[194] As discussed above, the terms of our subscription constrained our ability to analyze the complete commercial voter registration and history files at the registrant level.

[195] Roderick J. A. Little and Donald B. Rubin, *Statistical Analysis with Missing Data*, 2nd ed. (New York: John Wiley and Sons, 2002).

[196] Stephen Ansolabehere and Eitan Hersh, "Validation: What Big Data Reveal about Survey Misreporting and the Real Electorate." *Political Analysis* 20: 437-459.

[197] Roderick D. Little and Donald B. Rubin, *Statistical Analysis with Missing Data*, 2nd ed. (Hoboken, New Jersey: John Wiley and Sons, 2002), 41-43.

In: Voter Identification Laws: Issues and Analyses
Editor: Alanna Summerfield
ISBN: 978-1-63463-546-2

Chapter 2

BEST PRACTICES TO IMPROVE VOTER IDENTIFICATION REQUIREMENTS*

The Eagleton Institute of Politics (at Rutgers), The State University of New Jersey, and The Moritz College of Law (at The Ohio State University)

THE RESEARCH TEAM

This research report on Voter Identification Requirements in the 2004 election is part of a broader analysis that also includes a study of Provisional Voting, which has already been submitted to the EAC. Conducting the work was a consortium of The Eagleton Institute of Politics of Rutgers, The State University of New Jersey, and The Moritz College of Law of The Ohio State University.

The Eagleton Institute explores state and national politics through research, education, and public service, linking the study of politics with its day-to-day practice. It focuses attention on how contemporary political systems work, how they change, and how they might work better. Eagleton regularly undertakes projects to enhance political understanding and involvement, often in collaboration with government agencies, the media, non-profit groups, and other academic institutions.

The Moritz College of Law has served the citizens of Ohio and the nation since its establishment in 1891. It has played a leading role in the legal profession through countless contributions made by graduates and faculty. Its contributions to election law have become well known through its Election Law @ Moritz website. *Election Law @ Moritz* illuminates public understanding of election law and its role in our nation's democracy.

* This is an edited, reformatted and augmented version of a contracted report for the U.S. Election Assistance Commission, dated June 28, 2006.

Project Management Team

Dr. Ruth B. Mandel
Director.
Eagleton Institute of Politics
Board of Governors Professor of Politics Principal Investigator
Chair of the Project Management Team

Edward B. Foley
Robert M. Duncan/Jones Day Designated
Professor of Law
The Moritz College of Law
Director of Election Law @ Moritz

Ingrid Reed
Director of the New Jersey Project Eagleton Institute of Politics

Daniel P. Tokaji
Assistant Professor of Law
The Moritz College of Law

John Weingart Associate Director
Eagleton Institute of Politics

Thomas M. O'Neill
Consultant,
Eagleton Institute of Politics Project Director

Dave Andersen Graduate Assistant,
Eagleton Institute of Politics

John Harris
Graduate Assistant
Eagleton Institute of Politics

Donald Linky
Senior Policy Fellow
Eagleton Institute of Politics

Sara A. Sampson Reference Librarian,
Moritz College of Law

Tim Vercellotti
Assistant Research Professor
Assistant Director,
Center for Public Interest

Polling
Eagleton Institute of Politics

Laura Williams
The Moritz College of Law

PEER REVIEW GROUP

A draft of this report and the statistical analysis in its appendix were critiqued by a Peer Review Group. The comments of its members improved the quality of our work. While the Group as a whole and the comments of its members individually contributed generously to the research effort, any errors of fact or weaknesses in inference are the responsibility of the Eagleton-Moritz research team. The members of the Peer Review Group do not necessarily share the views reflected in our recommendations.

R. Michael Alvarez
Professor of Political Science California Institute of Technology

John C. Harrison
Massee Professor of Law
University of Virginia School of Law

Martha E. Kropf
Assistant Professor Political Science University of Missouri-Kansas City

Daniel H. Lowenstein
Professor of Law, School of Law University of California at Los Angeles

Timothy G. O'Rourke
Dean, Fulton School of Liberal Arts Salisbury University

Bradley Smith Professor of Law
Capital University Law School

Tim Storey
Program Principal
National Conference of State Legislatures

Peter G. Verniero
former Attorney General, State of New Jersey Counsel, Sills,
Cummis, Epstein and Gross, PC

REPORT AND RECOMMENDATIONS TO THE EAC VOTER IDENTIFICATION ISSUES

Report Background

The Help America Vote Act of 2002 (HAVA) (Public Law 107-252) authorizes the United States Election Assistance Commission (EAC) (Sec. 241, 42 USC 15381) to conduct periodic studies of election administration issues. The purpose of these studies is to promote methods for voting and administering elections, including provisional voting, that are convenient, accessible and easy to use; that yield accurate, secure and expeditious voting systems; that afford each registered and eligible voter an equal opportunity to vote and to have that vote counted; and that are efficient.

This study provides information on voter identification practices in the 2004 election. It makes recommendations for best practices to evaluate future proposals for voter ID requirements, including the systematic collection and evaluation of information from the states. The research was conducted by the Eagleton Institute of Politics at Rutgers, the State University of New Jersey, and the Moritz College of Law at the Ohio State University under a contract with the EAC, dated May 24, 2005. The work included a review and legal analysis of state statutes, regulations and litigation concerning voter identification and provisional voting as well as a statistical analysis of the relationship of various requirements for voter identification to turnout in the 2004 election. This report is a companion to a report on Provisional Voting submitted to the EAC on November 28, 2005 under the same contract.

EXECUTIVE SUMMARY AND RECOMMENDATIONS

Background and Methods

This report arrives at a time of considerable ferment over the issue of voter identification. The debate across the nation over requiring voters to produce a specific identification document before being permitted to cast a regular (as opposed to a provisional) ballot, has revealed supporters and opponents in polarized camps.

- Proponents of stricter identification requirements base their case on improving the security of the ballot by reducing opportunities for one kind of vote fraud --multiple voting or voting by those who are not eligible. The proponents argue that their goal is to ensure that only those legally entitled to vote do so, and do so only once at each election.
- Opponents seek to forestall more stringent identification requirements, such as government-issued photo ID, in order to ensure broad access to a regular ballot. They fear that some voters --such as, they argue, racial and ethnic minorities, the young, and elderly voters-- may lack convenient access to the required ID documents, or that such voters may be fearful of submitting their ID documents to official scrutiny and thus stay away from the polls.

- Both sides argue that their preferred policy will engender faith in the electoral process among citizens.

This report considers policy issues associated with the voter ID debate. It inquires whether empirical study can suggest a way to estimate the effects of different voter ID requirements on turnout. That analysis would constitute an important first step in assessing tradeoffs between ballot security and ballot access. The aim of this research is to contribute to the effort to raise the quality of the debate over this contentious topic. The tradeoffs between ballot security and ballot access are crucial. A voting system that requires voters to produce an identity document or documents may prevent the ineligible from voting. It may also prevent eligible voters from casting a ballot. If the ID requirement of a ballot protection system blocks ineligible voters from the polls at the cost of preventing eligible voters who lack the required forms of identification, the integrity of the ballot may not have been improved; the harm may be as great as the benefit.

As part of the project's effort to analyze the relationship between Voter ID requirements, turnout, and their policy implications, a statistical analysis examined the potential variation in turnout. This statistical study developed a model to illuminate the relationships between voter ID requirements and turnout. This model's findings and limitations suggest avenues for further research and analysis that may assist the EAC and the states as they explore policies to balance the goals of ballot integrity and ballot access.

The statistical analysis describes one possible way to estimate what might be the incremental effect on voters' access to the ballot of an increase in the rigor of voter identification requirements. We do not offer this statistical analysis as the last word, but rather as a preliminary word on the subject. Its findings must be regarded as tentative; the information (such as the specific reasons some potential voters are not allowed to cast a regular ballot) that that might permit greater certainty is simply not available. Indeed, as our recommendations indicate, the next step to improve understanding of the effects of stricter voter identification on turnout and on vote fraud is to collect more information on both topics systematically and regularly.

Making a statistical estimate of the effect of voting regulations on turnout is difficult. The dynamics of turnout are complex, much studied, and only partially understood. Some agreement exists, however, that three factors that exert substantial influence on voter turnout are:[1] the socioeconomic status of the potential voter; legal requirements to vote; and the political context of the election. By focusing on how voters identify themselves at the polls, this report emphasizes legal requirements. The statistical analysis also considers some of the socioeconomic, racial, and age characteristics of the electorate, as well as the political context in 2004 (such as whether a state was a battleground in the presidential race).

Examining tradeoffs between ballot security and ballot access requires some measure of the effectiveness of voter ID requirements in reducing multiple voting or voting by ineligible voters. The existing evidence on the incidence of vote fraud, especially on the kind of vote fraud that could be reduced by requiring more rigorous voter identification, is not sufficient to evaluate those tradeoffs.[2] Assessing the effectiveness of voter ID as a way to protect the integrity of the ballot should logically include an estimate of the nature and frequency of vote fraud. This research does not include consideration of vote fraud, nor does it estimate the possible effectiveness of various voter ID regimes to counter attempts at vote fraud. Our analysis also cannot take into account how many potential voters who did not turn out under comparatively stricter voter ID requirements might have been ineligible or eligible to vote.

Despite these qualifications regarding the quality of the available data and the limitations of statistical analysis, however, the different statistical methods and two different sets of data on turnout in 2004 election used in the study point to the same general finding. Stricter voter identification requirements (for example, requiring voters to present non-photo ID compared to simply stating their names) were correlated with reduced turnout in the models employed, as described in detail in Appendix C. [3] As explained below, these models find that a statistically significant relationship exists, even when controlling for other factors (such as whether the election was in a battleground state) that might affect turnout. (But note that in the model using the aggregate data, photo ID did not have a significant effect on turnout. The reason may have been that in this election, each state with a photo ID requirement provided an alternate way for those without a photo ID to cast a regular ballot.) Without knowing more about the effects of stricter voter ID on reducing multiple voting or voting by ineligible voters, however, the tradeoffs between ballot security and ballot access cannot be assessed.

Methodology

The report includes detailed information on the nature of the statutory requirements across the country in 2004 and on the statutes and court decisions that provide the legal context for the voter ID debate. We gathered information on the requirements in effect in the 50 states and the District of Columbia in that year. Based on our interpretation of state statutes, supplemented in some cases by conversations with state election officials, we divided the states' ID requirements into five categories. We believe each category is more rigorous than the one preceding, based on the demands they make on voters.[4] The categories range from "Stating Name" which we judge to be somewhat less demanding than "Signing Name." "Signature Match" requires poll workers to examine the signature and compare it to a sample, which is slightly more demanding than the voter simply signing. "Present ID" requires voters to offer some documentary evidence of their identity, ranging from a utility bill to a passport. It is more demanding than the previous three categories because it requires that the voter remember to bring this documentation to the polls. (Even a simple ID, such as a utility bill, may not be available to some renters or, say, those in group housing.) We regard a government "Photo ID" as the most rigorous requirement. Such identity documents may not be uniformly and conveniently available to all voters.

For each state, we identified both the "maximum" and "minimum" identification requirements. The term "maximum" refers to the most that voters may be *asked* to do or show at the polling place (putting aside cases in which particular voter's eligibility may be questioned pursuant to a state challenge process). The term "minimum," on the other hand, refers to the most that voters can be *required* to do or show, in order to cast regular ballot (again leaving aside a state challenge process). We have included "maximum" requirements in our analysis, and not simply "minimum" requirements, because simply asking voters to produce particular identifying information may have a deterrent effect, even if voters are ultimately allowed to cast a regular ballot without that identification. For example, in a state where voters are asked to show photo ID at the polling place, but still allowed to vote by completing an affidavit confirming their eligibility, the "maximum" of being asked to show photo ID may deter some voters even though the "minimum" would allow them to vote without photo ID.

It is worth emphasizing that, at the time of the 2004 election, there was *no* state that had a "minimum" requirement of showing photo ID – in other words, there was no state that required voters to show photo ID in order to cast a regular ballot. For this reason, our report does not measure the impact of laws, like those recently enacted in Indiana and Georgia, which require voters to show photo ID in order to cast a regular ballot without an affidavit exception.

To examine the potential variation on turnout rates associated with each type of voter ID requirements in effect on Election Day 2004, the statistical analysis drew on two sets of data. These were, first, aggregate turnout data at the county level for each state and, second, the reports of individual voters collected in the November 2004 Current Population Survey by the U. S. Census Bureau. Using two different data sets makes it possible to check the validity of one analysis against the other. It also provides insights not possible using only one of the data sets. The aggregate analysis cannot provide valid estimates on the effects of different ID requirements on particular demographic groups (e.g., the old, the young, African-Americans, the poor, or high school graduates). The Current Population Survey data does permit that kind of analysis, although it has the disadvantage of relying on self-reports by respondents about their registration status and experience in the polling place.

To understand legal issues that have been raised in recent litigation over voter ID requirements, we collected and analyzed the few major cases that have been decided so far on this issue. The decisions so far provide some guidance on the constitutional and other constraints as to voter ID requirements.

Summary of Findings

As voter identification requirements vary, voter turnout varies as well. This finding emerged from both the statistical analysis's aggregate data and the individual-level data, although not always for both the maximum and minimum sets of requirements. The overall relationship between the stringency of ID requirements and turnout was fairly small, but still statistically significant.

In the model used with the aggregate data in the statistical analysis, for the maximum ID requirements, the match-signature requirement and the provide-a- non-photo-ID requirement, but not the photo ID requirement, were all correlated with lower turnout compared to requiring that voters state their names. When the registration closing deadline was added as an independent variable in the aggregate analysis, signature match and non-photo id remained significant and negative predictors in the model.

The reduction in turnout was not the same for all demographic groups in the citizen voting age population.

The non-photo identification requirement showed the most significant and consistent correlation with reduced turnout. This result may be surprising given the intense debates surrounding photo identification requirements. The effect of photo ID requirements cannot, however, be assessed from the data the statistical analysis examined, since none of the states had laws in 2004 that conditioned voting on presentation of photo ID. Each of the five states that had photo ID as a "maximum" requirement (i.e., the most that voters could be asked to show at the polls) accepted another type of identification or an affidavit as a "minimum" requirement in the 2004 election (i.e., they were allowed to cast a regular ballot with something less than photo ID).

Significant questions about the relationship of voter identification requirements to turnout remain unanswered. The data examined in this project could not capture the dynamics of how identification requirements might lower turnout. If ID requirements dampen turnout, is it because individuals are aware of the requirements and stay away from the polls because they cannot or do not want to meet the requirements? Or, do the requirements result in some voters being turned away when they cannot meet the requirements on Election Day? Other factors that may also be correlated with stricter ID laws – such as less user-friendly voter registration systems – may actually be causing lower turnout. The CPS data do not include the information needed to answer this question. Knowing more about the "on the ground" experiences of voters concerning identification requirements could guide policy-makers at the state and local level in determining whether and at what point in the electoral cycle a concerted public information campaign might be most effective in helping voters to meet identification requirements. Such knowledge also could help in designing training for election judges to handle questions about, and potential disputes over, voter identification requirements.

Our analysis of litigation suggests that the courts will look more strictly at requirements that voters produce a photo ID in order to cast a regular ballot, than at non-photo ID laws. The courts have used a balancing test to weigh the legitimate interest in preventing election fraud against the citizen's right to privacy (protecting social security numbers from public disclosure, for example) and the reasonableness of requirements for identity documents. To provide both the clarity and certainty in administration of elections needed to forestall destabilizing challenges to outcomes, a best practice for the states may be to limit requirements for voter identification to the minimum needed to prevent duplicate registration and ensure eligibility.

The current lack of understanding of precisely how voter ID requirements affect turnout could be ameliorated by requiring the collection and reporting of additional data, including the reasons potential voters are required to cast a provisional ballot and the reasons for rejecting provisional ballots during the 2006 and subsequent elections. Also useful would be the results of surveys of voters on their experiences in meeting voter ID requirements and on what type of ballot they cast.[5] And, of course, more information is needed on the incidence and varieties of vote fraud, but that inquiry is outside the scope of this report.

Recommendations for Consideration and Action by the EAC

The dynamics of Voter ID requirements –how more rigorous voter ID requirements may affect the decision by potential voters to go or stay away from the polls-- are not perfectly understood. This lack of understanding should be recognized in the policy process in the states. The debate over voter ID in the states would be improved by additional research sponsored by the EAC.

The EAC should consider the following actions to improve understanding of the relationship between voter ID requirements and the two important goals of ensuring ballot access and ensuring ballot integrity.

1. Encourage or sponsor further research to clarify the connection between Voter ID requirements and the number of potential voters actually able to cast a ballot that is actually counted.
2. Recommend as a best practice the publication of a "Voting Impact Statement" by states as they assess their voter ID requirements to protect the integrity of the ballot. The analysis will help ensure that efforts to increase ballot security have a neutral effect on electoral participation by eligible voters. A "Voter Impact Statement" would estimate the number and demographics of 1) eligible, potential voters that may be kept from the polls or permitted to cast a provisional ballot by a stricter ID requirement; and 2) and assess the number of ineligible voters who will be prevented from voting by the stricter ID requirements.
3. Encourage or require the states in the 2006 election and beyond, to collect and report reliable, credible information on the relationship between ballot access and ballot security. EAC should publish an analysis of this information to provide a sound factual basis for the states to consider as they estimate the incidence of the kinds of vote fraud that more stringent ID requirements may prevent. The analysis should describe the dynamics of the voter ID process in preserving the security of the ballot. EAC might also use the information reported by the states to encourage further assessment by the states of the effectiveness of programs to ensure that all eligible voters have required ID and are permitted to vote in future elections. Well-designed longitudinal studies in the states can show the results of changing voter ID requirements on electoral participation over time. The studies should include precinct-level data to provide the fine-grained analysis that can provide a solid foundation for policy.
   I. Useful information could be supplied by state-sponsored surveys of voters conducted by local election officials. Such surveys would make clear why those who cast a provisional ballot were found ineligible to cast a regular ballot. The answers would illuminate the frequency with which ID issues divert voters into the provisional ballot line.
   II. Surveys to ask voters what they know about the voter id requirements would also provide useful context for evaluating the effect of various voter ID requirements on electoral participation.
   III. Spot checks by state election officials on how the identification process works at polling places could provide information on how closely actual practice tracks statutory or regulatory requirements. Such reports should be available to the public.
4. Encourage states to examine the time period allowed for voters who cast a provisional ballot because they lacked required ID to return with their identification. In eleven states, voters who had to cast a provisional ballot because they lacked the ID required for a regular ballot were permitted to return later with their ID. Their provision of this ID is the critical step in evaluating the ballots. The length of the period in which the voter may return with ID is important. In setting the time period for return, which now varies among the states from the same day to about two weeks, states should consider three factors: the convenience of the voter, the total time allowed to evaluate ballots6, and the safe harbor provision in presidential elections.

5. Recommendations to the states from EAC should reflect current judicial trends. Requirements that voters provide some identifying documentation have been upheld where photo ID is not the only acceptable form. Whether laws requiring photo ID will be upheld is less certain.

SUMMARY OF RESEARCH

Background and Approach of the Study

Voter ID requirements are just one set of rules governing voting that may affect turnout. Social scientists have long studied how election rules affect participation in elections. The general view today is that the individual citizen makes the choice of whether to vote in a way similar to other decisions that a rational citizen makes, by comparing costs and benefits. The benefits of voting are fairly stable and hard to specify given the remote probability that any one vote will make a difference in an election. But whatever the benefit as perceived by an individual voter, as the costs of voting (for example, time, hassle, acquisition of information) increase, the likelihood that a citizen will vote decrease. Not all groups in the population calculate the cost of participation in the same way, so that election laws (such as registration or identification requirements) may affect different groups differently.

A short summary of some of the social science literature illustrates what may be a broad consensus that the rules of elections affect turnout, but note the important differences in the details of what groups may be most affected.

- Bowler, Brockington and Donovan in “Election Systems and Voter Turnout: Experiments in the United States”. The Journal of Politics, 63:3 (August 2001) concluded that electoral systems help shape turnout by altering the benefits perceived by voters. For example, cumulative voting systems have 5% greater turnout than plurality systems
- The effect of registration systems has been the subject of many studies over the last 40 years. Kelley, Ayres, and Bowen in "Registration and Voting: Putting First Things First." American Political Science Review. 61:2 (June 1967) found that local variations in the rate of voting are most directly tied to variations in the rate of registering to vote, and that the rate of registering to vote in localities is most directly related to the laws and administration of the registration process. They concluded that the decline in voting over the past 80 years was due, in part, to the rise of registration laws.
- Brians and Grofman in "Election Day Registration's Effect on U.S. Voter Turnout." Social Science Quarterly. 82:1 (March 2001), found that relaxing registration laws produces higher turnout. In particular, they observed that relaxing registration laws is more likely to promote voter turnout among those with medium levels of income and education, rather than those at the lowest levels. Highton in "Easy Registration and Voter Turnout," Journal of Politics. 59:2 (May 1997), concluded similarly that registration laws affect voter turnout, but also observed that easier registration promotes turnout among those in lower socio-economic status.

- Mitchell and Wlezien. "The Impact of Legal Constraints on Voter Registration, Turnout, and the Composition of the American Electorate," Political Behavior. 17:2 (June 1995) agreed that easier registration promotes higher turnout, but also concluded that higher turnout from easier registration would be unlikely to change the composition of the electorate. Nagler in "The Effect of Registration Laws and Education on U.S. Voter Turnout." American Political Science Review. 85:4 (December 1991) found that registration laws decrease voter turnout by depressing the eligible electorate, but that lower educated people are not disproportionately impacted by these laws. But Rosenstone and Raymond E. Wolfinger in "The Effect of Registration Laws on Voter Turnout." American Political Science Review. 72:1 (March 1978) found that while registration laws did affect both voter turnout and the composition of the electorate, the sharpest effect of these restrictions was felt in the South and among the least educated.
- Squire, Wolfinger, and Glass in "Residential Mobility and Voter Turnout." *American Political Science Review*. 81:1 (March 1987) found that people who move constitute a major demographic group affected by registration laws. They estimated that altering laws to facilitate voting by recently moved people could increase turnout by 9%. Highton in "Residential Mobility, Community Mobility, and Voter Turnout." *Political Behavior*. 22:2 (June 2000) also found that people who move have lower turnout than stable residents, and estimated that the decline was more a result of registration laws than a loss of social connections.
- Highton and Wolfinger in "Estimating the Effects of the National Voter Registration Act of 1993." *Political Behavior*. 20:2 (June 1998) concluded that the Motor Voter laws led to a significant increase in voting; that eliminating voter purges for not voting also increases voting; and that these effects are felt most heavily by the young (under 30) and the mobile (moved within past 2 years). Knack, in "Does 'Motor Voter' Work? Evidence from State-Level Data." *Journal of Politics*., 57:3 (August 1995), also found that motor voter does lead to increased registration and voting, but that other parts of NVRA of 1993, like mail-in registrations, agency-based registrations, and limitations on voter purges had not been as influential two years after the passage of the act.

While voter ID may not have been the subject of as much research as the registration process, establishing the eligibility of a person to vote has long been part of the electoral process. Voters may have to identify themselves twice in the electoral process: when registering to vote and then when casting a ballot. The pressures felt by the voter arising from the need to check ID, even so simple a check as a signature match, can be greater at the polls on Election Day than at the time of registration. Poll workers may feel under pressure when faced with long lines and limited time.

Voter ID Requirements on Election Day

This analysis focuses on ID requirements on Election Day, but with an appreciation that the ID requirements at time of registration and on Election Day are inter-related. [7] The emphasis in this report is on Voter ID requirements on Election Day and afterwards as election judges evaluate provisional ballots. This is the critical period for the electoral system, the time when ballot access and ballot security are in the most sensitive balance.

The report looks at voter ID issues that go beyond the rather narrow identification requirements in HAVA. Much of the current debate in state legislatures over voter ID ranges beyond HAVA to require more rigorous documentation of identity for all would-be voters, not just those who had not registered in person and are casting a ballot for the first time. Current controversies in the states over voter ID seems to have been sparked in part by the HAVA requirements, but goes beyond those requirements, and sets the context for the analysis here.[8]

We recognize that the previously technical, rather dull subject of voter ID requirements has become fiercely partisan and divisive in many states. The polarization of the debate has raised the stakes over this issue, making dispassionate analysis both more valuable and more rare.[9] Voter ID is often described as the critical step in protecting the integrity of the ballot, the process to ensure that the potential voter is eligible and, if eligible, is permitted to cast one ballot and one ballot only. Truly protecting the integrity of the ballot, however, requires a perspective that takes in the entire voting process. It demands more than preventing the ineligible from voting, and should also ensure that all those who are eligible and want to vote can cast a ballot that counts. The protection effort must embrace all forms of voting, including absentee ballots, and consider each step in the process from registration through vote counting.

A voting system that requires voters to produce an identity document or documents may prevent the ineligible from voting. It may also prevent the eligible from casting a ballot. If the ID requirements block ineligible voters from the polls at the cost of preventing eligible voters who cannot obtain or have left at home the required forms of identification, the integrity of the ballot may not have been improved; the harm may be as great as the benefit. Ultimately, a normative evaluation of whether a state should adopt a stricter voter ID requirement (and, if so, what particular form that new requirement should take) will weigh value judgments as well as available factual evidence. Nonetheless, this report has proceeded on the premise that increased understanding of the factual evidence relating to the imposition of voter ID requirements, based on available data and statistical analysis of that data, can help inform the policy process.

Assessing the effectiveness of voter ID as a way to protect the integrity of the ballot should logically include an estimate of the nature and frequency of vote fraud. The EAC has commissioned a separate analysis of the incidence of vote fraud. Consequently, this research does not include consideration of vote fraud nor the possible effectiveness of various voter ID regimes to counter attempts at vote fraud. As a result, our study of the possible effects of voter ID requirements on turnout cannot take into account how many potential voters who did not turn out under comparatively stricter voter ID requirements might have been ineligible or eligible to vote.

In some states, voters lacking required ID, or who have ID that does not reflect their current address, are able to vote only by casting a provisional ballot.[10] Voter ID requirements that require voters to bring a document to the polls --rather than simply sign their names-- may divert more voters to the provisional ballot. Requiring poll workers to request and check ID, can put stress on the already demanding environment of the polling place. Scrutiny of ID can create lines at the polling places. Further delays can result when voters cast a provisional ballot and fill out the ballot envelope. Voters who cast a provisional ballot because they lack their ID on Election Day, and who then fail to return with the needed document or documents, will have their ballot rejected.[11] And, of course, the cost of processing provisional ballots is greater than the cost of regular ballots.

Each of these potential consequences of more elaborate voter identification processes can increase the chance of litigation. Long lines will, at best, discourage voters and at worst make voting seem a hassle, an impression that could keep more citizens (even those with ID) from the polls.

Evaluating the effect of different Voter ID regimes can be most effective when based on clear standards --legal, equitable, practical. The standards outlined here might be described as questions policy-makers should ask about Voter ID requirements. We suggest seven questions that address important dimensions of the problem.

1. Is the Voter ID system designed on the basis of valid and reliable empirical studies of the incidence of the sorts of vote fraud it is designed to prevent?[12]
2. How effective is the ID requirement in increasing the security of the ballot? How well can it be coordinated with a statewide voter database?[13]
3. How practical is the requirement? (Can it be administered smoothly by the staff and budget likely to be made available? How much additional training of polling place workers might be required?) Is it simple enough or can it be defined with sufficient clarity that poll workers throughout the state can administer it uniformly and with a minimum of local interpretation made on the fly under the pressure of Election Day?[14]
4. How cost-effective is the system? Does it demonstrably increase the security of the ballot affordably, measured in both monetary and other costs? To improve understanding of the non-monetary component of the costs, conducting a voter impact study might be appropriate. The voter impact study would examine, before the adoption of the regulation, the cost of compliance by the voter (such as the cost in time and money of acquiring a photo ID card), any offsetting benefits to voters, and the possible disparate effects of the regulation on various groups of voters.[15] A thorough, objective impact statement that demonstrated the nexus between the identification regime and the integrity of the ballot could provide protection against inevitable legal challenges.
5. If a side effect of the Voter ID regulation is likely to reduce turnout, generally or among particular groups, is it possible to take other steps to ameliorate the adverse consequences?[16]
6. Does it comply with the letter and spirit of Voting Rights Act?
7. The seventh question is the most difficult to answer. How neutral is the effect of the Voter ID requirement on the composition of the qualified and eligible electorate? Might it, intentionally or unintentionally, reduce the turnout of particular groups of voters or supporters of one party or another without an offsetting decrease in vote fraud?

Voter ID and Turnout

Based on research for this study by the Moritz College of Law, states had one of five types of maximum requirements in place on Election Day 2004. These are shown in Table 1, *Voter ID Requirements*. The five categories: at the polling place, voters were asked to either: state their names (10 states); sign their names (13 states and the District of Columbia); sign their names, to be matched to a signature on file (seven states); provide a form of identification that did not necessarily include a photo (15 states); or provide a photo identification (five states).[17] Using this information made it possible to code the states according to these requirements, and examine the assumption that voter identification requirements would pose an increasingly demanding requirement in this order: stating one's name, signing one's name, matching one's signature to a signature on file, providing a form of identification, and providing a form of photo identification, however, in all "photo ID" states in 2004, voters without photo ID could cast a regular ballot after signing an affidavit concerning their identity and eligibility or provide other forms of ID). The report refers to this set of ID requirements as "maximum," the most rigorous ID the voter can be asked to present at the polling place in order to cast a regular ballot.[18]

Election laws in several states offer exceptions to these requirements if potential voters lack the necessary form of identification. Laws in those states set a minimum standard – that is the minimum requirement that a voter may be required to satisfy in order to vote using a regular ballot. States can be categorized based on the minimum requirement for voting with a regular ballot. In 2004 the categories were somewhat different compared to the maximum requirement, in that none of the states required photo identification as a minimum standard for voting with a regular ballot. That is, voters who lacked photo ID would still be allowed to vote in all states, if able to meet another requirement. Four states required voters to swear an affidavit as to their identity (Florida, Indiana, Louisiana, and North Dakota). The five categories for minimum requirements were: state name (12 states), sign name (14 states and the District of Columbia), match one's signature to a signature on file (six states), provide a non-photo identification (14 states), or swear an affidavit (four states). The analysis also examined this array of minimum identification requirements to assess how they correlated with turnout: state name, sign name, match signature, provide non-photo identification, and, given the potential legal consequences for providing false information, swearing an affidavit. As noted above, *no* state had a "minimum" requirement of showing photo ID. This analysis therefore cannot estimate the effect of laws, such as those recently enacted in Indiana and Georgia that require voters to show photo ID in order to cast a regular ballot without an affidavit or other exception.

We recognize the difficulties in summarizing each state's voter ID requirements. The problem is illustrated by the number of footnotes to Table 1 below. The variety of statutory and regulatory details among the states is complex.

Moving beyond the statutes and regulations, we also recognize that the assignment of each state to one category may fail to reflect actual practice at many polling places. As in any system run by fallible humans, the voter ID process is subject to variation in practice.[19] Voters may have been confronted with demands for identification different from the directives in state statutes or regulation. It seems reasonable to conclude, however, that while actual practices may vary, the variance is around each state's legal requirement for ID. The analysis of the effect of state requirements on turnout must be viewed with some caution. We believe that the categories used in this report provide an acceptable level of discrimination among voter identification regimes.

Table 1. Voter ID Requirements[20]

State	Maximum Forms of ID Required 2004	Current ID Requirement for First-Time Voters	Current ID Requirements for All Other Voters	Verification Method for Provisional Ballots
Alabama	Provide ID	Provide ID	Provide ID	Address & Registration
Alaska	Provide ID	Provide ID	Provide ID	Signature
Arizona	Provide ID	Gov-issued Photo ID	Gov-issued Photo ID[1]	Address & Registration
Arkansas	Provide ID	Provide ID	Provide ID	Address & Registration
California	Sign Name	Sign Name	Sign Name	Signature
Colorado	Provide ID	Provide ID	Provide ID	Address & Registration
Connecticut	Provide ID	Provide ID	Provide ID	Affidavit
D.C.	Sign Name	Provide ID*	Sign Name	Address & Registration
Delaware	Provide ID	Provide ID	Provide ID	Affidavit
Florida	Photo ID[2]	Photo ID	Photo ID	Signature
Georgia	Provide ID	Gov. Issued Photo ID	Gov. Issued Photo ID	Affidavit
Hawaii	Photo ID^^	Photo ID	Photo ID^^	Affidavit
Idaho	Sign Name	Provide ID*	Sign Name	EDR
Illinois	Give Name	Provide ID*	Match Sig.	Affidavit
Indiana	Sign Name	Gov. Issued Photo ID	Gov. Issued Photo ID	Bring ID Later
Iowa	Sign Name	Provide ID*	Sign Name	Bring ID Later
Kansas	Sign Name	Sign Name	Sign Name	Bring ID Later
Kentucky	Provide ID	Provide ID	Provide ID	Affidavit
Louisiana	Photo ID	Photo ID	Photo ID^	DOB and Address
Maine	Give Name	Provide ID*	Give Name	EDR
Maryland	Sign Name	Provide ID*	Sign Name	Bring ID Later
Mass.	Give Name	Provide ID*	Give Name	Affidavit
Michigan	Sign Name	Provide ID*	Sign Name	Bring ID Later
Minnesota	Sign Name	Provide ID*	Sign Name	EDR
Mississippi	Sign Name	Provide ID*	Sign Name	Affidavit
Missouri	Provide ID	Provide ID*	Provide ID	Address & Registration
Montana	Provide ID	Provide ID*	Provide ID	Bring ID Later
Nebraska	Sign Name	Provide ID*	Sign Name	Affidavit
Nevada	Match Sig.	Provide ID*	Match Sig.	Affidavit
New Jersey	Match Sig.	Provide ID*	Match Sig.	Bring ID Later
New Mexico	Sign Name	Provide ID	Provide ID	Bring ID Later
New York	Match Sig.	Provide ID*	Match Sig.	Affidavit
NH	Give Name	Provide ID	Give Name	EDR
North Carolina	Give Name	Provide ID*	Give Name	Varies
North Dakota	Provide ID	Provide ID	Provide ID	No Registration
Ohio	Match Sig.	Provide ID	Provide ID	Address & Registration
Oklahoma	Sign Name	Provide ID*	Sign Name	Address & Registration
Oregon	Match Sig.	Provide ID*	Match Sig.	Signature
Penn.	Match Sig.	Provide ID[4]	Match Sig.	Address & Registration
Rhode Island	Give Name	Provide ID*	Give Name	Address & Registration
South Carolina	Photo ID[5]	Photo ID	Photo ID^^	Address & Registration
South Dakota	Photo ID[6]	Photo ID	Photo ID^^	Affidavit

Table 1. (Continued)

State	Maximum Forms of ID Required 2004	Current ID Requirement for First-Time Voters	Current ID Requirements for All Other Voters	Verification Method for Provisional Ballots
Tennessee	Provide ID	Provide ID[7]	Provide ID	Affidavit
Texas	Provide ID	Provide ID[8]	Provide ID	Bring ID Later
Utah	Give Name	Provide ID	Give Name	Bring ID Later
Vermont	Give Name	Provide ID	Give Name	Affidavit
Virginia	Provide ID	Provide ID	Provide ID	Affidavit
Washington	Sign Name	Provide ID	Provide ID	Address & Registration
West Virginia	Match Sig.	Provide ID	Match Sig.	Address & Registration
Wisconsin	Give Name	Provide ID	Give Name	Bring ID Later
Wyoming	Give Name	Provide ID	Give Name	Affidavit

* States applies only HAVA's ID requirement, applicable to first-time voters who registered by mail and did not provide applicable ID at the time of registration.

[1] Arizona voters who lack a photo ID may present 2 forms of ID with no photograph.

[2] Florida required a photo ID in 2004, but voters without that credential could sign an affidavit concerning their identity and eligibility and cast a regular ballot. Florida subsequently changed its law to require that voters present photo ID to cast a regular ballot, though voters without photo ID may still cast a provisional ballot by signing an affidavit, which ballot should ordinarily be counted.

[3] Louisiana required a photo ID in 2004. Voters without that credential could sign an affidavit concerning their identity and eligibility and cast a regular ballot.

[4] Pennsylvania requires ID of all first-time voters, whether they registered by mail or in-person.

[5] Voters lacking a photo ID could vote by providing another form of ID in 2004.

[6] Voters lacking a photo ID could vote by providing another form of ID in 2004.

[7] Tennessee voters must provide signature and address. In counties without computerized lists, the signature is compared to the registration card. In counties with computerized lists, the signature is compared to a signature on ID presented with the registration.

[8] Texas voters must present a current registration certificate. Those without a certificate can vote provisionally after completing an affidavit.

Relationship of Voter ID requirements to Turnout

The statistical analysis examined the potential variation in turnout rates based on the type of voter identification required in each state on Election Day 2004 using two sets of data: aggregate turnout data at the county level for each state, as compiled by the Eagleton Institute of Politics, and individual-level survey data included in the November 2004 Current Population Survey conducted by the U.S. Census Bureau.

The statistical analysis examined turnout among U.S. citizens of voting age in both the aggregate and the individual-level data. Determining citizenship status in the individual-level data simply involved restricting the analyses to individuals who identified themselves as citizens in the November 2004 Current Population Survey. (Those who said they were not citizens did not have the opportunity to answer the supplemental voting questions contained in the Current Population Survey.)

Findings of the Statistical Analysis

The analysis looked at the voter identification requirements in two ways, as a continuous variable and as a series of discrete variables. As a continuous variable the maximum voter identification requirements are ranked according to how demanding they were judged to be, with photo ID as the most demanding requirement. As discrete variables, the statistical analysis assume that stating name is the least demanding ID requirement and compare each other requirement to it.

The analysis treating the requirements as a continuous variable offers some statistical support for the premise that as the level of required proof increases, turnout declines. Averaging across counties in each state, statewide turnout is negatively correlated with maximum voter identification requirements ($r = -.30$, $p < .05$). In considering the array of minimum requirements, with affidavit as the most demanding requirement, however, the correlation between voter identification and turnout is negative, but it is not statistically significant ($r = -.20$, $p = .16$). This suggests that the relationship between turnout rates and minimum requirements may not be linear. Breaking down the turnout rates by type of requirement reveals in greater detail the relationship between voter identification requirements and voter turnout.

Table 2. Variation in 2004 State Turnout Based on Voter Identification Requirements

Maximum Requirement		Minimum Requirement	
Voter Identification Required in the States	Mean Voter Turnout for States in that Category	Voter Identification Required in the States	Mean Voter Turnout for States in that Category
State Name	64.2 %	State Name	63.0 %
Sign Name	61.1 %	Sign Name	60.4 %
Match Signature	60.9 %	Match Signature	61.7 %
Provide Non-Photo ID	59.3 %	Provide Non-Photo ID	59.0 %
Provide Photo ID	58.1 %	Swear Affidavit	60.1 %
Average Turnout (All States)	60.9 %		

This table displays the mean turnout using the aggregate county level data for each state in 2004.

The aggregate data show that 60.9 percent of the estimated citizen voting age population voted in 2004. Differences in voter turnout at the state level in 2004 varied based on voter identification requirements. Taking into account the maximum requirements, an average of 64.6 percent of the voting age population turned out in states that required voters to state their names, compared to 58.1 percent in states that required photo identification. A similar trend emerged when considering minimum requirements. Sixty-three percent of the voting age population turned out in states requiring voters to state their names, compared to 60.1 percent in states that required an affidavit from voters. Given the lack of a clear, consistent linear relationship between turnout and minimum identification requirements, however, we opted to treat the voter identification requirements as a series of dichotomous variables.[21] (Dichotomous variables reflect either the presence or absence of a characteristic. In the dummy variable for non-photo ID, a state would be coded as 1 if it required non-photo ID, and 0 otherwise.)

Voter identification requirements are just one factor that might affect voter turnout. Multivariate models that take into account other predictors of turnout can paint a more complete picture of the relationship between voter identification requirements and turnout. This analysis estimated the effects of voter identification requirements in multivariate models that also took into account the electoral context in 2004 and demographic characteristics of the population in each county. While the model takes account of several important variables, statistical models do not capture all the messiness of the real world. It is a simplification of a complex reality, and its results should be treated with appropriate caution.

The model also took into account such variables as:

- Was the county in a presidential battleground state?
- Was the county was in a state with a competitive race for governor and/or the U.S. Senate?
- Percentage of the voting-age population in each county that was Hispanic or African-American [22]
- Percentage of county residents age 65 and older
- Percentage of county residents below the poverty line

Another contextual factor to consider is voter registration requirements, such as the deadline for registration. As states set the deadline farther away from Election Day, the task of remembering to register to vote becomes more challenging. Thus our model takes into account the number of days between each state's registration deadline and the election.

The dependent variable in each model using the aggregate data was voter turnout at the county level, with turnout calculated as the percentage of the citizen voting-age population that voted in the 2004 election.

The results of this modeling suggest that the stricter voter identification requirements of matching one's signature to a signature on file with election authorities or presenting a non-photo ID are associated with lower turnout compared to turnout in states that required voters to simply state their name, holding constant the electoral context and demographic variables.

Contextual factors, such as whether the county was in a battleground state or whether that state had a competitive race for governor and/or U.S. Senate, were associated with increased voter turnout. The time between the closing date for registration and the election was correlated with a slight negative effect on turnout. As the percentage of Hispanics in the county's population increased, turnout declined. The percentage of senior citizens in the county and household median income were associated with higher turnout. The percentage of African-Americans in the county did not have a significant effect in the model. The percentage of senior citizens in the county and household median income showed a positive correlation with turnout. In this aggregate model, the percentage of African-Americans in the county was not associated with a significant difference in turnout.

The relationship of the minimum voter identification requirements to turnout was not demonstrated. None of the dummy variables for voter identification requirements were statistically significant. (A "dummy variable" represents a particular attribute and has the value zero or one for each observation, e.g. 1 for male and 0 for female.) Being a battleground state and having a competitive statewide race were significant and positive, as was the percentage of senior citizens in the county and household median income. The percentage of Hispanics in the county's population continued to be associated with reduced turnout, as was the number of days between the closing date for registration and the election.[23]

Analysis of the aggregate data at the county level generates some support for the hypothesis that stricter identification requirements are correlated with lower turnout. For the maximum requirements, a signature match and non-photo identification –but not photo identification-- were correlated at a significant level with lower turnout in 2004, compared to requiring that voters simply state their names.

Aggregate data, however, cannot fully capture the individual demographic factors that may figure into the decision to turn out to vote.[24] Voter identification requirements could have a relationship to the turnout of particular groups of voters, in ways that county-level aggregate data on turnout would not capture. To explore the effects of voter identification requirements on turnout more completely, it is important to examine individual-level data as well.

Individual-level Analysis

Individual-level turnout data exists in the November 2004 Current Population Survey conducted by the U.S. Census Bureau. The Census Bureau conducts the CPS monthly to measure unemployment and other workforce data, but the bureau adds a battery of voter participation questions to the November survey in even-numbered years to coincide with either a presidential or midterm Congressional election.

One of the of the CPS is the sheer size of the sample. The survey's Voting and Registration Supplement consisted of interviews, either by telephone or in person, with 96,452 respondents.[25] The large sample size permits analyses of smaller groups, such as Black or Hispanic voters or voters with less than a high school education. The statistical analysis in relying on the CPS is based on reports from *self-described* registered voters. Omitted are those who said they were not registered to vote, as are those who said they cast absentee ballots because the identification requirements for absentee ballots may differ from those required when one votes in person. Eliminated from the sample are respondents who said they were not U.S. citizens, who in this survey were not asked the voter registration and turnout questions. In addition to the voter identification requirements, the models include other socioeconomic, demographic, and political environment factors that might have influenced turnout in 2004.[26] The dependent variable in these analyses is whether a respondent said he or she voted in the November 2004 election.[27]

In the model, three of the voter identification requirements have a statistically significant correlation with whether survey respondents said they had voted in 2004. That is, compared to states that require voters only to state their names, the requirement to sign one's name, provide a non-photo ID, or photo ID in the maximum requirements or affidavit in the minimum is associated with lower turnout.

Of the other state factors, only the competitiveness of the presidential race showed a significant, correlation with increased turnout. In terms of demographic influences, African-American voters were more likely than white voters or other voters to say they had cast a ballot, while Asian-Americans were less likely than white or other voters to say they had turned out. Hispanic voters were not statistically different from white or other voters in terms of reported turnout. Consistent with previous research, income, and marital status all were positive predictors of voting. Women also were more likely to say they voted than men. Among the age categories, those ages 45 to 64 and 65 and older were more likely than those ages 18 to 24 to say they voted. Respondents who had earned a high school diploma, attended some college, graduated from college or attended graduate school were all more likely to say they voted than those who had not finished high school.

While the probit models provide statistical evidence for the relationship of voter identification requirements and other variables to turnout, probit coefficients do not lend themselves to intuitive interpretation.[28] Table 3 below shows predicted probabilities (calculated from the probit coefficients) of voting for each level of voter identification requirements while holding all other independent variables in the models at their means.[29]

Table 3. Predicted probability of voter turnout – all voters

	Maximum requirement	Minimum requirement
State name	91.7%	91.5%
Sign name	89.9%	90.2%
Match signature	Not significant	Not significant
Non-photo ID	89.0%	89.0%
Photo ID	88.8%	----
Affidavit	----	87.%5
Total difference from "state name" to "photo ID" or "affidavit"	2.9%	4.0%
N	54,973	

Figures represent the predicted probability of registered voters saying they voted as the identification requirement varies from stating one's name to providing photo identification or an affidavit , with all other variables held constant.

Data source: U.S. Census Bureau, Current Population Survey, Voting and Registration Supplement, November 2004.

Taking into account that signature matches were not a predictor of turnout, the differences in predicted probability decline from stating one's name to providing a photo identification or affidavit. Voters in states that required photo identification were 2.7 percent less likely to vote than voters in states where individuals had to give their names.[30] In terms of the minimum requirement, voters in states that required an affidavit at minimum were 4 percent less likely to turn out than voters in states where they had to give their names.

The differences were more pronounced for those with fewer years of education. Constraining the model to show predicted probabilities only for those with less than a high school diploma, the probability of voting was 5.1 percent lower in states that required photo identification as the maximum requirement and 7 percent lower in states that required an affidavit as the minimum requirement compared to states where stating one's name was the maximum or minimum requirement.

Race and ethnicity have generated particular interest in the debate over voter ID requirements.[31] The analysis using the aggregate data shed no light on the association between voter ID requirements and turnout for African-American and Hispanic voters. But in the models using the individual data, some significant relationships emerged for African-American, Hispanic and Asian citizens. For the entire population, the signature, non-photo identification and photo identification requirements all were associated with lower turnout compared to the requirement that voters simply state their names. These correlations translated into reduced probabilities of voting of about 3 to 4 percent for the entire sample, with larger differences for specific subgroups. For example, the predicted probability that Hispanics would vote in states that required non-photo identification was about 10 percentage points lower than in states where Hispanic voters gave their names. The difference was about 6 percent for African-Americans and Asian-Americans, and about 2 percent for white voters.

The model also showed that Hispanic voters were less likely to vote in states that required non-photo identification as opposed to stating one's name. Hispanic voters were 10 percent less likely to vote in non-photo identification states compared to states where voters only had to give their name.

More rigorous voter identification requirements were associated with lower turnout rates for Asian-American voters as well. Asian-American voters were 8.5 percent less likely to vote in states that required non-photo identification compared to states that require voters to state their names under the maximum requirements, and they were 6.1 percent less likely to vote where non-photo identification was the minimum requirement.

Conclusions of the Statistical Analysis

The statistical analysis found that, as voter identification requirements vary, voter turnout varies as well. This finding emerged from both the aggregate data and the individual-level data, although not always for both the maximum and minimum sets of requirements. The overall relationship between ID requirements and turnout for all registered voters was fairly small, but still statistically significant.

In the aggregate data, the match-signature requirement and the provide-a-non-photo ID requirement were correlated with lower turnout compared to requiring that voters state their names. But the photo-ID requirement did not have an effect that was statistically significant, possibly because in 2004 each state requiring a photo-ID provided an alternative way to cast a regular ballot for voters who lacked that document.

In the model using the individual-level data the signature, non-photo ID, and photo ID requirements were all correlated with lower turnout compared to the requirement that voters simply state their names (in the entire sample and for white voters, but the statistical significance may be an artifact of the very large sample size). That the non-photo identification requirement was the most consistent in terms of statistical significance across the groups is intriguing given the intense debates surrounding photo identification requirements.

Significant questions about the relationship between voter identification requirements and turnout remain unanswered. The data examined in the statistical analysis could not capture the dynamics of how identification requirements might lower turnout, nor could they rule out that other attributes of a state's electoral system might explain the statistically significant correlations that the study found. If ID requirements dampen turnout, is it because individuals are aware of the requirements and stay away from the polls because they cannot or do not want to meet the requirements? Or, do the requirements result in some voters being turned away when they cannot meet the requirements on Election Day , or forced to cast a provisional ballot that is not ultimately counted? The CPS data do not include measures that can answer this question. Knowing more about the "on the ground" experiences of voters concerning identification requirements could guide policy-makers at the state and local level in determining whether and at what point in the electoral cycle a concerted public information campaign might be most effective in helping voters to meet identification requirements. Such knowledge also could help in designing training for election judges to handle questions about, and potential disputes over, voter identification requirements.

LITIGATION OVER VOTER ID REQUIREMENTS

A handful of cases have challenged identification requirements in court in recent years. In general, requirements that voters provide some identifying documentation have been upheld, where photo ID is *not* the only acceptable form. Whether laws requiring photo ID will be upheld is more doubtful. To date, only two cases have considered laws requiring voters to show photo ID (*Common Cause v. Billups* and *Indiana Democratic Party v. Rokita*).. Cases challenging the mandatory disclosure of voters' Social Security numbers on privacy grounds have yielded mixed results.

Non-photo identification. For the most part, courts have looked favorably on requirements that voters present some form of identifying documents if the photo identification is *not* the only form accepted. In *Colorado Common Cause v. Davidson,* No. 04CV7709, 2004 WL 2360485, at *1 (Colo. Dist. Ct. Oct. 18, 2004), plaintiffs challenged a law requiring *all* in-person voters to show identification (not just first-time registrants). The court upheld this requirement against a constitutional challenge. Similarly, in *League of Women Voters v. Blackwell,* 340 F. Supp. 2d 823 (N.D. Ohio 2004), the court rejected a challenge to an Ohio directive requiring first-time voters who registered by mail to provide one of the HAVA-permitted forms of identification, in order to have their provisional ballots counted. Specifically, the directive provided that their provisional ballots would be counted if the voter (a) orally recited his driver's license number or the last four digits of his social security number or (b) returned to the polling place before it closed with some acceptable identification (including reciting those identification numbers). *Id.* This was found to be consistent with HAVA.

Photo ID. Since the 2004 election, two states have adopted laws requiring photo identification at the polls in order to have one's vote counted, without an affidavit exception: Georgia and Indiana.[32] Both these requirements were enacted in 2005 and both have been challenged in court. The Georgia law required voters attempting to cast a ballot in person present a valid form of photographic identification. O.C.G.A. § 21-2-417. On October 18, 2005, the District Court granted the plaintiffs' motion for a preliminary injunction, enjoining the application of the new identification requirements on constitutional grounds. In granting the injunction, the court held that plaintiffs' claims under both the Fourteenth Amendment (equal protection) and Twenty-Fourth Amendment (poll tax) had a substantial likelihood of succeeding on the merits at trial (*Common Cause v. Billups*, Prelim. Inj. 96, 104). In January

2006, Georgia enacted a modified version of its photo ID law, which the court has not yet ruled on. In the other state that has enacted a photo ID requirement (Indiana), legal challenges have also been filed. (*Indiana Democratic Party v. Rokita* and *Crawford v. Marion County Election Board*). On April 14, 2006, the district court granted defendants' motion for summary judgment, concluding that plaintiffs had failed to produce evidence showing that the state's ID law would have an adverse impact on voters. Another case of significance, for purposes of photo ID requirements, is *American Civil Liberties Union of Minnesota v. Kiffmeyer,* No. 04-CV-4653, 2004 WL 2428690, at *1 (D. Minn. Oct. 28, 2004). In that case, the court enjoined a Minnesota law that allowed the use of tribal photo ID cards, only for an Indian who lived on the reservation. 2004 WL 2428690, at *1. The Court found no rational basis for distinguishing based on whether or not the cardholder lives on the reservation. *Id.* at *1, 3. These decisions indicate that courts are likely to carefully scrutinize the evidence regarding the impact of photo ID requirements.

Privacy. In *Greidinger v. Davis*, 988 F.2d 1344 (4th Cir. 1993), the court struck down on due process grounds a Virginia law requiring disclosure of voters' social security numbers for voter registration. The social security numbers recorded in voter registration lists had been disclosed to the public and political parties that had requested the lists. The court found that the requirement to give the social security number effectively conditioned rights on the consent to an invasion of privacy. It concluded that this public disclosure of the social security numbers was not necessary to achieve the government's interest in preventing fraud. On the other hand, in *McKay v. Thompson*, 226 F.3d 752 (6th Cir. 2000), the court rejected privacy challenges based on both the Constitution and federal statutes, to a Tennessee law requiring social security numbers for voter registration since 1972. 226 F.3d at 755. Second, the NVRA only permits requiring the minimum amount of information necessary to prevent duplicate voter registration and to determine eligibility. The distinction appears to be between the use of Social Security numbers for internal purposes only, which was deemed permissible, and the disclosure of those numbers to the public which was not.

These decisions suggest that the courts will carefully scrutinize the evidence, where states require that voters produce a photo ID in order to cast a regular ballot. The courts have used a balancing test to weigh the legitimate interest in preventing election fraud against the citizen's right to privacy (protecting social security numbers from public disclosure, for example) and the reasonableness of requirements for identity documents. To provide both the clarity and certainty in administration of elections needed to forestall destabilizing challenges to outcomes, these early decisions suggest that best practice may be to limit requirements for voter identification to the minimum needed to prevent duplicate registration and ensure eligibility.

Developments Since 2004

Since the passage of HAVA, with its limited requirements for voter identification, and following the 2004 election, debate over voter ID has taken place in state legislatures across the country. That debate has not been characterized by solid information on the consequences of tightening requirements for voters to identify themselves before being permitted to cast a regular, rather than a provisional, ballot.

Better information might improve the quality of the debate. Answers to the following key questions are not available in a form that might satisfy those on both sides of the argument.

- What is the overall incidence of vote fraud?
- How does fraud take place in the various stage of the process: registration, voting at the polls, absentee voting, or ballot counting?
- What contribution can tighter requirements for voter ID make to reducing vote fraud?
- What would be the other consequences of increasingly demanding requirements for voters to identify themselves? This is the question addressed, within the limits of the available data, in the analysis in this report.

Answering these questions would provide the information needed for more informed judgement in the states as they consider the tradeoffs among the competing goals of ballot integrity, ballot access, and administrative efficiency. The Carter-Baker Commission recognized the tradeoffs when it tied recommendation for national ID to an affirmative effort by government to identify unregistered voters and make it easy for them to register.

State Voter Databases and Voter ID

With the implementation of the HAVA Computerized Statewide Voter Registration List, an application for voter registration for an election for Federal office may not be accepted or processed unless the application includes a driver's license number or last four digits of the Social Security number on the voter registration form. This information can be used to verify the identity of the registrant through interfacing with lists maintained by the Motor Vehicle office and Social Security office. If registrants do not have either a driver's license or Social Security number, the State will assign a unique identifier number to that person.

Some states are wrestling now with these unresolved issues. In New Jersey, for example, pending legislation would require that voters must be able to confirm their registration through a secure access to the Statewide Voter Registration List. It also requires voters to present ID at the polls in order to cast a regular ballot if the numbers recorded on the registration have not been verified (or if no verifiable number appears on the registration). It recognizes the HAVA requirement that if the number provided by the voter has not been verified and if the voter does not present ID at the polls, that voter may cast a provisional ballot. The bill does not specify they have to provide ID within 48 hours in order for their vote to count, as is the case with first-time mail-in registrants.

As some states gain experience in this area, the EAC would perform a useful service by making timely recommendations of best practices for all states to consider.

CONCLUSION

The analysis of voter ID requirements is complex. It takes into account important values associated with an electoral process, such as ballot access and integrity. The continuing effort to understand how voter ID requirements may affect turnout and the integrity of the ballot could benefit from additional factual information, including statistical analyses. Our research includes a statistical study of this kind. It indicated that the level of voter turnout in a state is correlated with the stringency of the voter ID requirement imposed by that state. Additional empirical research of this nature, with additional data collected by or for the EAC, would further illuminate the relationship between stricter voter ID rules and turnout, perhaps explaining if awareness of a strict ID requirement tends to discourage would-be voters from going to the polls. Or, additional research may shed light on whether, if voters did go to the polls, stricter Voter ID requirements will divert more voters into the line for provisional ballots. The consequence of increased reliance on provisional ballots can be longer lines at the polls and confusion, without necessarily a clear demonstration that the security of the ballot is correspondingly increased. [33]

The debate over voter ID in the states would be improved by additional research sponsored by the EAC. That might include longitudinal studies of jurisdictions that have changed voter ID requirements, as well as precinct-level analyses that would allow more finely tuned assessment of the correlation between stricter identification requirements and turnouts. Further research could also identify methods to eliminate the need for voters to bring specific identity documents with them to the polls, while assuring that each voter who casts a ballot is eligible and votes only once.

End Notes

[1] See, for example, Tom William Rice and Patrick J. Kenney, "Voter Turnout in Presidential Primaries." 1985. Political Behavior, 7: 101-112. Identification requirements are not the only legal restrictions on voting. States also differ, for example, in their registration requirements (including how long before the election registration must take place and the identity documents required register).

[2] The EAC has contracted with other researchers to study vote fraud issues.

[3] Appendix C: Tim Vercellotti, Eagleton Institute of Politics, Analysis of Effects of Voter Identification Requirements on Turnout. Using the aggregate data, photo ID did not have a significant effect on turnout, possibly because in the 2004 election every state requiring photo ID provided an alternative way to cast a regular ballot for those voters who lacked photo identification. The individual data from the Current Population Survey did show a significant effect, but only for the overall sample and for white voters, which may be an artifact of the large sample size.

[4] Even the most relaxed provisions for identification at the polls –anything stricter than the honor system used in North Dakota—will impose some burden on particular voters. Harvard Law Review 119:1146.

[5] Arizona held its first election with its new, stricter ID requirements on March 14, 2006. In at least one county (Maricopa) election officials handed a survey to voters that asked if they knew about the voter identification law and if they did, how they found out about it. Edythe Jensen, "New Voter ID Law Goes Smoothly in Chandler," Arizona Republic, March 15, 2006. More surveys of this kind can illuminate the dynamics of voter ID and voting in ways that are not possible now because of insufficient data.

[6] Our research on provisional voting reveals that states that provide more than a week to evaluate provisional ballots end up counting substantially more of those ballots than states that provide less than a week.

[7] As the Carter-Baker Commission noted, photo ID requirements for in-person voting do little to address the problem of fraudulent registration by mail, especially in states that do not require third-party organizations that register voters to verify ID. Commission on Federal Election Reform, pp 46-47.

[8] Harvard Law Review 119:1127: "Legislators hoping to stiffen their state antifraud laws have taken their cue from identification provisions buried in HAVA."

[9] "Of the various electoral procedure laws passed in the fifty states since the 2000 and 2004 presidential elections and those still being debated in state legislatures and local media, few arouse more potent partisan feelings than voter identification laws." Harvard Law Review 119:1144. John Fund's 2004 book, Stealing Elections:

How Voter Fraud Threaten Our Democracy, cites (pages 16 – 17) a Rasmussen Research poll that asked respondents if they were more concerned with voting by ineligible participants or with disenfranchisement of eligible voters. Sixty-two percent of Kerry supporters, but only 18 percent of Bush supporters, worried more about disenfranchisement; 58 percent of Bush supporters, but only 19 percent of Kerry supporters were more concerned with voter fraud.

[10] For example, the Florida voter ID law adopted after the 2004 election and pre-cleared by the Department of Justice, permits voters who cannot meet the ID requirements to sign an affidavit on the envelope of a provisional ballot, which will be counted if the signature matches that on the voter's registration form.

[11] The EAC's Election Day Study found "improper ID," to be the third most common reason for a provisional ballot to be rejected. "Improper ID" was cited by 7 states responding to the survey, compared to 14 mentions for voting in the wrong precinct. Election Day Study, Chapter 6, p. 5.

[12] "Often where the battle over voter identification is most heated, real evidence of voter fraud proves scarce: in Georgia, for example, the Secretary of State averred that she had never encountered a single instance of voter impersonation at the polls. State laws might sometimes impose tighter restrictions on in-person voting than on absentee ballots, which yield the greatest incidence of, and provide the easiest avenue for, voter fraud. . ." Harvard Law Review 127:1144 (2006)

[13] See the final section of this report for a brief overview of possible effects of a statewide voter database on voter identification issues.

[14] In New York, in 2004, disparities in training and voting information were made apparent in a study finding elections officials had wildly varying interpretations of what the state's voter identification requirement actually was. Tova Wang, "Warning Bell in Ohio," December 5, 2005. Website, the Foundation for National Progress.

[15] "Absent clear empirical evidence demonstrating widespread individual voter fraud, legislatures need to fashion narrowly tailored voter identification provisions with an eye toward the inevitable and well-grounded constitutional challenges that will arise in the courts. Only as states grow more adept at administering elections will courts likely demonstrate greater willingness to uphold strict identification requirements." Harvard Law Review 127:1144 (2006)

[16] For example, the Carter-Baker Commission coupled its recommendation for a national voter ID card to a call for an affirmative effort by the states to reach out and register the unregistered, that is, to use the new Voter ID regime as a means to enroll more voters. Similarly, Richard Hasen has suggested combining a national voter ID with universal registration. See his "Beyond the Margin of Litigation: Reforming U.S. Election Administration to Avoid Electoral Meltdown," 62 Washington and Lee Law Review 937 (2005).

[17] Oregon conducts elections entirely by mail. Voters sign their mail-in ballots, and election officials match the signatures to signatures on file. For the purposes of this analysis, Oregon is classified as a state that requires a signature match.

[18] As noted above, our analysis does not consider additional requirements that particular voters may be subjected to as part of an official challenge process, in the event that their eligibility is called into question.

[19] One state election official told us that, "We have 110 election jurisdictions in Illinois, and I have reason to believe [the voter ID requirements] are administered little bit differently in each one. We wish it weren't that way, but it probably is."

[20] See Appendix 1 for a more detailed summary, including citations and statutory language, of the identification requirements in each state.

[21] The voter identification requirements are coded as a series of dummy variables, coding each variable as one if the requirement existed in a given state, and zero otherwise. This yielded five dichotomous variables for maximum requirements (state name, sign name, match signature, non-photo identification, or photo identification), and five dichotomous variables for minimum requirements (state name, sign name, match signature, non-photo identification, or providing an affidavit). Omitted is the variable for stating one's name so that it could serve as the reference category in comparison with the other four identification requirements in each of the statistical analyses.

[22] The U.S. Census projections for 2003 provided the data for the percentage of the voting-age population in each county that was Hispanic or African-American and for the percentage of county residents age 65 and older.

[23] This test incorporated a series of interactions between the maximum and minimum voter identification requirements and the percentage of African-Americans and Hispanics living in the counties. In each case the interactions did not improve the fit of the models to the data. See tables A-1 and A-2 in the appendix of Vercellotti's paper in the appendices.

[24] For example, previous research has found that education is a powerful determinant of turnout (Wolfinger and Rosenstone 1980, but see also Nagler 1991).24 Married people also are more likely to vote than those who are

not married (Alvarez and Ansolabehere 2002; Alvarez, Nagler and Wilson 2004; Fisher, Kenny, and Morton 1993).

[25] It is important to note that the Census Bureau allows respondents to answer on behalf of themselves and others in the household during the interview. While proxy reporting of voter turnout raises the possibility of inaccurate reports concerning whether another member of the household voted, follow-up interviews with those for whom a proxy report had been given in the November 1984 CPS showed 99 percent agreement between the proxy report and the information given by the follow-up respondent (U.S. Census Bureau 1990).

[26] The models are estimated using probit analysis, which calculates the effects of independent variables on the probability that an event occurred – in this case whether a respondent said he or she voted and using robust standard errors to control for correlated error terms for observations from within the same state.

[27] The U.S. Census Bureau reported, based on the November 2004 CPS, that 89 percent of those who identified themselves as registered voters said they voted in 2004 (U.S. Census Bureau 2005). Previous research has shown that, generally speaking, some survey respondents overstate their incidence of voting. Researchers speculate that over-reports may be due to the social desirability that accompanies saying one has done his or her civic duty, or a reluctance to appear outside the mainstream of American political culture (U.S. Census Bureau 1990). It is also possible that voting is an indication of civic engagement that predisposes voters to agree to complete surveys at a higher rate than non-voters (Flanigan and Zingale 2002). Hence the voter turnout rates reported in the CPS tend to be up to 10 percentage points higher than the actual turnout rate for the nation (Flanigan and Zingale 2002). Even with this caveat, however, the CPS serves as a widely accepted source of data on voting behavior.

[28] A probit model is a popular specification of a generalized linear regression model, using the probit link function.

[29] In the case of dichotomous independent variables, holding them at their mean amounted to holding them at the percentage of the sample that was coded 1 for the variable (Long 1997).

[30] The voter turnout percentages may seem disproportionately high compared to the turnout rates reported in the aggregate data analysis. It is important to consider that the turnout rates in the aggregate data were a proportion of all citizens of voting-age population, while the turnout rates for the individual-level data are the proportion of only registered voters who said they voted.

[31] Incorporating discrete variables for Hispanics, African-Americans, and Asian-Americans into one model carries the implicit assumption that the remaining variables, including education and income, will influence each of these groups in a similar manner in terms of deciding whether to vote. These assumptions are not always born out by the data (see Leighley and Vedlitz, 1999.) To isolate the effects of voter identification and other variables on voter turnout within specific racial and ethnic groups, the sample is divided into sub-samples and the model re-run to calculate the data discussed and shown in Tables 5, 6, and 7 in Appendix C.

[32] Indiana's law does allow voters without ID to cast provisional ballots, and then to appear before the county board of elections to execute an affidavit saying that they are indigent and unable to obtain the requisite ID without payment of a fee. But in contrast to other states, voters cannot cast a ballot that will be counted by submitting an affidavit at the polls, affirming that they are the registered voter and are otherwise eligible to vote.

[33] In this connection, the Brennan Center's response to the Carter-Baker Commission report observes that, "while it might be true that in a close election "a small amount of fraud could make the margin of difference," it is equally true that the rejection of a much larger number of eligible voters could make a much bigger difference in the outcome." Response to the Report of the 2005 Commission on Federal Election Reform, The Brennan Center for Justice at NYU School of Law and Spencer Overton, On Behalf Of The National Network on State Election Reform, September 19, 2005.

INDEX

A

B

C

D

E

F

G

H

I

J

L

M

N

O

P

Q

R

S

T

U

V

W

Y